SO YOU WANT TO
SING COUNTRY

So You Want to Sing

A Guide for Professionals

A Project of the National Association of Teachers of Singing

So You Want to Sing: Guides for Performers and Professionals is a series of works devoted to providing a complete survey of what it means to sing within a particular genre. Each contribution functions as a touchstone work for not only professional singers, but students and teachers of singing. Titles in the series offer a common set of topics so readers can navigate easily the various genres addressed in each volume. This series is produced under the direction of the National Association of Teachers of Singing, the leading professional organization devoted to the science and art of singing.

So You Want to Sing Music Theater: A Guide for Professionals, by Karen S. Hall, 2013.

So You Want to Sing Rock 'n' Roll: A Guide for Professionals, by Matthew Edwards, 2014.

So You Want to Sing Jazz: A Guide for Professionals, by Jan Shapiro, 2015.

So You Want to Sing Country: A Guide for Performers, by Kelly K. Garner, 2017

SO YOU WANT TO SING COUNTRY

A Guide for Performers

Kelly K. Garner

Allen Henderson
Executive Editor, NATS

Matthew Hoch
Series Editor

A Project of the National Association of
Teachers of Singing

ROWMAN & LITTLEFIELD
Lanham • Boulder • New York • London

Published by Rowman & Littlefield
A wholly owned subsidiary of The Rowman & Littlefield Publishing Group, Inc.
4501 Forbes Boulevard, Suite 200, Lanham, Maryland 20706
www.rowman.com

Unit A, Whitacre Mews, 26-34 Stannary Street, London SE11 4AB

British Library Cataloguing in Publication Information Available

Library of Congress Cataloging-in-Publication Data

Names: Garner, Kelly K., author.
Title: So you want to sing country : a guide for performers / Kelly K. Garner.
Description: Lanham, Maryland : Rowman & Littlefield, [2017] | Series: So you
    want to sing | Includes bibliographical references and index.
Identifiers: LCCN 2016025572 (print) | LCCN 2016026884 (ebook) | ISBN
    9781442246409 (pbk. : alk. paper) | ISBN 9781442246416 (electronic)
Subjects: LCSH: Singing—Instruction and study. | Country music—Instruction
    and study. | Country music—History and criticism.
Classification: LCC MT820 .G23 2017 (print) | LCC MT820 (ebook) | DDC
    783/.0642143—dc23
LC record available at https://lccn.loc.gov/2016025572

♾™ The paper used in this publication meets the minimum requirements
of American National Standard for Information Sciences—Permanence of
Paper for Printed Library Materials, ANSI/NISO Z39.48-1992.

Printed in the United States of America

CONTENTS

FIGURES

FOREWORD

So You Want to Sing Country: A Guide for Performers is the fourth book in the NATS/Rowman & Littlefield "So You Want to Sing" series and the first book to fall under my editorship. And what a joy it was to work with Dr. Kelly Garner on this endeavor! Her experience, passion, and deep knowledge of the subject matter have coalesced into the valuable resource that you hold in your hands. This book has truly been a labor of love for her, and its content has been distilled over the course of many years in the industry and as a teacher of singing.

I hadn't met Dr. Garner before working with her on this project, but it turns out that we have an important connection to one another: Kelly is a born-and-bred Alabamian and an alumna of Auburn University, where I currently serve as an associate professor of voice and coordinator of voice studies. In the introduction to this book, she speaks of a Southerner's childhood in which she was steeped in country music. As she moved forward through her schooling, she found opportunities to continue her passion for singing country through commercial music and jazz performance degrees from Belmont University, Middle Tennessee State University, and the University of Miami, as well as many years of experience in the country music industry. Finding someone who is equally at home as a professor and industry professional is rare, and she has important wisdom to share with performers and teachers of singing who are eager to learn more about the country music genre. Perhaps most importantly, Dr. Garner's experience with other contemporary commercial music (CCM) styles informs the perspective of her writing: she understands how country "fits" into the commercial music industry as a whole.

Beginning with this volume, we are also pleased to welcome a third common chapter to the series: "Using Audio Enhancement Technology" by Matthew Edwards (author of *So You Want to Sing Rock 'n' Roll*). This chapter will stand alongside the voice science and vocal health chapters by Dr. Scott McCoy and Dr. Wendy LeBorgne. Dr. Edwards is highly regarded as a specialist in this topic, and all future "So You Want to Sing" books on amplified CCM topics will now include this chapter so that the reader can benefit from his expertise.

The collected volumes of the "So You Want to Sing" series offer a valuable opportunity for performers and teachers of singing to explore new styles and important pedagogies. I am confident that voice specialists, both amateur and professional, will benefit from Dr. Garner's important resource on country music. It has been a privilege to work with her on this project.

Matthew Hoch

ACKNOWLEDGMENTS

To my parents, James R. Garner and Martha Yancey Garner, for their constant love, support, and tireless assistance to help me manage a busy schedule and lots of transition through the past five years. I love you!

To my aunt and copy editor, Dr. Nancy Hoagland, for reading through this work with me and catching all my mistakes. Thank you!

To my fabulous colleagues at Belmont University. What an honor and privilege it is to teach alongside you.

To my current and former students. You are the reason I love being an educator! What a privilege to help you develop your artistry and careers. You inspire me! I love my students!

To my series editor, Dr. Matthew Hoch, for your guidance and direction in this process and for helping me push toward the finish line!

To Allen Henderson and the NATS organization, thank you for giving me the opportunity to be one of the writers in this very important book series.

To my friend, Jennifer Kitchens, for compiling and editing the index. Thank you!

To my big dog, Clarence, for his unconditional love and for being a constant reminder that the simple things in life are sometimes the most important!

The content for chapter 1 and appendix C is drawn primarily from the following resources: Kingsbury and Nash's *Will the Circle Be Unbroken: Country Music in America* (2006); Kingsbury's *The Grand Ole Opry History of Country Music: 70 Years of the Songs, the Stars, and the Stories* (1995); Malone and Neal's *Country Music, USA* (3rd ed., 2013); and Neal's *Country Music: A Cultural and Stylistic History* (2013). Full citations are listed in the bibliography.

INTRODUCTION

When the National Association of Teachers of Singing (NATS) approached me about writing the country book in their "So You Want to Sing" series, I had a feeling that my life was about to come full circle. You see, I was the little girl who back in the early 1970s would wear red Roy Rogers cowboy boots and sit directly in front of the television set in rural northeast Alabama watching the *Country Boy Eddie Show* on WBRC Channel 6 out of Birmingham. This television show had discovered the talents of Tammy Wynette and many others during its popular run. I was also from a family that could appreciate good music, especially the music that had been created in the very hills and valleys that we walked over every day. My Uncle Charles in particular had a love for Patsy Cline and Jim Reeves. So as you can imagine, I began hearing and learning about country music from the time when I was only a very small child.

The evolution of my career has been varied. I grew up singing in church. My grandparents' church, Mt. Olive Baptist Church, was the first stage I graced at the ripe old age of three. It was located on top of Sand Mountain on Highway 278 in Altoona, Alabama, and overlooked a beautiful valley bordered by rolling hills and a lake. This is property that my family once owned and still is bordered by the existing farm.

There were usually around fifty people attending the church services, and even though small, there was a sweet spirit and love for music that could not be denied. I also grew up singing in my home church in Piedmont, Alabama. This congregation was somewhat larger but again was an environment that encouraged me to love the music of the land. Piedmont, as you may know, is the French word for "foothills," and in the picturesque setting of the hills and valleys, there was no doubt that we were nestled into the tail end of the Appalachians, a mountain chain rich in the heritage of country music.

I began my college career at Gadsden State Community College, where my mother and grandmother taught mathematics. After receiving my associate's degree, I transferred to Auburn University and finished my BSE in secondary math education. This step in my evolution as a musician is quite important because as a member of the singing group Auburn University Singers, I was called upon by the director to sing a Patsy Cline song. Strangely enough, I knew this was not going to be a difficult task. I had been singing along with Patsy as long as I could remember. One of the songs I remember doing was "I Fall to Pieces," and with AU Singers, it became a popular crowd-pleaser at many of our events.

After graduating from Auburn, I decided to move to Nashville and finish a BM degree in commercial voice with a performance emphasis at Belmont University. I had been a double major in music and math education at Auburn for a couple of years, so I only had about two years left to finish an undergraduate degree in music. A friend of mine at Auburn had told me about Belmont University and how they had a degree that was in commercial or popular music. I decided to give it a try! While at Belmont, I studied all the styles including classical, jazz, R&B, pop, rock, gospel, and country with several different teachers. I first began studying classical voice with Majorie Halbert. She gave me such a complete foundation of vocal pedagogy, and I continued to study with her even though I also began studying with commercial teachers Carolyn Binkley and Bruce Bennett, all of whom spoke of "speech-level" singing and connectivity of the voice. Bruce introduced me to improvisation and discussed the concept of developing a "palette of colors" in tone production.

Upon graduation from Belmont, I was offered an opportunity to sign an exclusive artist recording contract with Diadem Music Group. This was a smaller gospel label but was an environment where I learned many things about how to make the kind of music I wanted to make. While working on the record, one of the ways I made a living was by singing demos for songwriters, trying to sound like certain artists to increase their chances of getting a song recorded. Two of the artists I was regularly asked to "sound like" were Faith Hill and Wynonna Judd. It seemed to be an easy task for me and was a great way to pay the rent.

During this postgraduation time in my life, I also made my living by being a music copyist for orchestrators and by getting booked to sing on choral music "octavo" sessions with seven other studio singers. It was during these sessions that I learned another very important piece of information as a singer. I started to hear the other studio singers use a term I didn't think I had heard before or at least didn't understand. On particular passages in the music, if it was in a certain part of their range, they would tell each other to "mix it." I began to learn by listening to their tone production and placement. I would take notice of the section they were talking about and would try to figure out how they were indeed "mixing" it. To this day, I do more "mixing" in my own vocal production than anything else. I learned very quickly what a useful tool it is to "mix" and how it can be a "vehicle" to get around in the voice easily, especially across the upper bridge. This is a technique we will explore further in a later chapter.

After touring and traveling for quite a few years with the recording we had made at Diadem, I decided to come off the road full time and take a worship leading position back at my home church, First Baptist in Piedmont, Alabama. After two years of church work, I moved back to Nashville and took an exclusive staffwriter position at Centergy Music Group. Niles Borop, my publisher and mentor, spent the next five years teaching me how to write a good song and, more importantly, as you will see later, how to recognize a good song. The publishing company was predominantly a gospel company, but we also wrote country songs when we knew an artist was planning a new record and looking for songs.

After being with the publisher for a couple of years, I began to see many artists record my songs. One song was nominated for a Dove Award as Southern Gospel Recorded Song of the Year and a BMI Award nomination for Most Performed Gospel Song. Because of the industry success and performing experience I had acquired, Belmont

University contacted me in the spring of 2001 and wanted to know if I would be interested in teaching commercial voice for the School of Music. I decided to give it a try and was developing young artists at Belmont for the next five years. It was during this time at Belmont that I was asked to teach and revamp the country and pop/rock vocal styles classes.

In 2006, I was given the opportunity to build a recording studio, Big Dog Studios, and a production company, Kelly Garner Productions, LLC. Within three years from the production company's inception, I had produced twenty-two artists and had as many as eighty-eight songs on the desk at one time. Several of these artists were recording country music, as well as other styles. In 2009, I was involved with so many artists and their songs, it became apparent that I needed to start a publishing arm for my production company. Yellow Tree Music Group, a small music publishing company, was founded and eventually employed twelve exclusive writers and nineteen affiliated writers. Our catalog includes songs in the style of gospel, church print, and country and continues to this day.

In 2011, I came to the conclusion that I missed being an educator and working with young students on a daily basis. Because of this, I decided to move my business with me to Miami, Florida, where I began to pursue a DMA degree in jazz voice performance with a cognate in music technology from the University of Miami's Frost School of Music, Department of Studio Music and Jazz. I graduated in 2014 with a completed dissertation entitled "Vocal Recording Techniques for the Modern Digital Studio."

In March 2014, I received an invitation from Dean Cynthia Curtis at Belmont University to rejoin the music faculty for the following fall semester. I accepted the position of lecturer in commercial voice in the School of Music at Belmont University, teaching applied commercial voice, performance seminars, studio singers, pop-rock vocal styles, and country vocal styles and in 2015, was promoted to assistant professor of commercial voice.

I hope you enjoy reading this work as much as I have enjoyed writing it. I consider it to be quite an honor to contribute to such a work and to be an author in the book series. Those of us working in this field will continue to pool our research and our efforts to hopefully move the education of these styles and techniques forward.

ONLINE SUPPLEMENT NOTE

So You Want to Sing Country features an online supplement courtesy of the National Association of Teachers of Singing. Visit the link below and click on the button for the So You Want to Sing Series to discover additional exercises and examples, as well as links to recordings of the songs referenced in this book.

http://www.nats.org/So_You_Want_To_Sing_Book_Series.html

A musical note symbol ♪ in this book will mark every instance of corresponding online supplement material.

❶

THE EVOLUTION
OF COUNTRY MUSIC

A HISTORY LESSON

The evolution of country music made a path straight through the living room of the typical Appalachian family around the turn of the twentieth century.[1] Usually in the evening, just after "suppertime," the family would gather and begin to sing familiar tunes and folk songs. Some family members would play instruments and others would sing. The stories of the people in rural America were told by the lyrics of the folk song or ballad. The mouthpieces, or storytellers of these songs, were the singers. They would not need any sheet music or charts as most musicians do today. They only needed their memories. The songs they would sing are songs that had come over on the boat with their European ancestors. These are songs that had been passed on orally for as long as they could remember. When the recording industry began to rise up in the 1920s, it became widely popular for generally two reasons. People were interested in singing about either a time or moment in their lives they would like to remember or for a lifestyle they wished to possess.

The story lines of the country song seemed to bring out the best in people. It was more than just a song; it was the language of the land. The people of Appalachia seemed to understand the emotion held in certain songs better than people from other regions. The "suppertime" family entertainment of these mountain people was a phenomenon, one that began to catch fire in the hearts of all Americans. The country song emerged as a vehicle for telling stories but was also a form of community fellowship and family fun. To be quite honest, the living room of these Appalachian families was probably the first country music stage. As time passed and the recording industry developed, this stage became much bigger and further reaching than anyone would have ever imagined. Radio (and later TV shows) began to disseminate country music to anyone who owned a receiver. We will now take a stroll through history discussing some of the very first country music singers and the contributions of each subsequent generation.

FIRST GENERATION—THE EARLY YEARS (1920s)

Prior to 1923, the genre we know as country music did not exist. It was first referred to as "hillbilly music" because of its rural origins among mostly white, Southern, working-class musicians. This music was intended to be consumed, or listened to, by a very similar audience. During the early years, the songs that were sung came directly from the social and economic conditions of the country music audience. Workers began to leave the farming life that they had known and move to urban areas where they could make more money. Many of these Appalachian people had come to the cities to work in the cotton mills and had brought their music with them. Eventually though, these people began to miss different aspects of life on the farm and found themselves wanting to sing songs about the lifestyle that they had once known. ♪

The conclusion of World War I also contributed to the development of country music, with soldiers coming back from deployment with an expanded world outlook but a desire to hear and sing about subjects that were nostalgic and represented their idea of "home." In Hollywood, stars of the silver screen such as Roy Rogers and Gene Autry gave a face to cowboy songs, while the jazz genre began to invade the music of the "barn dance" with what would be called western swing. ♪

Immigrants to the Southern Appalachian Mountains of North America brought the music and the musical instruments that their families had used in Europe for three hundred years. Because of the proximity of Southern Appalachia, the Atlanta music scene began to play a major role in the formation of this genre with country music's earliest recordings. Okeh Records began issuing hillbilly music recordings like "Little Log Cabin in the Lane" by Fiddlin' John Carson as early as 1923. This first record was followed by Columbia Records releasing Samantha Bumgarner's "Old Familiar Tunes" in 1924 and RCA Victor Records releasing the Carter Family and Jimmie Rodgers in 1927. Bumgarner and Eva Davis were the first female musicians to record and release country songs. "Hillbilly" musicians, like Cliff Carlisle, were also part of the movement, recording blues tunes throughout the 1920s. ♪

Atlanta would remain a major recording center for two decades and a major performance center for four decades leading all the way up to the first country music TV shows on local Atlanta stations in the 1950s. In 1923, when Okeh Records' talent scout Ralph Peer traveled to Atlanta, he was actually looking for black music—what he would find and eventually record was Fiddlin' John Carson and the release of the first documented hillbilly hit record. Believe it or not, some record companies in Atlanta turned away early artists such as Fiddlin' John Carson, but others realized that his music would fit perfectly with the lifestyle of America's farming community. There were a couple songs recorded on June 30, 1922, for Victor Records and released in April 1923 that were considered to be the very first commercial recordings, what was considered to be country music at the time. These songs were entitled "Arkansas Traveler" and "Turkey in the Straw" by fiddlers Henry Gilliland and A. C. (Eck) Robertson. Vernon Dalhart was the first country singer to have a nationwide hit in May 1924 with "Wreck of the Old 97." The flip side of Dalhart's record was "Lonesome Road Blues," which also became very popular. ♪

Uncle Dave Macon was an important figure in the early evolution of country as he was one of the first vaudeville-style "entertainers." He would add his antics to his stage show, including spinning his banjo around and jumping up and down during a song while still singing and playing. His song "Bile Them Cabbage Down" was the first recording of what would become known as a classic country music "shout tune"—this was the kind that an entire vaudeville show's cast would sing together at the end of the show. In some modern jazz arrangements, this type of element is known in today's market as a "shout chorus." ♪

The steel guitar began to be utilized in country music as early as 1922 when Jimmie Tarlton met famed Hawaiian guitarist Frank Ferera on the West Coast. Frank was a Hawaiian of Portuguese decent who came to the United States in 1914 as an entertainer at the Panama Pacific Exhibition. He claimed to have introduced the Hawaiian guitar to Americans.

Deford Bailey was one of the most popular performers of the Grand Old Opry in the late 1920s and was the first African American country star (see appendix C). ♪

Ralph Peer, a talent scout and sound recordist, captured Jimmie Rodgers and the Carter Family's historic recording sessions on August 1, 1927, in Bristol, Tennessee, in a vacant hat warehouse. A very similar occurrence to what these recording sessions might have been like is depicted in the movie *O Brother Where Art Thou?* (see appendix C). ♪

The stock market crash of 1929 and the ensuing era known as the Great Depression also contributed to the development of country music. Most country music fans of that time were seeking a reprieve from the drudgery of their daily lives. Listening to country music was a way of escape for them, but they also seemed to be able to identify with the rural topics about which country songs were written.

Musical Sources

Traditional ballads, songs that told a story, were considered to be the oldest source of this musical heritage and were handed down orally from generation to generation. These romanticized songs from the British Isles were sought out and compiled by song collectors Cecil Sharpe, Maud Karpeles, and Olive Dame Campbell. These collections were published into songbooks such as *English Folk Songs from the Southern Appalachians* (1917). Even though few of the early country singers actually recorded any of the songs from this tradition, publishing these collections was vitally important to raising public awareness of the rich musical culture in southern Appalachia.

Cowboy songs began to gain recognition thanks to folklorists and collectors who were working in the American West. N. Howard "Jack" Thorpe collected the first book of "lyrics only" cowboy songs in his 1908 volume, *Songs of the Cowboy*. Two years later, John Lomax published

Cowboy Songs and Other Frontier Ballads, a volume that contained both lyrics and music.

Gospel hymns also provided a source of music for early country singers. Traveling preachers hosted revivals and camp meetings where congregational singing gained popularity. A new style of hymn began to emerge that included repeated phrases, catchy rhythms, and short refrain melodies that were repeated many times. Composers such as Fanny Crosby ("Pass Me Not, O Gentle Savior") and P. P. Bliss ("Almost Persuaded") specialized in this new style of the gospel hymn.

An industry began to grow around these new gospel hymns at the turn of the twentieth century. Publishers began to produce inexpensive paperback hymnals filled with newly composed and established favorites. The books that included just lyrics might sell for ten to fifteen cents, while books with lyrics and music sold for twenty-five to thirty-five cents per copy. Many publishers of these hymns, including the popular James D. Vaughan Company, would hire professional quartets to travel and tour throughout the region, singing the songs that were included in these books in order to advertise the collections. Some editions of these collections printed the songs in standard notation, but the more popular versions included a system of different shapes, such as triangles and squares, representing different pitches in the scale. This system was known as "shape notes." There were two different types of "shape note" systems appearing in print: one was a four-note system that emerged around 1800 and another seven-note system that developed several decades later. The seven-note system was the version that became widely used for hymnal publication and was quite popular among the first generation of country singers. ♪

Music teachers, such as my great-grandfather, Charles A. Kilpatrick, and Lum Howard, would teach one- or two-week singing schools in various communities across the Appalachian region. Lum Howard was the father of my "second" grandmother, Mrs. Eucile "Ceil" Maddox. These singing school teachers would teach the local residents to read shape notes in hopes that they would take the musical knowledge back to their families and church congregations. I heard many stories while I was growing up from Mrs. Maddox about her father traveling all over the state of Alabama, teaching singing schools and leading what they would call "all-day singings." I attended quite a few of these "all-day singings" while I was growing up in my grandparents' church, Mt. Olive Baptist in Altoona, Alabama. I was even called upon occasionally by Mrs. Maddox to lead a song. This meant that I would pick out a song in one of the paperback songbooks and go down to the front and "direct" or conduct the song. I usually chose my song from the Vaughan, Tennessee, or Stamps-Baxter songbook. I would sometimes even sit in the "class," as they would call it, down in the front section of the congregation where the semi-professional singers and the traveling quartets would sit. Many of the performers and recording stars in early country music attended these events and knew many of these songs by heart, but they would also draw from the published songbooks to learn certain songs they wanted to perform in their own shows and performances.

The blues was also an important contributor to the unique sound of country music. In typical blues style, African American performers would normally sing short verses over a repeated blues chord progression. This style became known within the country genre as "down-home" blues or country blues. The subject of the lyrics was usually bemoaning "good love gone bad" and was laced with double entendres or sexual metaphors. Blues singers would usually play for crowds that had a lively "house party" atmosphere and would sometimes take turns improvising on choruses with other performers. Blues was not exclusive to African Americans. Some white performers in the early development of country music would sing songs that lyrically and musically came from the rich blues tradition. There was also the presence of "jug" bands, where performers would blow across the top of a ceramic jug to create bass notes. The earliest recorded folk tunes were songs like Mamie Smith's "Crazy Blues." Her record was so popular that record executives launched recording expeditions into the South to find more blues artists. During these expeditions, they not only found blues artists but also quite a few country artists who contributed to the development of singing in a country style. ♪

Jazz emerged out of some of the same popular New Orleans dance styles that influenced country music. By World War I, bands were taking some rhythmic influences from ragtime and adding a new element called swing. This new genre involved unequal, "laid-back" subdivisions of the beat and featured improvisation from performers. The term "laid-back" subdivisions more specifically refers to playing eighth subdivisions as if they were the last eighth note in a triplet subdivision of each beat. Sitting the usual "straight eighth" on the final division or note of a triplet will make the rhythm "swing." Early country musicians were very influenced by the concept of swing and very aware of artists like Louis Armstrong, Jelly Roll Morton, King Oliver, and Fletcher Henderson's dance band. ♪

Tin Pan Alley was a neighborhood in New York City located between Fifth and Sixth avenues on West 28th Street that was known for original material. Many early country music entertainers used it as a place to find material. The name "Tin Pan Alley" came from music publishers hiring entertainers to advertise and "bang out" songs on pianos. Many early country singers saw themselves simply as entertainers instead of hillbilly musicians, and because of this, they would emulate many of the popular singers of the day, learning their songs.

Traveling medicine and minstrel shows were also very influential in the development of country music. The medicine show was run by traveling salesmen who were selling elixirs and miraculous cures. These salesmen would hire entertainers to travel with them in an attempt to draw a crowd. This was a way for budding country artists to hone their craft while traveling with the medicine show. Minstrel shows were a little different in that they were essentially traveling theater troupes. They would entertain local audiences with folk-like skits, speeches, songs, dances, and humorous dialogue. Both black and white performers would perform in "blackface," which they achieved by using burnt cork to darken their faces and hands. They presented extreme racial stereotypes and caricatures of African American identity. These characters would try unsuccessfully to put on high-class airs and sing longingly about the happy days spent on the slave plantation. Many aspects of the minstrel show were extremely racist, but historians have pointed out that even the African American performers would do so in blackface. Perhaps this was a way for the African American performers to draw attention to social injustices that desperately needed reform. Several early country performers took songs such as "Turkey in the Straw," "Old Zip Coon," and "Old Dan Tucker" straight from the minstrel stage. Many historians have suggested that the popular country barn dance programs were minstrel shows without the use of blackface. ♪

As country performers would draw from many of these sources to find much of the material they would perform, they would do so learning the songs by ear or by using some of the inexpensive paperback songbooks mentioned earlier. However, after using the songs and working them into their performances over a period of time, the arrangements would begin to take on the character of the artist and sound completely different from the way they were first intended. Ralph Peer wanted uncopyrighted material that he could copyright himself, for that was where he thought the money was going to be in this hillbilly music business.

The Recording Effect

Before the invention of recording, music was only consumed in the moment of the performance. There was no way to rewind or relive it. Each musical moment would happen once before the live audience and then was gone like a vapor. For people in rural settings, music came from traveling performers, from members of the community, or from members of their immediate family performing for each other. When Thomas Edison invented the phonograph in 1877, the way music would be received, exchanged, and consumed by the public would be forever changed. He invented it with the intention to record speech as a novelty or to dictate business correspondence. The phonograph used a stylus to record or "cut" sound waves into a rotating cylinder. In 1888, a new device came along, invented by Emile Berliner, which was called a gramophone. It would record onto a flat disk instead of a rotating cylinder. Record labels eventually called recordings made by black performers "race" records and recordings made by white artists a variety of titles, including "old familiar tunes" or "olde time tunes." However, the term that was eventually used most frequently for white records was the label "hillbilly" music. ♪

The process of recording continued to be refined with the dawn of the twentieth century and would see mass reproduction of sound recordings start to become extremely popular with the public. By World War I, record players could cost anywhere from $15 to $175. By 1917, patents that had protected the phonograph and gramophone technology had expired, which meant that smaller labels and manufacturers could compete. One year later, sales of records and record players went as high as $158 million. In 1922, record sales alone peaked at $100 million but began to decline sharply because of oversaturation and radio broadcast offering a free alternative to record sales.

When the industry started to sink in sales, record labels started recording artists like Mamie Smith with the song "Crazy Blues." When the Okeh label started to see success from this record, all the other record labels began to seek out similar untapped talent in remote areas. Both blues and country music suddenly emerged as commercially viable genres. Many have suggested that even though they deemed country music commercially viable, it was still somewhat untainted from commercialization. The mass appeal that country music was experiencing from the public seems to be connected to the fact that the style was raw and almost exactly the same music that had been played in the living rooms of Appalachia. ♪

The Radio Dial

Radio had been a bit of a research project during World War I. Experimental broadcast of concerts and sporting events took place in 1919, but by 1920 the first commercial radio station was on the air. By 1922, there were eighty-nine radio stations operating across the South, mostly owned by corporations that initially used them for advertising. They knew they needed to add something in between advertising to hold the public's attention, so radio as we know it was born. By 1930, one out of every three homes had a radio in the central family room. By 1932, two out of every five homes had radios, but that number would climb to four out of five by 1938. According to Kingsbury, people listened to the radio an average of five and a half hours every day. The emergence of radio gave the public a cheaper alternative to buying recorded disks.

The *Atlanta Journal*'s radio station, WSB, which stood for "Welcome South, Brother," went on the air on March 16, 1922, with a 100-watt transmitter. It was upgraded to 500 watts within a few months and on a clear night could be heard in Canada and Mexico. WSB reached an estimated two million listeners during this time. Local entertainer Fiddlin' John Carson, accompanied by a string band on September 9, 1922, would be the first broadcast of what would be called country music. ♪

WBAP (We Build a Program) in Fort Worth, Texas, was owned by the Fort Worth Star-Telegram Company and went on the air May 2, 1922. On January 4, 1923, the station aired a broadcast of an old-time fiddler on a square dance program and officially began the barn dance phenomenon. Even though these first two stations play a significant role, the stations with the biggest impact on country music going forward would be Chicago's WLS and Nashville's WSM. WLS was owned by Sears and Roebuck, and the call letters stood for "World's Largest Store." They would broadcast the first official "National Barn Dance" on April 19, 1924. In Nashville, WSM was owned by the National Life and Accident Insurance Company. Their call letters stood for "We Shield Millions," referring to their company's core business. They began broadcasting on October 5, 1925, with a 1,000-watt transmitter, which was a very powerful signal for that time. On November 28 of the same year, they aired an unscheduled performance of old-time champion fiddler Uncle Jimmy Thompson, and the public support was tremendous. The station had been contemplating doing a barn dance and decided to go ahead after the outpouring of support for Thompson. WSM launched its regularly scheduled barn dance on December 26, 1925, and it would eventually become the legendary Grand Ole Opry. The Grand Ole Opry is still, to this day, the most highly coveted performance venue of country music's best-known singers and musicians.

SECOND GENERATION (1930s–1940s)

Radio became an even more popular source of entertainment during the 1930s and 1940s. This was thought of as the second generation of country music. "Barn dance" shows began all over the South, as far north as Chicago and as far west as California. During this time, cowboy songs and western music, which had been recorded in the 1920s, began to be popularized by Hollywood films. Bob Wills, born into a long line of fiddlers, grew up in West Texas hearing both frontier fiddle music and the emotive sounds of black field workers. In 1930, he and guitarist Herman Arnspiger teamed up with Milton Brown in Fort Worth, Texas, to form a trio that, in 1931, would become the Light Crust Doughboys. They would soon become the most popular string band in the Southwest. Wills had also appeared in Hollywood Westerns, which helped his appeal with the public. Bob Wills concocted a mix of country and jazz that started out as dance hall music but would eventually become known as "western swing." In 1938, Wills was one of the first to add electric guitar to his band. Two other musicians in western swing that were quite popular and appeared in films were Spade Cooley and Tex Williams. At the height of its popularity, western swing rivaled the popularity of big band swing music. ♪

In 1939, country musicians like Johnny Barfield began to record "boogie," or "boogie-woogie" as some would call it. Shortly after he recorded his version of "Boogie Woogie," he introduced it to an audience in a show at Carnegie Hall. The Great Depression continued to affect the consumption of music and cut into the number of records that were being sold. During hard times like these, radio was simply a cheaper alternative for working-class families. The Grand Ole Opry continued to thrive through the 1930s, and some of the Opry's most popular stars included Uncle Dave Macon, Roy Acuff, and African American harmonica player DeFord Bailey. Additionally, in 1934, WSM's signal was at 50,000 watts and could be heard across the country. On the musical front, many musicians were performing and recording songs in any number of styles. Moon Mullican played western swing but also recorded songs that could be called rockabilly. Besides western swing, boogie-woogie, and rockabilly, between 1947 and 1949, "crooning" would become popular in country, and an artist named Eddy Arnold would place eight songs in the top ten in country but would also eventually cross over into the pop market. ♪

Singing Cowboys and Western Swing

Cowboy songs had been recorded since the 1920s but were eventually popularized by Hollywood "Westerns" during the 1930s and 1940s. The "stars of the silver screen" rescued hillbilly music from its "cornball" reputation with their noble horses, big white hats, trusty sidekicks, and rugged but noble independence. However, just as the movie version of the cowboy hero was not a literal depiction of a working cowboy, the musical style of the singing cowboy was heavily influenced by people who were not actually cowboys at all. The emerging musical style of the singing cowboy in the 1930s was primarily a creation of the Hollywood film industry.

Some of the most famous singing cowboys of the era were Gene Autry and Roy Rogers. Autry collaborated regularly with a group of musicians called Sons of the Pioneers. They supplied songs for his films and significantly contributed to his commercial success (see appendix C). ♪

Other singing cowboys emerged in the late 1930s; the third most influential singing cowboy of the movies, after Gene Autry and Roy Rogers, was Tex Ritter. He grew up in Texas and became interested in cowboy songs and folklore while studying at the University of Texas (see appendix C). One of his big hits was "Get Along Little Dogies" (1935), an actual cowboy song that was often dumped into the midst of different Hollywood movies. A year later, he signed with a start-up movie studio as their singing cowboy star and began producing the same sensationalized cowboy movies and songs that Autry and Rogers had been making famous. ♪

The singing cowboy style began to be found in places other than the Hollywood movies. Female singers were also beginning to be a part of the "singing cowboy" scene. Some singers would simply contribute to their family groups, but then suddenly a female star emerged who would open the door for females and change country music for all time. An Arkansas native, Patsy Montana (born Ruby Blevins) went to college at UCLA and while there met Stuart Hamblen, a cowboy singer with a local radio station. A few years later, while in Chicago at the World's Fair, on a whim she decided to audition at WLS. She was instantly hired as a singer and fiddler with the Prairie Ramblers and, in 1935, recorded her history-making song with the Prairie Ramblers, "I Want to Be a Cowboy's Sweetheart." This important song sold a million copies and was the biggest hit up to that time for a female hillbilly singer. It included bright, sassy yodeling; cowboy-themed lyrics; and a swing beat and would pave the way for women to have successful solo careers in country music. Although she recorded for another decade, this song would remain her signature hit. ♪

Changing Instrumentation

In the early years, drums were not used by country musicians because they were thought to be too loud and not considered to be a "pure" instrument. However, by 1935, western swing big band leader Bob Wills had made the decision to add drums to the Texas Playboys. Even into the mid-1940s, the Texas Playboys' drummer was not allowed to appear on stage at the Grand Ole Opry. Rockabilly groups were frequently using drums by 1955, but the Louisiana Hayride show kept their "unused" drummer backstage as late as 1956. By the early 1960s, it was rare if a country band did not appear onstage with a drummer.

Bob Wills started using electric guitar in his band around 1938, but it would take another decade for Arthur Smith to garner a top-ten hit with his recording of "Guitar Boogie." This hit was important because it also crossed over to the pop chart and introduced people to the sound and recording potential of the electric guitar. For decades thereafter, session players in Nashville would prefer the warm tones of the Gibson and Gretsch archtop but the "hot lick" Fender style eventually became the signature guitar sound associated with country music.

Hillbilly Boogie

In 1939, Johnny Barfield played and recorded a song called "Boogie Woogie" at Carnegie Hall. This gave country musicians a new term as they began to record more and more of what was called "boogie." It was first referred to as hillbilly boogie or "okie" boogie but was later renamed "country boogie." This danceable style of music quickly became popular in late 1945 and includes a lively feel with fast tempo, blues chord progression, swing rhythm, highly energized bass line in constant motion, piano, and syncopated rhythms with an emphasis on subdivision. Black musicians began to transform what was known as boogie into jump blues, while white musicians began to incorporate it into their country and honky-tonk music. When the Delmore Brothers released "Freight Train Boogie," it was considered to be influential in moving country music and blues toward rockabilly. Arthur Smith's "Guitar Boogie" was recorded in the style of country boogie as well as many songs recorded by artists Merrill Moore and Tennessee Ernie Ford. Hillbilly boogie remained popular well into the 1950s and it remains a small subgenre of country music today. ♪

Bluegrass

As World War II was coming to a close, string band music, also known as "mountaineer" music, began to emerge from the primitive traditions in Appalachia. This precursor of bluegrass became associated with notions of old-time, traditional, backwoods, and anti-modern perspectives. Bill Monroe, the "father of bluegrass," began playing with his brothers Charlie (guitar) and Birch (fiddle), known as the Monroe Brothers, until they split in 1938. Shortly after the split, Bill formed his new band, the Blue Grass Boys. In 1939, the term "bluegrass" finally emerged when Bill Monroe, introduced by Roy Acuff, appeared with Lester Flatt and Earl Scruggs on the Grand Ole Opry stage as Bill Monroe and the Blue Grass Boys. When they performed the new style on the Opry stage, many were unsure as to what to call it, but Bill Monroe was from the "bluegrass" state of Kentucky and his group was called the "Blue Grass Boys." So, to put it simply, the name just stuck. His band played at a breakneck speed with much syncopation, and he sang in higher keys than was common for most male singers. The vocal style usually associated with bluegrass is a smooth, straight tone with a slightly forward placement into the mask area of the face. ♪

Carter and Ralph Stanley were born in the remote Clinch Mountain territory, and they sang in a Primitive Baptist church where instruments weren't allowed; yet, by the end of their high school years, they were regulars on a local radio station. As early fans of Bill Monroe, the Stanley Brothers became the first of many devotees to expand the new sounds of bluegrass. Their signature sound in their early Columbia recordings was a mournful mountain vocal style, stacked up in unique three-part vocal harmonies. They recorded their most remembered sides for Mercury between 1953 and 1958, even though the bluegrass market had been somewhat diminished in the shadow of the rock-and-roll movement. Even though the folk revival brought some popularity back, the partnership ended when Carter died in 1966 at just forty-one years of age. Ralph forged on with his own band, which included newcomer Larry Sparks. This new group of his became a launching pad for other musicians, such as Keith Whitley and Ricky Skaggs, in the years to come. In 2001, Ralph Stanley appeared as the patriarchal figure in the musical cast of *O Brother, Where Art Thou?* ♪

Folk

Following World War II, country music was called "hillbilly" among the industry crowd and "folk" in the general public and trades. In 1944,

Billboard magazine started referring to "hillbilly" as "folk songs and blues" and, in 1949, began using the term "country" or "country and western." Country music and western music were frequently played on the same radio stations, thus another reason the genre was called "country and western" music during this period of time.

Some of the songs that appeared in the country market, but lacked the hillbilly or vocal twang associations usually identified with country, were usually categorized in the American folk tradition. Another term that was eventually used for this folksy sound was "Americana."

Guitarist and songwriting legend from Kentucky Merle Travis was a proponent of folk music with a virtuosic style of fingerpicking. Tennessee Ernie Ford also created an exaggerated stage character "hillbilly" image for himself as a folksy musician from Bristol, Tennessee. Ford's vocals were smooth, resonant, and nuanced, entirely unlike the honky-tonk singing of the same era. One of Ford's biggest hits was a Merle Travis song entitled "Sixteen Tons." More popular singers, like Tennessee Ernie Ford, began to take folk-inspired songs with topics that were very country and pair them with music that was entirely from the popular tradition. ♪

Gospel

Gospel remained a popular component of country music through the 1930s and 1940s. Red Foley, the biggest country star following World War II, had one of the first million-selling gospel hits with "Peace in the Valley." He also was known to sing songs in other styles such as boogie, blues, and rockabilly. Many other artists would eventually bridge the gap between gospel and country, doing country albums and gospel albums side by side. As mentioned previously, gospel had a great effect on the development of country. Many country music musicians and artists either got their start performing in the church or at least were influenced by the soulful, blues-infused renditions associated with gospel music. ♪

New Radio Stars Emerge

World War II changed everything. Servicemen and -women were taking the music they loved with them around the world. Publishing companies were beginning to set up shop in Nashville, and musicians were shedding their hillbilly associations in favor of the images of cowboys and western entertainers. This trend held course until Elvis Presley emerged onto the scene in 1954 and changed popular music for all time. But from the early 1940s until 1954, country music was shaped by its radio stars and a new style called honky-tonk.

Several Grand Ole Opry stars would still be with the show for several decades. Minnie Pearl, famous for the price tag dangling off her hat and her signature "Howdeeee," would stay with the Opry for five decades. Little Jimmy Dickens joined the Opry in 1948 and was still performing in the 2010s. Roy Acuff and Red Foley both hosted national broadcast segments of the Opry and continued to make hit records. They were heavily influenced by the hillbilly and folk traditions but sang with very little twang in their voices and focused on storytelling ballads, sentimental songs, and gospel hymns.

The most influential artist to come alongside them in the mid-1940s was Eddy Arnold. Arnold, the son of a sharecropper from Henderson, Tennessee, started his career touring with western swing and polka bandleader Pee Wee King as his lead singer. In 1943, he started singing on Nashville's WSM; put together his band, the Tennessee Plowboys; and signed a recording contract with RCA Victor. One year later, Arnold would host a segment on the Opry every week and would soon be crowned the undisputed biggest country star of his generation (see appendix C). He accumulated eighteen number-one songs between 1946 and 1955. His band consisted of fiddle, steel guitar, guitar, and upright bass with occasional piano and mandolin. He was known as a "crooner" with silky-smooth vocals that won him a large female following. ♪

Honky-Tonk

The poor white population in Texas and Oklahoma began to create another type of stripped-down and raw musical sound. It had its roots in western swing, ranchera music of Mexico and the border states (particularly Texas), and the blues of the American South. It became known across the land as honky-tonk and came with a variety of moods, utilizing a basic instrumental ensemble of fiddle, acoustic rhythm guitar, electric lead guitar, upright or acoustic bass, steel guitar, and eventually, drums.

The rhythm guitar players would use a "sock rhythm" style of playing where they would hold the strings on the neck of the guitar while striking the strings on the body. The percussive sound was similar to a drum kit's "high hat" and created a "chuck" sound on two and four. The "honky-tonk" term refers to the types of venues where the music was played and to an attitude and philosophy represented by the artists and songs within the style. Bob Wills and his Texas Playboys described this music as being a little bit of everything: black and white, and just loud enough to get you to not think and keep ordering the whiskey. East Texan Al Dexter had hits with "Honky Tonk Blues" and later with the recording of "Pistol Packin' Mama." Usually associated with bar room establishments, the "honky-tonk" songs were performed by artists such as Ernest Tubb, Kitty Wells, Ted Daffan, Floyd Tillman, the Maddox Brothers and Rose, Lefty Frizzell, and Hank Williams (see appendix C). ♪

Kitty Wells, one of the few country singers actually born in Nashville, sang one of the biggest hits ever associated with this subgenre, "It Wasn't God Who Made Honky Tonk Angels." This song was an "answer song" to Hank Thompson's "The Wild Side of Life" (1952), which chastises a woman for abandoning her proper domestic role as a wife to go back to the honky-tonk. These answer songs brought the discussion of gender roles to the forefront (see appendix C). This "honky-tonk" sound and subgenre of country would later be considered as "traditional" country. ♪

Later in his career, Hank Williams's song "Honky Tonkin'" suddenly changed from just a song into a verb that would describe patrons going down to the local tavern or roadhouse for a night of drinking, dancing, and carousing. The music would focus on the personal relationships and lives of the people who would frequent these places. There were up-tempo drinking songs, laments that described human misery, as well as redemption-based gospel songs. So many of the honky-tonk artists recorded the gospel songs right alongside the "live fast, love hard, die young" songs. Vocals took on the same naturalized sound that had started to be used in some western swing records in the early 1940s. Some of the artists' vocals would have a bright, nasal tone that added to the twang of honky-tonk music. Honky-tonk also included some western-swing style piano and soon became the next generation of dance-hall music in the Southwest. Hank William's unique style not only had a tremendous influence on country music, he also inspired many pioneers of rock-and-roll such as Elvis Presley, Jerry Lee Lewis, Chuck Berry, and Ike Turner. Williams also provided a musical blueprint and style for another young up-and-coming honky-tonk artist, George Jones. Jones, first inspired by Williams, would later go on to become a legend in his own right (see appendix C).

THIRD GENERATION (1950s–1960s)

By the early 1950s, most bands in country music were playing a mixture of western swing, country boogie, and honky-tonk. Artists like Hank Williams had contributed to the popularity of this combination but a shift in the style and sound of this music was about to take place. By 1953, Hank Williams was dead and with him passed the era of honky-tonk. Rockabilly began to gain popularity and reached its peak around the year 1956. The Nashville Sound started to develop in the mid-1950s and by the 1960s had turned country music into a multimillion-dollar industry centered in Nashville, Tennessee.

The Nashville Sound was characterized by its use of big orchestra and something of a cosmopolitan spin on country music. Because of this drastic shift from the norm, there was somewhat of a traditionalist back-lash within the separate genres. Just like the British invasion prompted a return to "old values" in rock and roll, many lost enthusiasm for the music that was being produced in Nashville. Out of this departure came a new genre known as country rock.

Webb Pierce was one of the most popular chart-topping country artists of the 1950s. He had thirteen singles, spent 113 weeks at number one, and had a total of forty-eight singles chart during this decade. Thirty-one of these singles reached the top ten and twenty-six reached the top four. "Western" music was influenced by the cowboy ballads and Tejano music rhythms of the southwestern United States and northern Mexico. This style reached its peak in popularity in the late 1950s, most notably with the song "El Paso," first recorded by Marty Robbins in September 1959. ♪

Even though there were many similarities in instrumentation and origin, the country music scene, for the most part, did not associate with the folk revival and folk rock during this era. For example, the Byrds were not received well during their performance when they played the

Grand Ole Opry. Politics was thought to have played a big part in this response. Folk revivalists were seen as progressive activists, whereas country music audiences were typically more culturally conservative. When the folk revival died out, only a few folk artists, such as Burl Ives, John Denver, and Gordon Lightfoot, would cross over into the country music scene.

Rockabilly

Rockabilly emerged during the 1950s as a new form of country but would not peak until 1956 with what could be called "the year of rockabilly." Rockabilly was a mixture of rock-and-roll and hillbilly music. The three instruments most commonly used in this style were electric guitar, acoustic guitar, and acoustic bass. Rockabilly incorporated twelve-bar blues, swing rhythms, "boogie" patterns, percussive rhythms, exaggerated vocal expressions, and slap-back echo and reverberation added in the recording process. There was also an unbridled enthusiasm and careless energy associated with this style. The song lyrics of rockabilly were usually about teen romance, sex, or partying.

In 1953, Elvis Presley, a young truck driver, walked into Sam Phillips's studio in Memphis to record a song. Phillips's secretary took notice of Elvis and convinced Phillips to bring him back to the studio in 1954. Elvis had grown up a fan of country music artists Hank Snow, Roy Acuff, and Ernest Tubb, among others. Elvis's style was steeped in Southern gospel, black gospel, and the music of other black R&B musicians. Elvis mixed together every style that he loved: country, blues, pop, and gospel. He recorded "That's Alright Mama" and then came back within a few days and recorded "Blue Moon of Kentucky." Elvis changed it from a waltz to a driving four-beat pattern and added in grunts and growls, while slap bass and electric guitar "tore up" the studio. He knew this tune from having been a longtime fan of country music and Bill Monroe. He began his career in the rockabilly genre, as rock and roll was not yet in existence, but it was during this period that Elvis Presley would convert to country music with the hit "Heartbreak Hotel." In 1958, Elvis Presley acknowledged the influence of rhythm and blues on his style, saying, "The colored folk have been singin' and playin' it just the way I'm doing it now, man, for more years than I know." Elvis also admitted that his music was just "hopped-up country." The musical style blended the traditions of both black and white music. ♪

Two other big songs in the rockabilly genre were Johnny Cash's "I Walk the Line" and Carl Perkins's "Blue Suede Shoes." Johnny Cash, in particular, is both an enigma and an icon in country music. His records sounded like nothing else on the radio, country or pop. The arrangements were stark, and Cash's deep voice was instantly recognizable. ♪

Many of Cash's fans liked his music but not country music. Some of them think that he is more connected to rock than to country. Others only know Cash for the tunes he recorded in the 1990s and 2000s. During this time his music was far removed from mainstream country; nonetheless, his music is deeply embedded in the country music industry and has been a big part of its evolution over the years. Cash made a major career shift in the late 1960s when he recorded a pair of live albums inside Folsom and San Quentin prisons. These two performances happened at the peak of the country-rock phenomenon and established Cash as a brooding, "man in black" outlaw character.

The Ozark Jubilee was broadcast from Springfield, Missouri, on ABC-TV and radio from 1955 to 1960, giving country music even more national television exposure. The television program showcased the biggest country stars including some rockabilly artists and other local artists from the Ozarks. In 1956, Webb Pierce said that it was almost impossible to sell country music in a place like New York City. He went on to explain that in modern times television takes us everywhere, and that country music recordings and sheet music sell as well in large cities as they do anywhere else.

In the late 1950s and early 1960s, young teen crooners came onto the scene in country music. They tended to be clean-cut young men with a rock-and-roll sound. One of these young men to make it in country music was Sonny James. Born and raised in Hackleburg, Alabama, he grew up traveling and performing with his family, much like the Everly Brothers (see appendix C). After serving in the Korean War, he followed the same career path as many other country musicians, appearing on the *Louisiana Hayride* and then on television's *Ozark Jubilee*. His biggest hit came in 1957 with the song "Young Love." It went number one on both the pop and country charts. James joined the Grand Ole Opry in the early 1960s and a decade later scored sixteen number-one hits in a row. My friend Mrs. Ceil Maddox (the woman I mentioned earlier in this chapter whose father taught singing schools) was also from the same town in Alabama and would tell stories about being in the house the day Sonny James was born and rocking him when he was a baby. She was a good friend to his family, as well as to my family. Sonny James is a good example of the circles of gospel music and country music overlapping. The music community during this period of time was very small and family oriented. The boundary lines between country and gospel were sometimes blurred as country musicians would perform and listen to gospel music and vice versa. ♪

By the end of the decade, a backlash of traditional artists began to shift the industry away from the rock-and-roll influences of the mid-1950s. Some of the influential artists leading this charge were Ray Price, Marty Robbins, and Johnny Horton. Marty Robbins, born in Glendale, Arizona, represented two important aspects of country music with his recording "El Paso," heading into the era of the Nashville Sound. First, the arrangement was not drenched in orchestral strings, and second, it typified a fascination with cowboys, the Wild West, and how it had influenced the American culture. This sound was typical of Columbia Records during a time when they were establishing some of their artists like Robbins and Johnny Cash as "outsiders," playing more hard-edge country music with a tendency toward older, traditional influences.

The Nashville and Countrypolitan Sounds

Beginning in the mid-1950s, a new sound began to take the country by storm. Thanks to producers Chet Atkins, Paul Cohen, Owen Bradley, and Billy Sherrill, the Nashville Sound delivered a more diverse audience and helped revive country music from a commercially lean period. The Nashville Sound was characterized by 1950s popular stylings, a prominent and smooth vocal, a string section, and a vocal chorus. Instrumental soloing was not emphasized as much and was traded for more of the typical "licks" from the country musicians. Some of the leading artists of the Nashville Sound included Jim Reeves, Skeeter Davis, The Browns, Patsy Cline, and Eddy Arnold. The "slip note" piano style of session musician Floyd Cramer was also an important element during this time period.

Though she looked like a rodeo queen and cussed like a sailor, Patsy Cline possessed one of the most sophisticated vocal talents to ever come out of Nashville. She is revered for the power and expressiveness of her voice, not to mention her strong-willed personality. Cline was born in Winchester, Virginia, as Virginia Patterson Hensley. She grew up in a working-class white family in a small town with sharp divisions of race and class (see appendix C). Being from the "poor" side of town, her taste for country music, colorful clothes, and brazen personality made all the society ladies in town look down on her. This was a slight that Patsy never forgot. She married Gerald Cline in 1953 and took a modified version of her middle name and his last name as her stage name. She got her big break in 1954 when she appeared in Washington, D.C., on the television show of country music promoter Connie B. Gay. From there, she signed a recording contract with a company from California, 4 Star Records, but the label's owner, Bill McCall, would only let her record songs for which he owned the copyright. Many believe this limitation in her choice of songs is what might have hampered her early career. In 1956, she had a hit single, "Walking after Midnight," that was more or less a honky-tonk rendition of a pop song. With no other hits following, her career floundered within a few years. But McCall agreed for her to start working with Owen Bradley through a collaboration deal with Decca Records. By 1960, her deal with 4 Star had ended and Decca picked her up. She began to be able to record songs by the top songwriters in Nashville and was soon inducted into the Grand Ole Opry. Over the next few years, her career soared as she and Owen Bradley cultivated her Nashville Sound into a full-scale crossover phenomenon. Bradley encouraged her to abandon the brash vocal style she had used in live performances in favor of a more expressive, nuanced vocal style. The results of her new vocal stylings were recordings such as "I Fall to Pieces" and "She's Got You," songs that crossed over into pop radio. Cline became the poster child for a new brand of country, a style that was more widely accepted and embraced by a much wider audience. Her producers began to ask her to wear elegant evening gowns and cultivate a more sophisticated image. Patsy wanted to wear cowgirl fringe and sing covers of Hank Williams and Bill Monroe songs. This caused some tension between Cline and producer Bradley, but the result was an appeal to a much broader audience. On March 5, 1963, Cline sang a benefit concert in Kansas City and then boarded a plane for Nashville with band members Hawkshaw Hawkins, Cowboy Copas, and manager/pilot Randy Hughes. The plane crashed just ninety miles outside of Nashville, killing everyone on board. Her music stayed in the public spotlight for a few more years as her label released several posthumous records. Her music drifted out of the spotlight in the 1970s when the industry started to shift away from the Nashville Sound. Several high-profile artists brought her music back a few years later. Loretta Lynn, one of Patsy's dearest female friends in the music industry, recorded an album of her songs called *I Remember Patsy*. Three years later, writer and entertainment executive Ellis Nassour published a biography of her. Eventually k.d. lang covered several of her songs, and in 1985, a Hollywood film starring Jessica Lange entitled *Sweet Dreams* was released. The film chronicled her career and troubled relationships, including her marriage to second husband Charlie Dick. ♪

Jim Reeves left a mark on the male country vocal that would never be extinguished. Originally from Panola County, Texas, Reeves, a former baseball player, began his career as a hillbilly singer. He signed a recording contract with an independent label in 1952 and spent the next several years touring, recording honky-tonk songs, and performing on the *Louisiana Hayride*. After recording a few hits such as "Mexican Joe," he was asked to join the Grand Ole Opry and signed a recording contract with RCA (see appendix C). At RCA, producer Chet Atkins added backup vocals and a sleeker, more sophisticated arrangement to go along with his smooth vocals. The formula that Atkins used seemed to work, and in 1957, Reeves had his first crossover hit with "Four Walls." This recording topped the country charts and went to number eleven on the pop charts. The formula of downplaying the twang, steel guitar, and honky-tonk elements was essentially the same formula of the teen crooner artists who crossed over to pop. ♪

The musicians who played on the crossover hits were the same ones who played on the rockabilly and rock-and-roll hits. These Nashville players were also the ones who played on the country hits. The difference was just in production style, arrangement, and the audience to which the different styles were pitched. For instance, the Nashville Sound recordings were not pitched to the teen audience.

Nashville's pop song structure began to morph country music into a subgenre known as Countrypolitan. Countrypolitan targeted mainstream markets and sold well throughout the later 1960s and early 1970s. This success was remarkable during a time when most of American popular music was being overshadowed by the British Invasion. Some of the top artists in Countrypolitan included Tammy Wynette, Lynn Anderson, and Charlie Rich, as well as former "hard country" artists Ray Price and Marty Robbins (see appendix C).

While visiting Nashville, Opry star Porter Wagoner heard Tammy Wynette and offered her a spot singing on one of his tours. Wynette then moved to Nashville in 1965 and signed with Billy Sherrill, a producer with Epic Records and the person responsible for shaping the "classic" country sound. She was called the "First Lady of Country"; her first hit was "Apartment No. 9," but her best-known song was "Stand by Your Man." This song was one of the best-selling hit singles by a country female until Dolly Parton came out with "9 to 5." Many of her hits dealt with classic themes of loneliness, divorce, and the difficulties of man-woman relationships. During the late 1960s and early 1970s, Wynette charted twenty-three number-one songs. Along with Loretta Lynn and Dolly Parton, Tammy Wynette is given credit for defining the role of women in country music during the 1970s. ♪

In spite of the Nashville Sound's popularity and broad appeal, many traditional country artists began to emerge during this period and dominate the genre; some of the artists who were a part of this movement include Loretta Lynn, Merle Haggard, Buck Owens, Porter Wagoner, and Sonny James (see appendix C).

Loretta Lynn's songs focused on blue-collar women's issues with themes about philandering husbands and persistent mistresses, topics usually inspired by issues she faced in her own marriage with Doolittle Lynn. In song after song, Loretta Lynn always managed to speak up for women and women's rights. She pushed the boundaries in the conservative genre of country music by singing about birth control ("The Pill"), repeated childbirth ("One's on the Way"), and being widowed by the draft during the Vietnam War ("Dear Uncle Sam"). In 1980, her best-selling 1976 autobiography *Coal Miner's Daughter* was made into an Academy Award–winning film starring Sissy Spacek and Tommy Lee Jones. ♪

Country Soul and Crossover

In 1962, Ray Charles made an unexpected turn with his pop music audience and started to focus his attention on country and western music. He suddenly found himself on top of the *Billboard* pop chart with the song "I Can't Stop Loving You" and recorded the groundbreaking album entitled *Modern Sounds in Country and Western Music*. Charles is a good example that it was not only the Nashville Sound that was trying to cross over to other genres. He started in pop and crossed over into the country market. ♪

The Bakersfield Sound

Hardcore honky-tonk and western swing finally got together and created another subgenre of country music by 1966. Because of where it originated, 112 miles north-northwest of Los Angeles in Bakersfield, California, it was referred to as the "Bakersfield Sound." It relied on electric instruments and amplification, in particular the Telecaster electric guitar, and was heavily influenced by one-time West Coast residents Bob Wills and Lefty Frizzel. More than other subgenres of country during this era, it was described as having a sharp, driving, no-frills, edgy flavor. Some of the artists who led the way with this style were Buck Owens, Merle Haggard, Tommy Collins, Gary Allen, and Wynn Stewart, all eventually formulating their own brand and interpretation (see appendix C).

Buck Owens's signature style was based on simple storylines, infectious choruses, a twangy electric guitar, an insistent drum track placed forward in the mix, and high two-part vocal harmonies sung by Owens and his guitarist, Don Rich. ♪

Along with Buck Owens, Merle Haggard and his band the Strangers helped create the Bakersfield Sound. A songwriter, singer, guitarist, fiddler, and instrumentalist, Haggard's sound was characterized by the unique twang of the Fender Telecaster, a traditional country steel guitar sound, new vocal harmony styles in which words were minimal, and a rough edge not heard on the more polished Nashville Sound records of the same era. By the 1970s, Haggard had begun to align with the growing outlaw movement and has continued to record and release successful albums into the 2000s. In 1997, Merle Haggard was inducted into the Country Music Hall of Fame.

Country Rock

The late 1960s in American music produced a unique blend of sounds as a result of the traditionalist backlash within the separate genres of music. In the aftermath of the British Invasion, many desired a return to the "old values" of rock and roll. At the same time, there was a lack of enthusiasm in the country sector for Nashville-produced music. What resulted was a cross-bred genre known as country rock. Early innovators in this new style of music in the 1960s and 1970s included Bob Dylan, who was the first to revert to country music with his 1967 album, *John Wesley Harding*, and even more with that album's follow-up, *Nashville Skyline*. Other artists that got in on the action were Gene Clark from the Byrds, Gram Parsons from Sweetheart of the Rodeo, the Flying Burrito Brothers, Clarence White, Michael Nesmith of the Monkees, the Grateful Dead, Neil Young, the Allman Brothers, the Marshall Tucker Band, and the Eagles. The Rolling Stones even got into the style with songs like "Honky Tonk Women" and "Dead Flowers."

Gram Parsons's work in the early 1970s was known for its purity and for his appreciation of aspects of traditional country music. He was given the title of "Father of Country Rock," but his career was cut tragically short by his death in 1973. His legacy was carried on by his protégée and duet partner, Emmylou Harris, who would release her debut solo album in 1975. This album in particular was a blend of country, rock and roll, folk, blues, and pop.

After the initial blending of some of these polar opposite genres, other brand-new genres soon resulted, such as southern rock, heartland rock, and alternative country. In the decades that followed, artists such as Juice Newton, Alabama, Hank Williams Jr., Shania Twain, Brooks & Dunn, Faith Hill, Garth Brooks, Dwight Yoakam, Dolly Parton, Rosanne Cash, and Linda Ronstadt moved country further and further toward a heavy rock influence.

Decline of Western Music and the Cowboy Ballad

By the late 1960s, the cowboy ballad and western music was beginning to decline. Popular western recording stars released albums only to have moderate success while rock and roll was dominating music sales. The Hollywood recording studios were even beginning to drop most of their western artists. The geographic shift in country music production to the city of Nashville also played a major role in the change. The Nashville Sound, country rock, and rockabilly music styles dominated over both "cowboy" artists and the more recent Bakersfield Sound. The latter was limited to certain artists such as Buck Owens, Merle Haggard, and a few others. During this process, country and western music as a genre lost most of its southwestern, ranchera, and Tejano musical influences. Nevertheless, when the new genre of "outlaw country" music emerged from Texas and Oklahoma and became popular in the 1970s, the once-forgotten cowboy ballad and honky-tonk music would be resurrected and reinterpreted.

FOURTH GENERATION (1970s–1980s)

Music produced in the fourth generation (1970s–1980s) included outlaw country and country pop or soft pop, with roots in the Countrypolitan sound, folk music, and soft rock. Between 1972 and 1975, singer/guitarist John Denver released a series of highly successful songs blending country and folk-rock musical styles. During the early 1980s, country artists continued to see their records perform well on the pop charts. In 1980, a style of "neocountry disco music" was popularized. During the mid-1980s, a group of new artists began to emerge who rejected the more polished country-pop sound that had been prominent on radio and the charts in favor of more traditional "back-to-basics" production.

Outlaw Country

Outlaw country was a combination of the traditional western and honky-tonk musical styles of the late 1950s and 1960s. One artist who was included in this subgenre is Ray Price. His band, the Cherokee Cowboys, included both Willie Nelson and Roger Miller. A big part of the outlaw country movement was the anger of an alienated subculture in the nation. This along with the outlaw country sound revolutionized the genre of country music during this time period. The term "outlaw country" is traditionally associated with Hank Williams Jr., Willie Nelson, Waylon Jennings, Kris Kristofferson, Michael Martin Murphey, and the later career resurgence of Johnny Cash, with a few female vocalists such as Jessi Colter and Sammi Smith. The best example of this sound is found in the 1976 album *Wanted! The Outlaws* (see appendix C). ♪

Better known as Hank Williams Jr. or Bocephus, Randall Hank Williams's musical style is considered to be a blend of southern rock, blues, and traditional country. He is the son of legendary country singer Hank Williams and began his career by following in his father's footsteps, singing his father's songs and imitating his style.

Willie Nelson was born during the Great Depression and was raised by his grandparents. He wrote his first song at the age of seven and joined his first band at ten. During his high school years, he played guitar and sang lead vocals for a band called Bohemian Polka. In 1958, he moved to Houston, Texas, after signing a contract with D Records. During this time, he wrote songs that would be country standards, including "Funny How Time Slips Away," "Hello Walls," "Pretty Paper," and "Crazy." In 1960, he moved to Nashville and later signed a publishing contract with Pamper Music, which allowed him to join Ray Price's band as a bassist. During the mid-1980s, while recording hit albums like *Honeysuckle Rose* and hit singles like "On the Road Again," "To All the Girls I've Loved Before," and "Pancho and Lefty," he joined the supergroup the Highwaymen, along with singers Johnny Cash, Waylon Jennings, and Kris Kristofferson. ♪

During the 1990s and 2000s, Nelson continued touring extensively and released albums every year. Reviews ranged from positive to mixed. He explored genres such as reggae, blues, jazz, and folk.

Waylon Arnold Jennings was born in Littlefield, Texas, just north of Lubbock, in 1937. He began playing guitar at eight and began performing on KVOW radio at the age of twelve. His first band was called the Texas Longhorns. His father drove a truck for a living and "picked" Jimmie Rodgers tunes on guitar for fun. From then on, Waylon turned to music with every chance he got, trying to imitate his favorite singer, Ernest Tubb. He once even broke off a broomstick so that he could play air-guitar. In 1958, Buddy Holly arranged Jennings's first recording session and then hired him to play bass. In Clear Lake, Iowa, Jennings gave up his seat on the ill-fated flight that crashed and killed Buddy Holly, J. P. Richardson, and others. The day of the flight was later known as "the Day the Music Died." Jennings formed a rockabilly club band called

the Waylors and recorded for independent Trend Records and A & M
Records but then achieved creative control with RCA Victor. ♪

Country Pop

A subgenre that first came about in the 1970s, country pop or soft
pop had its roots in the Countrypolitan sound, folk music, and soft
rock. Although the term first referred to country songs and artists that
crossed over to top 40, country pop artists are now more likely to cross
over into adult contemporary. It started with pop singers who had hits
on the country charts. Some of these artists were Glen Campbell, Bob-
bie Gentry, John Denver, Olivia Newton-John, Anne Murray, Marie
Osmond, B. J. Thomas, the Bellamy Brothers, and Linda Ronstadt (see
appendix C).

Between 1972 and 1975, singer/guitarist John Denver released a series
of enormously successful songs blending country and folk-rock musical
styles and was named Country Music Entertainer of the Year in 1975.
Some of the songs he released were "Rocky Mountain High," "Sunshine
on My Shoulders," "Annie's Song," "Thank God I'm a Country Boy," and
"I'm Sorry." In 1974, an Australian pop singer, Olivia Newton-John, won
the Best Female Country Vocal Performance as well as the Country Music Association's most coveted award for females, Female Vocalist of the
Year. In response to her winning this award and the new trend, George
Jones, Tammy Wynette, and a few other traditional Nashville country artists formed the short-lived Association of Country Entertainers in 1974. ♪

George Glenn Jones, born in Saratoga, Texas, on September 12,
1931, first heard country music when he was seven and was given a
guitar at the age of nine. Jones learned how to sing country music by
imitating his idols, Roy Acuff, Hank Williams, and Lefty Frizzell. He
was destined to sing sad songs one way or another because when he was
born his doctor dropped him and broke his arm. Jones achieved international fame for his long list of hits, including "White Lightning," which,
in 1959, launched his career as a singer. Jones was also known for his
distinct voice and phrasing but received his inspiration from Hank Williams. For the last twenty years of his life, Jones was frequently referred
to as the greatest living singer in country music. ♪

Born in Sevier County, Tennessee, Dolly Rebecca Parton (known as
Dolly Parton) is a singer-songwriter, instrumentalist, actress, author,

businesswoman, and philanthropist known primarily for her work in country music. She began writing serious songs when she was about seven years of age. Her career began as a child performer on the radio and then by recording a few singles at the age of thirteen. Relocating to Nashville at age eighteen in 1964, her first commercial successes were as a songwriter.

In 1999, she was inducted into the Country Music Hall of Fame. She has composed more than three thousand songs, the best known of which include "I Will Always Love You" (a two-time U.S. country chart-topper for Parton, as well as an international pop hit for Whitney Houston). ♪

During the mid-1970s, Dolly Parton was considered to be a very successful mainstream country artist who managed to launch a high profile campaign to cross over into pop music. In 1977, her hit "Here You Come Again" topped the U.S. country singles chart and also reached number three on the pop singles charts. Parton's male counterpart, Kenny Rogers, had an entirely different approach: he pushed his music toward the country charts after a successful career in pop, rock, and folk music. Kenny's hit "Lucille" topped the country charts and reached number five on the U.S. pop singles charts. Both Parton and Rogers would simultaneously continue to have success on the country and pop charts well into the 1980s. Crystal Gayle, Ronnie Milsap, and Barbara Mandrell were recording artists who also found success on the pop charts. ♪

As a member of the Country Music Hall of Fame, Kenneth Donald "Kenny" Rogers has charted more than 120 hit singles across various music genres. Though most of his success has been with country audiences, he was a pop singer early in his career but made a shrewd move to country music in the 1970s. His gritty voice was perfectly suited to country music's story songs.

A country music singer and pianist, Ronnie Lee Milsap was one of country music's most popular and influential performers of the 1970s and 1980s. He became country music's first successful blind singer, and was one of the most successful and versatile country "crossover" singers of his time. Milsap appealed to both country and pop music markets with hit songs that incorporated pop, R&B, and rock-and-roll elements. ♪

A 2009 Country Music Hall of Fame inductee, Barbara Ann Mandrell was born in Houston, Texas, on December 25, 1948. She is known for a series of top-ten hits and TV shows in the 1970s and 1980s that helped her become one of country's most successful female vocalists during that era.

Mandrell's proficiency with the steel guitar is what led her into a professional performing career. Joe Maphis and Chet Atkins heard twelve-year-old Barbara play the steel guitar at an annual trade show in Chicago in 1960. Since Barbara was living in California at the time, Maphis recommended her to start playing on the Town Hall Party in Los Angeles. By the time she hit Nashville in 1969, her versatility as a musician was taking priority over her ambition to become a lead vocalist. Recording for Columbia and producer Billy Sherrill, she began to create a sound that was closer to the Motown and Memphis sound than it was to country. Nonetheless, whatever style she chose to record, she became one of the superstars of country music. Like Johnny Cash, she was brilliant at self-promotion and was extraordinarily skilled at getting her name before the widest possible audience. Her weekly television show in the early eighties presented her and her sisters to a large audience who enjoyed all styles of music, including country. It was said that her show looked more like Las Vegas than Nashville, but she would include tunes that showcased the full range of her abilities. The songs ranged from sexy to religious and she would include dance routines as well as her ability to play one instrument after another. ♪

In 1975, author Paul Hemphill stated in the *Saturday Evening Post*, "Country music isn't really country anymore; it is a hybrid of nearly every form of popular music in America." During the early 1980s, country artists continued to see their records perform well on the pop charts. Willie Nelson and Juice Newton each had two songs in the top five of the *Billboard* Hot 100 in the early eighties: Nelson charted "Always on My Mind" (number five, 1982) and "To All the Girls I've Loved Before" (number five, 1984), and Newton achieved success with "Queen of Hearts" (number two, 1981) and "Angel of the Morning" (number four, 1981). Four country songs topped the *Billboard* Hot 100 in the 1980s: "Lady" by Kenny Rogers, from late fall 1980, "9 to 5" by Dolly Parton, "I Love a Rainy Night" by Eddie Rabbitt (the latter two back-to-back at the top in early 1981), and "Islands in the Stream," a duet by Dolly Parton and Kenny Rogers in 1983, which was written by Barry, Robin, and Maurice Gibb of the Bee Gees. Newton's "Queen of Hearts" almost reached number one, but was kept out of the spot by the pop ballad juggernaut "Endless Love" by Diana Ross and Lionel Richie. Although there were few crossover hits in the latter half of the 1980s, one song—Roy Orbison's "You Got It," from 1989—made the top ten of both the *Billboard* "Hot Country Singles" and Hot 100 charts. The record-setting, multi-platinum group Alabama was named Artist of the Decade for the 1980s by the Academy of Country Music.

Quartet Groups

Until the emergence of the Statler Brothers, the Oak Ridge Boys, and Alabama, quartets usually just performed for other artists as backing vocals. However, in the 1970s and 1980s, these groups became some of the most popular bands and musical superstars.

The Statler Brothers were boyhood friends who sang gospel music together while they were still in high school in Staunton, Virginia. They first called themselves the Kingsmen and sang in the same style as the Statesmen Quartet and the Blackwood Brothers. They eventually selected the name Statler and traveled throughout the Upper South singing a mixture of country, pop, and gospel. They started touring with Johnny Cash in 1964 and stayed with him for eight-and-a-half years. Although known as a gospel quartet, they always performed a variety of styles. ♪

The Oak Ridge Boys also came to country music from a background in gospel. Their beginnings date back to 1945 when named for a nearby atomic energy plant and founded by Wally Fowler in Knoxville, Tennessee. After going through many personnel changes in the sixties, they began to be a bit controversial in the gospel field with their long hair, flashy apparel, mix of secular and gospel material, and their sexy choreography on stage. They began incorporating some country songs into their Las Vegas show in the seventies and eventually produced hits in the country market such as "Ya'll Come Back Saloon," "Leaving Louisiana in the Broad Daylight," "Trying to Love Two Women," and the biggest hit of all, "Elvira." This was a fifties-style rockabilly tune that vaulted to the top of the country chart, crossed over into pop radio, and won them a Grammy. ♪

Alabama cultivated a large audience of young and old listeners with a style that was part country and part pop-rock with a hint of southern rock. Unlike many other "group" bands, the members of Alabama did not come from other genres. They succeeded with the same sound they were playing as teenagers in the clubs of Myrtle Beach, South Carolina. The group focused on close harmonies along with the mellow lead singing of Randy Owen. ♪

The Nitty Gritty Dirt Band had the biggest hit of their careers in 1970 with the song "Mr. Bojangles," but their blend of youth and country music came together in 1972 when they recorded the album *Will the Circle Be Unbroken*. They had started out as a jug band in Orange County, California, in the mid-1960s, but like other young bands they were ultra-eclectic, playing everything from mountain music and bluegrass to hard rock. ♪

Neocountry

In 1980, the film *Urban Cowboy* popularized a style of "neocountry disco music." This movie also included more traditional songs such as "The Devil Went Down to Georgia" by the Charlie Daniels Band. Sales in record stores shot straight up to $250 million in 1981; by 1984, nine hundred radio stations began programming country or neocountry pop on a full-time basis. However, as trends sometimes go, by 1984 sales had dropped below 1979 figures. ♪

Truck-Driving Country

Truck-driving country music is a fusion of honky-tonk, country rock, and the Bakersfield Sound. Its lyrics focus on a truck driver's lifestyle, but it has the tempo of country rock and the emotion of honky-tonk. Truck-driving country songs often talk about trucks and love. Some of the artists who sing truck-driving country songs include Dave Dudley, Red Sovine, Dick Curless, Red Simpson, Del Reeves, the Willis Brothers, and Jerry Reed. Dudley is often called the father of truck-driving country. ♪

Neotraditionalist Movement

During the mid-1980s, a group of artists began to emerge who rejected the more polished country-pop sound that had been prominent on radio and the charts. Instead, their sound was more traditional with "back-to-basics" production. This movement was led by Randy Travis as his 1986 debut album *Storms of Life* sold four million copies and was *Billboard*'s year-end top country album of 1987. Many of the artists during the latter half of the 1980s drew on traditional honky-tonk, bluegrass, folk, and western swing. Travis Tritt, Keith Whitley, Alan Jackson, Ricky Skaggs, Patty Loveless, Kathy Mattea, George Strait, and the Judds were some of the artists who exemplified this sound (see appendix C).

Randy Bruce Traywick was born in Marshville, North Carolina, on May 4, 1959, but was known professionally as "Randy Travis." He was a singer, songwriter, guitarist, and actor who was heralded as being the bright new hope of traditionalism. His sound was somewhat reminiscent of Lefty Frizzell. Considered a pivotal figure in the history of country music, Travis broke through in the mid-1980s with the release of his album *Storms of Life*, which sold more than four million copies. This was the album that established him as a major force in the neotraditional country movement. ♪

George Strait, a genuine cowboy, grew up on a ranch near Pearsall, Texas, on May 18, 1952, and is known as the "King of Country" and one of the most influential and popular recording artists of all time. He is known for his neotraditionalist country style, cowboy looks, and being one of the first major country artists to bring country music back to its roots and away from the pop country era in the 1980s. He never got into the outlaw mania, even though Austin was only thirty miles away. Instead, he wanted his music to reflect shuffle beat and Texas swing rhythms he had grown up with, including the vocal stylings of men like Ray Price, George Jones, and Merle Haggard. ♪

Ricky Lee Skaggs, born on July 18, 1954, wedded country music and bluegrass, working in the industry as a singer, musician, producer, and composer, to become one of the most influential mainstream stars of the 1980s. He primarily plays mandolin; however, he also plays fiddle, guitar, mandocaster, and banjo. ♪

The Judds were a colorful storybook country music duo composed of Naomi Judd and her daughter, Wynonna Judd (born in 1964), who effortlessly projected downhome charm and uptown glamour from the moment they hit the country scene in 1983.

In 1984, the Judd's number-one recording of "Mama He's Crazy" brought fresh harmonies and an acoustic sound to the country music audience. With Naomi making a point to stress family orientation and Appalachian origins, they were sometimes referred to as traditionalists with songs like "Grandpa, Tell Me 'bout the Good Old Days." ♪

FIFTH GENERATION (1990s)

During the fifth generation (1990s), country music became a worldwide phenomenon thanks to Garth Brooks. The Dixie Chicks became one of the most popular country bands in the 1990s and early 2000s. Country music was aided by a significant expansion of FM radio in the 1980s by adding numerous higher-fidelity FM signals to rural and suburban areas. Before the 1980s, country music was mainly heard on rural AM radio stations, but talk radio eventually overtook AM. The country music stations that were able to stay on AM developed the classic country format for their audiences. At the same time, beautiful music stations already in rural areas began abandoning the format to adopt country music as well. This availability of country music led producers to polish their product for a wider audience. Another force leading to changes in the country music industry was the changing sound of rock music, which was also being influenced by the alternative rock scene. A number of "classic rock" artists, especially Southern rock ones such as Charlie Daniels and Lynyrd Skynyrd, are more closely associated with the modern country music scene than that of the modern rock scene.

Clint Black was born in Long Branch, New Jersey, but grew up in Houston where he absorbed the sounds of pop-rock and honky-tonk country. Being blessed with good looks and a strong resemblance to Roy Rogers helped him greatly during the unfolding age of music videos. From this time forward, Black built his style and image as a pop-country performer (see appendix C). ♪

Troyal Garth Brooks was known for his remarkable ability to fuse the dynamics of rock culture with the traditional ways of country music. This uncanny ability to blur the lines between rock and country earned him his popularity with the public.

Brooks was a genius at fusing musical styles and cultural symbols—rock and country, cowboy costumes, and rock concert mannerisms and staging devices. He used a wireless microphone that would allow him to roam freely and would also employ ropes and pulleys that would fly him across the stage like Peter Pan. He was a master at marketing—his major at Oklahoma State University—and was known for self-promoting and offering his albums to his fans directly at below-market prices. Many of the attendees who Garth lured to his concerts were people who had never listened to country music before. Some of them were simply intrigued by what they had heard about the staging and trappings that took place during his concerts. For traditionalists, he became the bane of their existence, some even calling him "anti-Hank." Even though he was a totally different performer than Hank Williams, songs such as "The Dance," "If Tomorrow Never Comes," "Unanswered Prayers," and "Friends in Low Places" had memorable melodies and lyrically told the types of stories that seemed to attract a new generation of country listeners. ♪

Trisha Yearwood, a banker's daughter from Monticello, Georgia, became one of the most respected vocalists in country music when she launched her first album and single in 1991. This first hit in 1991 was a mid-tempo story song called "She's in Love with the Boy." ♪

Vince Gill started out wanting to play like Chet Atkins. At age ten, the young Oklahoman got a Gibson ES 335 just so he could get that Chet Atkins sound. He then started working in the country music industry in the early 1980s, but his career didn't really start to climb until he recorded the album *When I Call Your Name* in 1989 (see appendix C). ♪

Other artists that experienced success during this time included Clint Black, Sammy Kershaw, Aaron Tippin, Travis Tritt, Kenny Chesney, Mark Chesnut, Alan Jackson, and the newly formed duo of Brooks & Dunn. George Strait's career began in the 1980s but continued to have widespread success during the 1990s and beyond. Toby Keith began his career as a pop-oriented country singer in the 1990s but evolved into more of an outlaw country artist in the late 1990s with *Pull My Chain* and its follow-up, *Unleashed*. Female artists during this time period included Reba McEntire, Patty Loveless, Faith Hill, Martina McBride, Deana Carter, LeAnn Rimes, Mindy McCready, Lorrie Morgan, Shania Twain, and Mary Chapin Carpenter. All of these ladies released platinum-selling albums during the 1990s.

Born the youngest child with four older sisters, Alan Eugene Jackson was born on October 17, 1958, and grew up in the small town of Newnan, Georgia. He is known for blending traditional honky-tonk and mainstream country sounds and penning many of his own hits. In 2001, Jackson recorded "Where Were You When the World Stopped Turning?"—a sensitive and heartfelt song written about the 9/11 disasters in New York. It was a masterpiece of compassion and became an enormous hit and commercial success for Jackson. ♪

Keith Urban was born in New Zealand but started his country music career in Brisbane, Australia. He moved to Nashville in the early nineties just as the commercial boom in country music was beginning to peak. His abilities as a guitar player earned him respect as a session musician and helped him make some inroads in a genre that is sometimes reluctant to accept outsiders. Keith signed with Capitol Records and started to create hits with songs that were anchored by electric guitar hooks and heavy studio processing. Most of his songs are radio friendly with optimistic lyrics about love, such as "Somebody Like You" and "Sweet Thing." There is little connection between Urban and groups like Rascal Flatts to hard-core country styles, but nonetheless, they make an attempt to pay homage to the traditions of country with their songwriting craft and instrumental/vocal virtuosity. Bands like this are often paired with a rock group in concerts, which allow them to act like country music ambassadors, broadening the listening audience for country radio. ♪

Brooks & Dunn is a country music duo consisting of Kix Brooks and Ronnie Dunn and was founded in 1990 by the suggestion of Tim DuBois. Prior to this, both members were solo recording artists. The duo's material is known for containing influences of honky-tonk, mainstream country, and rock, as well as the contrast between their singing voices and onstage personalities. ♪

Reba McEntire began her career in the music industry as a high school student singing in the Kiowa High School band, on local radio shows with her siblings, and at the rodeos to which they would travel. While a sophomore in college, she performed the national anthem at the National Rodeo in Oklahoma City and caught the attention of country artist Red Steagall, who brought her to Nashville, Tennessee. She signed a contract with Mercury Records a year later in 1975, released her first solo album in 1977, and released five additional studio albums under the label by 1983. ♪

In the early nineties, McEntire, Garth Brooks, and Clint Black established sales records for CDs and box office receipts that surpassed those attained by entertainers in any other field of music.

Faith Hill grew up attending an all-white school but was fascinated with black gospel music, even frequently attending African American church services. A 1975 performance by Elvis Presley was the first concert she had ever attended, but it was a Reba McEntire concert ten years later that convinced her to pursue stardom. She was also obsessed with the singing of Aretha Franklin, wanting to soak up as much of her as possible. Hill's first two albums, *Take Me As I Am* (1993) and *It Matters to Me* (1995), established her as a popular country singer. ♪

Singer and actor, Samuel Timothy "Tim" McGraw's rough-around-the-edges delivery is instantly identifiable as he blends traditional and contemporary country in a rock-style concert manner without alienating the country purist. His recording of the song "Indian Outlaw" was the first hit to really inaugurate his career as a superstar. McGraw's style of contemporary country is a sound not suited for every country listener, but his fans follow him and purchase his music faithfully. Taylor Swift wrote a song about him, "Tim McGraw," and released it as her first single in 2006. In this song, she transforms McGraw from a superstar "hat" act into the new patriarch of contemporary country music. ♪

Martina McBride was signed to RCA Nashville in 1991 and made her debut the following year as a neotraditionalist country singer with the single "The Time Has Come." Over time, she developed a pop-styled crossover sound similar to that of Shania Twain and Faith Hill and has had a string of major hit singles on the *Billboard* country chart and occasionally on the adult contemporary chart. Five of these singles went to number one on the country chart between 1995 and 2001, and one peaked at number one on the adult contemporary chart in 2003. ♪

LeAnn Rimes made her breakthrough into country music in 1996 with her debut album, *Blue*, which reached number one on the Top Country Albums chart and was certified multi-platinum in sales by the Recording Industry Association of America (RIAA). The album's leadoff single, "Blue," became a top ten hit and Rimes gained national acclaim for her similarity to Patsy Cline's vocal style. She was only thirteen at the time. ♪

Singer/songwriter Shania Twain's good looks were a big part of her packaging that would allow husband and producer Mutt Lange to turn her into the most commercially successful female artist in country music history. Twain has since become one of the world's best-selling artists of all time, having sold more that seventy-five million albums worldwide. Her numerous accolades very quickly garnered her the title "queen of country pop." ♪

The Dixie Chicks came to mainstream country after a lengthy experience in Texas as bluegrass musicians. The Erwin sisters (Emily on five-string banjo and Martie on fiddle) had played bluegrass music in Dallas since 1984 as teenagers. In 1989, they joined with Laura Lynch and Robin Macy to create the first version of the Dixie Chicks. Their name came from a song performed by the rock band Little Feat. Between 1989 and 1993 they moved from singing on the street corners to opening for such major acts like Garth Brooks and performing for President Clinton's inaugural ball. ♪

Amid all the activity of these popular artists, in the early to mid-1990s, country western music was influenced by the popularity of line dancing. By the end of the decade, however, at least one line dance choreographer complained that good country line-dancing music was no longer being released. In contrast, artists such as Don Williams and George Jones, who had had more or less consistent chart success through the 1970s and 1980s suddenly had their record sales fall rapidly around 1991 as these new artists began to rise.

SIXTH GENERATION (2000s–PRESENT)

The sixth generation (2000s–present) is exemplified by country singer Carrie Underwood. The influence of rock music in country has become more overt during the late 2000s and early 2010s. Attempts to combine punk and country were pioneered by Jason and the Scorchers, and in the 1980s Southern Californian cowpunk scene with bands like the Long Riders. Hip-hop also made its mark on country music with the emergence of country rap. Most of the best-selling country songs of this era, however, were in the country pop genre, such as those by Lady Antebellum, Florida Georgia Line, and Taylor Swift.

Lady Antebellum is a country music group formed in Nashville, Tennessee, in 2006, which quickly became known for their male/female close harmonies fused with seventies rock-influenced instrumentation. The group is composed of Hillary Scott (lead and background vocals), Charles Kelley (lead and background vocals, guitar), and Dave Haywood (background vocals, guitar, piano, mandolin). Scott is the daughter of country music singer Linda Davis, and Kelley is the brother of pop singer Josh Kelley. ♪

Bluegrass singer-songwriter and musician Alison Maria Krauss was the real groundbreaker and one of the first true superstars to emerge in the bluegrass idiom. She entered the music industry at an early age, winning local talent contests by the age of ten. Krauss began experimenting with bluegrass music around 1983, when she was only twelve years old, playing fiddle in and around her hometown. By 1986, she had formed her own band, Union Station, recorded her first album, *Too Late to Cry*, for Rounder Records, and was beginning to realize that she could sing as well as she could play. Despite her instrumental abilities, her voice became her claim to fame. She later released her first album with Union Station as a group in 1989.

She has released fourteen albums, appeared on numerous soundtracks, and helped renew interest in bluegrass music in the United States. Her soundtrack performances have led to further popularity, including the *O Brother Where Art Thou?* soundtrack, an album also credited with raising American interest in bluegrass, and the *Cold Mountain* soundtrack, which led to her performance at the 2004 Academy Awards. ♪

Richard Marx crossed over with his *Days in Avalon* album, which features five country songs and several singers and musicians. Alison Krauss sang background vocals to Marx's single "Straight from My Heart." Also, Bon Jovi had a hit single, "Who Says You Can't Go Home," with Jennifer Nettles of Sugarland. Kid Rock's collaboration with Sheryl Crow, "Picture," was a major crossover hit in 2001 and began Kid Rock's transition from hard rock to a country-rock hybrid that would later produce another major crossover hit, 2008's "All Summer Long." Darius Rucker, former frontman for the 1990s pop-rock band Hootie & the Blowfish, began a country solo career in the late 2000s, one that to date has produced three albums and several hits on both the country charts and the *Billboard* Hot 100. Singer-songwriter Unknown Hinson became famous for his appearance in the Charlotte television show *Wild, Wild South*, after which Hinson started his own band and toured in southern states. Other rock stars who featured a country song on their albums were Don Henley and Poison.

Jennifer Nettles is known primarily for her role as lead vocalist of Sugarland, but before Sugarland's inception, she also fronted Atlanta-based bands Soul Miner's Daughter and the Jennifer Nettles Band. She also charted as a duet partner on the country version of rock band Bon Jovi's 2006 single "Who Says You Can't Go Home," a number-one hit on the *Billboard* country charts. ♪

Country singer Carrie Underwood was born in Muskogee, Oklahoma, but was raised in nearby Checotah, where her family owned a farm. She started singing in church as a child and performed all through high school. Underwood earned a journalism degree from Northeastern State University and while in college competed in beauty pageants and continued to sing in local venues. In 2005, Underwood was the winner of the fourth season of *American Idol* and has since become one of the most prominent recording artists of the last ten years. She has had worldwide sales of more than sixty-four million records and has received six Grammy Awards. Underwood became the only solo country artist to have a nimber-one hit on the *Billboard* Hot 100 chart from 2000 to 2009 with her first single "Inside Your Heaven" and also broke *Billboard* chart history as the first country music artist ever to debut at number-one on the Hot 100. She also made history by becoming the seventh woman to win Entertainer of the Year at the Academy of Country Music Awards, and the first woman in history to win the award twice, as well as twice consecutively. ♪

In addition to Underwood, *American Idol* launched the careers of Kellie Pickler, Josh Gracin, Bucky Covington, Kristy Lee Cook, Danny Gokey, Scotty McCreery, and Lauren Alaina. The series *Nashville Star* launched the careers of Miranda Lambert and Chris Young. *Can You Duet?* produced the duos Steel Magnolia and Joey + Rory.

Brad Paisley was known as a neotraditionalist and gave hope to those who liked the old country sounds. In the last years of the 1990s, Paisley, a devoted disciple of Buck Owens, emerged as the chief torchbearer of hard-core country sounds. Born in 1972 and growing up in rural West Virginia, he could hardly avoid hearing the sounds of genuine country music. His first introduction came from his grandfather, who played Merle Travis-style guitar. He received more training as a musician on the famous *Wheeling Jamboree*, where he played for eight years (see appendix C). ♪

Miranda Lambert, from Lindale, Texas, grew up playing in old-fashioned honky-tonks where she honed her vocal, guitar, and songwriter skills while gaining credibility in the alternative scene. In 2003, she got her big break as a third-place finalist on the reality talent contest *Nashville Star* and later signed to Epic Records. ♪

Teen sitcoms also have had an impact on modern country music, launching the careers of young artists like actress Jennette McCurdy in 2008. She was best known as the sidekick, Sam, on the teen sitcom *iCarly* and released her first single, "So Close," following that with the single "Generation Love" in 2011. Another teen sitcom star, Miley Cyrus (better known as Hannah Montana), also had a crossover hit in the late 2000s with "The Climb" and another with "Ready, Set, Don't Go," a duet with her father, Billy Ray Cyrus. Actress Hayden Panettiere also began recording country songs as part of her role on the TV series *Nashville*. Jana Kramer, an actress in the teen drama *One Tree Hill*, released a country album in 2012 that produced two hit singles in 2013.

Zac Brown Band is a country music band based in Atlanta, Georgia, on the Southern Ground Artists label. Their sound has evolved through the years into a part of the wave of Oceanside country that incorporates a range of reggae influences. ♪

Singer-songwriter Taylor Swift was one of the most commercially successful artists of the late 2000s and early 2010s. Her family moved to the Nashville area from Wyomissing, Pennsylvania, when she was a young teenager for the express purpose of furthering her musical career. She also supposedly rejected an early recording contract and held out for a deal that would afford her more creative control. Where some of her critics would challenge her singing, the one undisputed quality was her songwriting.

Swift released her debut single, "Tim McGraw," at age sixteen. That same year, in 2006, Taylor released her first studio album, *Taylor Swift*, which spent 275 weeks on *Billboard* 200. This was one of the longest runs of any album on that chart. In 2008, Taylor Swift released her second studio album, *Fearless*, which made her the second-longest number one charted on *Billboard* 200. Just behind Adele's *21*, this was also the second best-selling album within the past five years. ♪

The influence of rock music in country has become more obvious during the late 2000s and early 2010s with emerging artists like Eric Church, Jason Aldean, and Brantley Gilbert. Aaron Lewis, former frontman for the rock group Staind, had a moderately successful entry into country music in 2011 and 2012. Also rising in the late 2000s and early 2010s was the insertion of rap and spoken-word elements into country songs with artists such as Cowboy Troy and Colt Ford. They have focused almost exclusively on country rap (also known as "hick hop") while other, more mainstream artists (such as Big & Rich and Jason Aldean) have used it on occasion. In the 2010s, bro-country became popular, a genre noted primarily for its themes of drinking, partying, girls, and driving. Artists associated with this subgenre of country music include Luke Bryan, Jason Aldean, Blake Shelton, and Florida Georgia Line, whose song "Cruise" became the best-selling country song of all time.

ALT-COUNTRY

Jason and the Scorchers attempted to combine punk and country, while in the 1980s, the Southern Californian cowpunk scene was defined by bands like the Long Ryders. These styles merged fully in Uncle Tupelo's 1990 LP *No Depression*. This record is credited as being the first alt-country album, and it gave its name to the online notice board and magazine that underpinned the movement. People associated with Uncle Tupelo formed three major bands in the genre: Wilco, Son Volt, and Bottle Rockets. Other influential bands included Blue Mountain, Whiskeytown and Ryan Adams, Blood Oranges, Bright Eyes, Lucinda Williams, and Drive-by Truckers. Some alt-country songs have been crossover hits, including Ryan Adams's "When the Stars Go Blue." This song charted when it was performed by Tim McGraw. ♪

NOTE

1. Chapter 1 and Appendix C (the biographies) rely on the following resources: Kingsbury and Nash's *Will the Circle Be Unbroken: Country Music in America* (2006); Kingsbury's *The Grand Ole Opry History of Country Music: 70 Years of the Songs, the Stars, and the Stories* (1995); Malone and Neal's *Country Music, USA* (3rd ed., 2013); and Neal's *Country Music: A Cultural and Stylistic History* (2013).

2

SINGING COUNTRY AND VOICE SCIENCE

Scott McCoy

This chapter presents a concise overview of how the voice functions as a biomechanical, acoustic instrument. We will be dealing with elements of anatomy, physiology, acoustics, and resonance. But don't panic: the things you need to know are easily accessible, even if it has been many years since you last set foot in a science or math class!

All musical instruments, including the human voice, have at least four things in common, consisting of a *power source*, *sound source* (vibrator), *resonator*, and a system for *articulation*. In most cases, the person who plays the instrument provides power by pressing a key, plucking a string, or blowing into a horn. This power is used to set the sound source in motion, which creates vibrations in the air that we perceive as sound. Musical vibrators come in many forms, including strings, reeds, and human lips. The sound produced by the vibrator, however, needs a lot of help before it becomes beautiful music—we might think of it as raw material, like a lump of clay that a potter turns into a vase. Musical instruments use resonance to enhance and strengthen the sound of the vibrator, transforming it into sounds we identify as a piano, trumpet, or guitar. Finally, instruments must have a means of articulation to create the nuanced sounds of music. Let's see how these four elements are used to create the sounds of singing.

PULMONARY SYSTEM:
THE POWER SOURCE OF YOUR VOICE

The human voice has a lot in common with a trumpet: both use flaps of tissue as a sound source, both use hollow tubes as resonators, and both rely on the respiratory (pulmonary) system for power. If you stop to think about it, you quickly realize why breathing is so important for singing. First and foremost, it keeps us alive through the exchange of blood gases—oxygen in, carbon dioxide out. But it also serves as the storage depot for the air we use to produce sound. Most singers rarely encounter situations in which these two functions are in conflict, but if you are required to sustain an extremely long phrase, you could find yourself in need of fresh oxygen before your lungs are totally empty.

Misconceptions about breathing for singing are rampant. Fortunately, most are easily dispelled. We must start with a brief foray into the world of physics in the guise of Boyle's Law. Some of you no doubt remember this principle: the pressure of a gas within a container changes inversely with changes of volume. If the quantity of a gas is constant and its container is made smaller, pressure rises. But if we make the container get bigger, pressure goes down. Boyle's law explains everything that happens when we breathe, especially when we combine it with another physical law: *nature abhors a vacuum*. If one location has reduced pressure, air flows from an area of higher pressure to equalize the two, and vice versa. So if we can create a zone of reduced air pressure by expanding our lungs, air automatically flows in to restore balance. When air pressure in the lungs is increased, it has no choice but to flow outward.

As we all know, the air we breathe goes in and out of our lungs. Each lung contains millions and millions of tiny air sacs called *alveoli*, where gases are exchanged. The alveoli also function like ultra-miniature versions of the bladder for a bag pipe, storing the air that will be used to set the vocal folds into vibration. To get the air in and out of them, all we need to do is make the lungs larger for inhalation and smaller for exhalation. Always remember this relationship between cause and effect during breathing: we inhale because we make ourselves large; we exhale because we make ourselves smaller. Unfortunately, the lungs are organs, not muscles, and have no ability on their own to accomplish this feat. For this reason, your bodies came from the factory with special muscles designed to enlarge and compress your entire thorax (rib cage), while simultaneously moving your lungs. We can classify these muscles in two main categories: any muscle that has the ability to increase the volume capacity of the thorax serves an *inspiratory* function; any muscle that has the ability to decrease the volume capacity of the thorax serves an *expiratory* function.

Your largest muscle of inspiration is called the *diaphragm* (figure 2.1). This dome-shaped muscle originates from the bottom of your sternum (breastbone) and completely fills the area from that point around your ribs to your spine. It's the second-largest muscle in your body, but you probably have no conscious awareness of it or ability to directly control

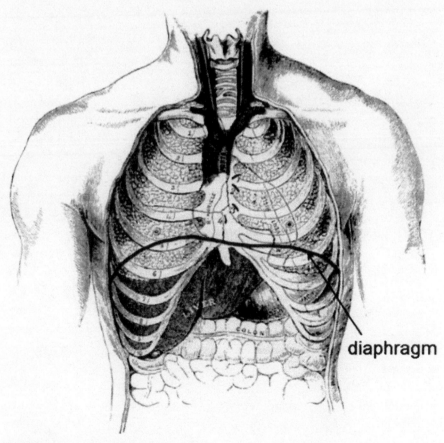

diaphragm

Figure 2.1. Location of diaphram
Dr. Scott McCoy

it. When we take a deep breath, the diaphragm contracts and the central portion flattens out and drops downward a couple inches into your abdomen, pressing against all of your internal organs. If you release tension from your abdominal muscles as you inhale, you will feel a gentle bulge in your upper or lower belly, or perhaps in your back, resulting from the displacement of your innards by the diaphragm. This is a good thing and can be used to let you know you have taken a good inhalation.

The diaphragm is important, but we must remember that it cannot function in isolation. After you inhale, it relaxes and gently returns to its resting position through an action called *elastic recoil*. This movement, however, is entirely passive and makes no significant contribution to generating the pressure required to sustain phonation. Therefore, it makes no sense at all to try to "sing from your diaphragm"—unless you intend to sing while you inhale, not exhale!

Eleven pairs of muscles assist the diaphragm in its inhalatory efforts, which are called the *external intercostal* muscles (figure 2.2). These muscles start from ribs one through eleven and connect at a slight angle downward to ribs two through twelve. When they contract, the entire thorax moves up and out, somewhat like moving a bucket handle. With the diaphragm and intercostals working together, you are able to increase the capacity of your lungs by about three to six liters, depending on your gender and overall physical stature; thus, we have quite a lot of air available to power our voices.

Eleven additional pairs of muscles are located directly under the external intercostals, which, not surprisingly, are called the *internal intercostals* (figure 2.2). These muscles start from ribs two through twelve and connect upward to ribs one through eleven. When they contract, they induce the opposite action of their external partners: the thorax is made smaller, inducing exhalation. Four additional pairs of expiratory muscles are located in the abdomen, beginning with the *rectus* (figure 2.2). The two rectus abdominis muscles run from your pubic bone to your sternum and are divided into four separate portions, called *bellies* of the muscle (lots of muscles have multiple bellies; it is coincidental that the bellies of the rectus are found in the location we colloquially refer to as our belly). Definition of these bellies results in the so-called ripped abdomen or six-pack of body builders and others who are especially fit.

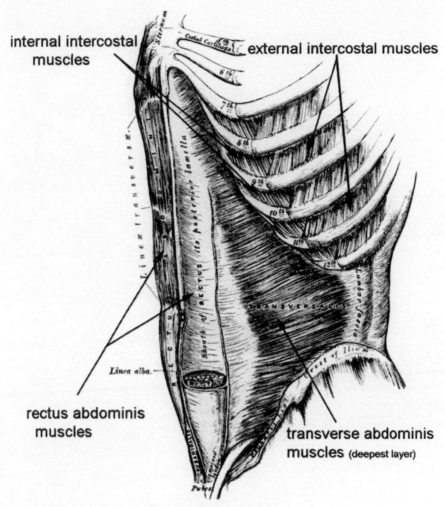

internal intercostal muscles

external intercostal muscles

rectus abdominis muscles

transverse abdominis muscles (deepest layer)

Figure 2.2. Intercostal and abdominal muscles
Dr. Scott McCoy

The largest muscles of the abdomen are called the *external obliques* (figure 2.3), which run at a downward angle from the sides of the rectus, covering the lower portion of the thorax, and extend all the way to the spine. The *internal obliques* lie immediately below, oriented at an angle that crisscrosses the external muscles. They are slightly smaller, beginning at the bottom of the thorax, rather than extending over it. The deepest muscle layer is the *transverse abdominis* (figure 2.3), which is

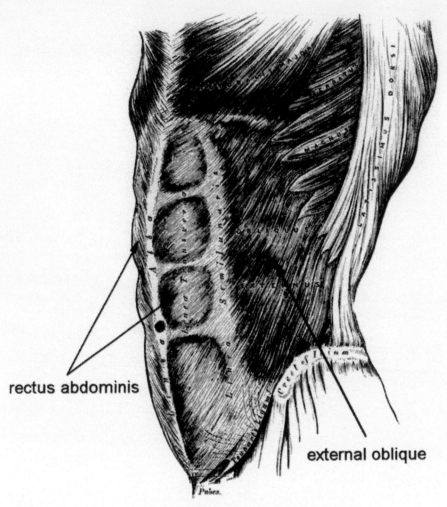

rectus abdominis

external oblique

Figure 2.3. External oblique and rectus abdominus muscles
Dr. Scott McCoy

oriented with fibers that run horizontally. These four muscle pairs completely encase the abdominal region, holding your organs and digestive system in place while simultaneously helping you breathe.

Your expiratory muscles are quite large and can produce a great deal of pulmonary or air pressure. In fact, they easily can overpower the larynx. Healthy adults generally can generate more than twice the pressure that is required to produce even the loudest sounds; therefore, singers must develop a system for moderating and controlling airflow and breath pressure. This practice goes by many names, including breath support, breath control, and breath management, all of which rely on the principle of *muscular antagonism*. Muscles are said to have an antagonistic relationship when they work in opposing directions, usually pulling on a common point of attachment, for the sake of increasing stability or motor control. You can see a clear example of muscular antagonism in the relationship between your biceps (flexors) and triceps (extensors) when you hold out your arm. In breathing for singing, we activate inspiratory muscles (e.g., diaphragm and external intercostals) during exhalation to help control respiratory pressure and the rate at which air is expelled from the lungs.

One of the things you will notice when watching a variety of singers is that they tend to breathe in many different ways. You might think that voice teachers and scientists, who have been teaching and studying singing for hundreds if not thousands of years, would have come to agreement on the best possible breathing technique. But for many reasons, this is not the case. For one, different musical and vocal styles place varying demands on breathing. For another, humans have a huge variety of body types, sizes, and morphologies. A breathing strategy that is successful for a tall, slender woman might be completely ineffective in a short, robust man. Our bodies actually contain a large number of muscles beyond those we've already discussed that are capable of assisting with respiration. For an example, consider your *latissimi dorsi* muscles. These large muscles of the arm enable us to do pull-ups (or pull-downs, depending on which exercise you perform) at the fitness center. But because they wrap around a large portion of the thorax, they also exert an expiratory force. We have at least two dozen such muscles that have secondary respiratory functions, some for exhalation and some for inhalation. When we consider all these possibilities, it is no surprise at all that there are many ways to breathe that can produce beautiful singing. Just remember to practice some muscular antagonism—maintaining a degree of inhalation posture during exhalation—and you should do well.

LARYNX: THE VIBRATOR OF YOUR VOICE

The larynx, sometimes known as the voice box or Adam's apple, is a complex physiologic structure made of cartilage, muscle, and tissue.

Biologically, it serves as a sphincter valve, closing off the airway to prevent foreign objects from entering the lungs. When firmly closed, it also is used to increase abdominal pressure to assist with lifting heavy objects, childbirth, and defecation. But if we gently close this valve while we exhale, tissue in the larynx begins to vibrate and produce the sounds that become speech and singing.

The human larynx is a remarkably small instrument, typically ranging from the size of a pecan to a walnut for women and men, respectively. Sound is produced at a location called the *glottis*, which is formed by two flaps of tissue called the *vocal folds* (aka vocal cords). In women, the glottis is about the size of a dime; in men, it can approach the diameter of a quarter. The two folds are always attached together at their front point but open in the shape of the letter V during normal breathing, an action called *abduction*. To phonate, we must close the V while we exhale, an action called *adduction* (just like the machines you use at the fitness center to exercise your thigh and chest muscles).

Phonation is only possible because of the unique multilayer structure of the vocal folds (figure 2.4). The core of each fold is formed by muscle, which is surrounded by a layer of gelatinous material called the *lamina propria*. The *vocal ligament* also runs through the lamina propria, which helps to prevent injury by limiting how far the folds can be stretched for high pitches. A thin, hairless epithelial layer that is constantly kept moist with mucus secreted by the throat, larynx, and trachea surrounds all of this. During phonation, the outer layer of the fold glides independently over the inner layer in a wavelike motion, without which phonation is impossible.

We can use a simple demonstration to better understand the independence of the inner and outer portions of the folds. Explore the palm of your hand with your other index finger. Note that the skin is attached quite firmly to the flesh beneath it. If you poke at your palm, that flesh acts as padding, protecting the underlying bone. Now explore the back of your hand. You will observe that the skin is attached quite loosely— you easily can move it around with your finger. And if you poke at the back of your hand, it is likely to hurt; there is very little padding between the skin and your bones. Your vocal folds combine the best attributes of both sides of your hand. They provide sufficient padding to help reduce impact stress, while permitting the outer layer to slip like the skin on the back of your hand, enabling phonation to occur. When you are sick

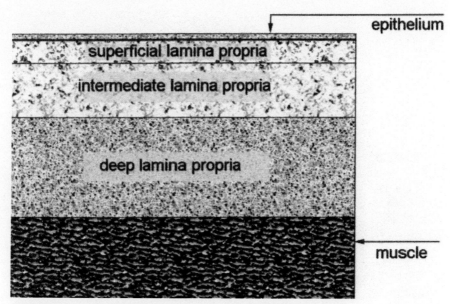

Figure 2.4. Layered structure of the vocal fold
Dr. Scott McCoy

with laryngitis and lose your voice (a condition called *aphonia*), inflammation in the vocal folds couples the layers of the folds tightly together. The outer layer no longer can move independently over the inner, and phonation becomes difficult or impossible.

The vocal folds are located within the five cartilaginous structures of the larynx (figure 2.5). The largest is called the *thyroid* cartilage, which is shaped like a small shield. The thyroid connects to the *cricoid* cartilage below it, which is shaped like a signet ring—broad in the back and narrow in the front. Two cartilages that are shaped like squashed pyramids sit atop the cricoid, called the *arytenoids*. Each vocal fold runs from the thyroid cartilage in front to one of the arytenoids at the back. Finally, the *epiglottis* is located at the top of the larynx, flipping backward each time we swallow to prevent food and liquid from entering our lungs. Muscles connect between the various cartilages to open and close the glottis and to lengthen and shorten the vocal folds for ascending and descending pitch, respectively. Because they sometimes are used to identify vocal function, it is a good idea to know the names of the muscles that control the length of the folds. We've already mentioned that

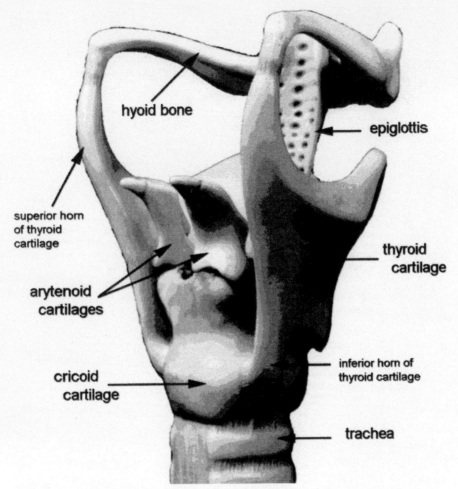

Figure 2.5. Cartilages of the larynx, viewed at an angle from the back
Dr. Scott McCoy

a muscle forms the core of each fold. Because it runs between the thyroid cartilage and an arytenoid, it is named the *thyroarytenoid* muscle (formerly known as the *vocalis* muscle). When the thyroarytenoid, or TA muscle, contracts, the fold is shortened and pitch goes down. The folds are elongated through the action of the *cricothyroid*, or CT muscles, which run from the thyroid to cricoid cartilage.

Vocal color (timbre) is created by the combined effects of the sound produced by the vocal folds and the resonance provided by the vocal tract. While these elements can never be completely separated, it is useful to consider the two primary modes of vocal fold vibration and their resulting sound qualities. The main differences are related to the relative thickness of the folds and their cross-sectional shape (figure 2.6). The first option depends on short, thick folds that come together with nearly square-shaped edges. Vibration in this configuration is given a variety of names, including *mode 1, thyroarytenoid* (TA) *dominant, chest mode,* or *modal voice.* The alternate configuration uses longer, thinner folds that only make contact at their upper margins. Common names include *mode 2, cricothyroid* (CT) *dominant, falsetto mode,* or *loft voice.* Singers vary the vibrational mode of the folds according to the quality of sound they wish to produce.

Before we move on to a discussion of resonance, we must consider the quality of the sound that is produced by the larynx. At the level of the glottis, we create a sound not unlike the annoying buzz of a duck call. That buzz, however, contains all the raw material we need to create speech and singing. Vocal or glottal sound is considered to be *complex,* meaning it consists of many simultaneously sounding frequencies (pitches). The lowest frequency within any tone is called the *fundamental,* which corresponds to its named pitch in the musical scale. Orchestras tune to a pitch called A-440, which means it has a frequency of 440 vibrations per second, or 440 *Hertz* (abbreviated Hz). Additional frequencies are included above the fundamental, which are called *overtones.* Overtones in the glottal sound are quieter than the fundamental. In voices, the overtones usually are whole number multiples of the fundamental, creating a pattern called the *harmonic series* (e.g., 100Hz, 200Hz, 300Hz, 400Hz, 500Hz, etc. or G2, G3, C4, G4, B4—note that

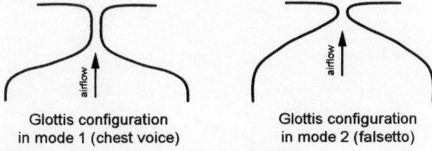

Glottis configuration in mode 1 (chest voice)

Glottis configuration in mode 2 (falsetto)

Figure 2.6. Primary modes of vocal fold vibration
Dr. Scott McCoy

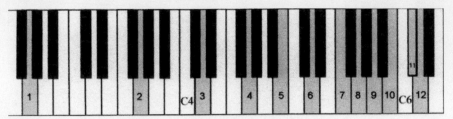

Figure 2.7.   Natural harmonic series, beginning at G2
Dr. Scott McCoy

pitches are named by the international system in which the lowest C of the piano keyboard is C1; middle-C therefore becomes C4, the fourth C of the keyboard) (figure 2.7).

Singers who choose to make coarse or rough sounds as might be appropriate for rock or blues often add overtones that are *inharmonic*, or not part of the standard numerical sequence. Inharmonic overtones also are common in singers with damaged or pathological voices.

Under most circumstances, we are completely unaware of the presence of overtones—they simply contribute to the overall timbre of a voice. In some vocal styles, however, harmonics become a dominant feature. This is especially true in *throat singing* or *overtone singing*, as is found in places like Tuva. Throat singers tune their vocal tracts so precisely that single harmonics are highlighted within the harmonic spectrum as a separate, whistle-like tone. These singers sustain a low-pitched drone and then create a melody by moving from tone to tone within the natural harmonic series. You can learn to do this too. Sustain a comfortable pitch in your range and slowly morph between the vowels /ee/ and /oo/. If you listen carefully, you will hear individual harmonics pop out of your sound.

The mode of vocal fold vibration has a strong impact on the overtones that are produced. In mode 1, high-frequency harmonics are relatively strong; in mode 2, they are much weaker. As a result, mode 1 tends to yield a much brighter, brassier sound.

VOCAL TRACT: YOUR SOURCE OF RESONANCE

Resonance typically is defined as the amplification and enhancement (or enrichment) of musical sound through *supplemental vibration*. What does this really mean? In layman's terms, we could say that resonance makes instruments louder and more beautiful by reinforcing the original vibrations of the sound source. This enhancement occurs in two primary ways, which are known as forced and free resonance (there is nothing pejorative in these terms: free resonance is not superior to forced resonance). Any object that is physically connected to a vibrator can serve as a forced resonator. For a piano, the resonator is the soundboard (on the underside of a grand or on the back of an upright); the vibrations of the strings are transmitted directly to the soundboard through a structure known as the bridge, which also is found on violins and guitars. Forced resonance also plays a role in voice production. Place your hand on your chest and say *ah* at a low pitch. You almost certainly felt the vibrations of forced resonance. In singing, this might best be considered your *private* resonance; you can feel it and it might impact your self-perception of sound, but nobody else can hear it. To understand why this is true, imagine what a violin would sound like if it were encased in a thick layer of foam rubber. The vibrations of the string would be damped out, muting the instrument. Your skin, muscles, and other tissues do the same thing to the vibrations of your vocal folds.

By contrast, free resonance occurs when sound travels through a hollow space, such as the inside of a trumpet, an organ pipe, or your vocal tract, which consists of the pharynx (throat), oral cavity (mouth), and nasal cavity. As sound travels through these regions, a complex pattern of echoes is created; every time sound encounters a change in the shape of the vocal tract, some of its energy is reflected backward, much like an echo in a canyon. If these echoes arrive back at the glottis at the precise moment a new pulse of sound is created, the two elements synchronize, resulting in a significant increase in intensity. All of this happens very quickly—remember that sound is traveling through your vocal tract at more than seven hundred miles per hour.

Whenever this synchronization of the vocal tract and sound source occurs, we say that the system is *in resonance*. The phenomenon occurs at specific frequencies (pitches), which can be varied by changing the position of the tongue, lips, jaw, palate, and larynx. These resonant frequencies, or areas in which strong amplification occurs, are called *formants*. Formants provide the specific amplification that changes the raw, buzzing sound produced by your vocal folds into speech and singing. The vocal tract is capable of producing many formants, which are labeled sequentially by ascending pitch. The first two, F1 and F2, are used to create vowels; higher formants contribute to the overall timbre and individual characteristics of a voice. In some singers, especially those who train to sing in opera, formants three through five are clustered together to form a super formant, eponymously called the *singer's formant*, which creates a ringing sound and enables a voice to be heard in a large theater without electronic amplification.

Formants are vitally important in singing, but they can be a bit intimidating to understand. An analogy that works really well for me is to think of formants like the wind. You cannot see the wind, but you know it is present when you see leaves rustling in a tree or feel a breeze on your face. Formants work in the same manner. They are completely invisible and directly inaudible. But just as we see the rustling leaf, we can hear, and perhaps even feel, the action of formants through how they change our sound. Try a little experiment. Sing an ascending scale beginning at B-flat3, sustaining the vowel /ee/. As you approach the D-natural or E-flat of the scale, you likely will feel (and hear) that your sound becomes a bit stronger and easier to produce. This occurs because the scale tone and formant are on the same pitch, providing additional amplification. If you change to an /oo/ vowel, you will feel the same thing at about the same place in the scale. If you sing to an /oh/ or /eh/ and continue up the scale, you'll feel a bloom in the sound somewhere around C5 (an octave above middle-c); /ah/ is likely to come into its best focus at about G5.

To remember the approximate pitches of the first formants for the main vowels, ee-eh-ah-oh-oo, just think of a C-Major triad in first inversion, open position, starting at E4: ee = E4, eh = C5, ah = G5, oh = C5, and oo = E4 (figure 2.8). If your music theory isn't strong, you could use the mnemonic "**e**very **c**hild **g**ets **c**andy **e**agerly." These pitches might vary by as much as a minor third higher and lower but no farther: once a formant changes by more than that interval, the vowel that is produced *must* change.

Formants have absolutely no preference for what they amplify—they are indiscriminate lovers, just as happy to bond with the first harmonic as the fifth. When men or women sing low pitches, there almost always will be at least one harmonic that comes close enough to a formant to produce a clear vowel sound. The same is not true for women with high voices, especially sopranos, who routinely must sing pitches that have a

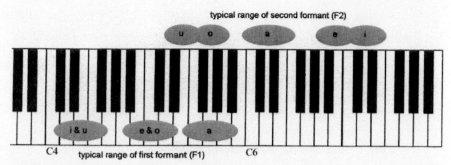

Figure 2.8. Typical range of first and second formants for primary vowels
Dr. Scott McCoy

fundamental frequency *higher* than the first formant of many vowels. Imagine what happens if she must sing the phrase "and I'll leave you forever," with the word "leave" set on a very high, climactic note. The audience won't be able to tell if she is singing *leave* or *love* forever; the two will sound identical. This happens because the formant that is required to identify the vowel /ee/ is too far below the pitch being sung. Even if she tries to sing *leave*, the sound that comes out of her mouth will be heard as some variation of /ah/.

Fortunately, this kind of mismatch between formants and musical pitches rarely causes problems for anyone but opera singers, choir sopranos, and perhaps ingénues in classic music theater shows. Almost everyone else generally sings low enough in their respective voice ranges to produce easily identifiable vowels.

Second formants also can be important, but more so for opera singers than everyone else. They are much higher in pitch, tracking the pattern oo = E5, oh = G5, ah = D6, eh = B6, ee = D7 (you can use the mnemonic "**e**very **g**ood **d**ad **b**uys **d**iapers" to remember these pitches) (figure 2.8). Because they can extend so high, into the top octave of the piano keyboard for /ee/, they interact primarily with higher tones in the natural harmonic series. Unless you are striving to produce the loudest unamplified sound possible, you probably never need to worry about the second formant; it will steadfastly do its job of helping to produce vowel sounds without any conscious thought or manipulation on your part.

If you are interested in discovering more about resonance and how it impacts your voice, you might want to install a spectrum analyzer on your computer. Free (or inexpensive) programs are readily available for download over the Internet that will work with either a PC or Mac computer. You don't need any specialized hardware—if you can use Skype or FaceTime, you already have everything you need. Once you've installed something, simply start playing with it. Experiment with your voice to see exactly how the analysis signal changes when you change the way your voice sounds. You'll be able to see how harmonics change in intensity as they interact with your formants. If you sing with vibrato, you'll see how consistently you produce your variations in pitch and amplitude. You'll even be able to see if your tone is excessively nasal for the kind of singing you want to do. Other programs are available that will help you improve your intonation (how well you sing in tune) or enhance your basic musicianship skills. Technology truly has advanced sufficiently to help us sing more beautifully.

MOUTH, LIPS, AND TONGUE: YOUR ARTICULATORS

The articulatory life of a singer is not easy, especially when compared to the demands placed on other musicians. Like a pianist or brass player, we must be able to produce the entire spectrum of musical articulation, including dynamic levels from hushed pianissimos to thunderous fortes, short notes, long notes, accents, crescendos, diminuendos, and so on. We produce most of these articulations the same way instrumentalists do, which is by varying our power supply. But singers have another layer of articulation that makes everything much more complicated; we must produce these musical gestures while simultaneously singing words.

As we learned in our brief examination of formants, altering the resonance characteristics of the vocal tract creates the vowel sounds of language. We do this by changing the position of our tongue, jaw, lips, and sometimes palate. Slowly say the vowel pattern ee-eh-ah-oh-oo. Can you feel how your tongue moves in your mouth? For /ee/, it is high in the front and low in the back, but it takes the opposite position for /oo/. Now slowly say the word *Tuesday*, noting all the places your tongue comes into contact with your teeth and palate and how it changes shape as you produce the vowels and diphthongs. There is a lot going on in there—no wonder it takes so long for babies to learn to speak!

Our articulatory anatomy is extraordinarily complex, in large part because our bodies use the same passageway for food, water, air, and sound. As a result, our tongue, larynx, throat, jaw, and palate are all interconnected with common physical and neurologic points of attachment. Our anatomical Union Station in this regard is a small structure called the *hyoid bone*. The hyoid is one of only three bones in your entire body that do not connect to other bones via a joint (the other two are your *patellae*, or kneecaps). This little bone is suspended below your jaw, freely floating up and down every time your swallow. It is a busy place, serving as the upper suspension point for the larynx, the connection for the root of the tongue, and the primary location of the muscles that open your mouth by dropping your jaw.

Good singing—in any genre—requires a high degree of independence in all these articulatory structures. Unfortunately, nature conspires against us to make this difficult to accomplish. From the time we were born, our bodies have relied on a reflex reaction to elevate the palate and raise the larynx each time we swallow. This action becomes habitual: palate goes up, larynx also lifts. But depending on the style of music we are singing, we might need to keep the larynx down while the palate goes up (opera and classical), or palate down with the larynx up (country and bluegrass). As we all know, habits can be very hard to change, which is one of the reasons that it can take a lot of study and practice to become an excellent singer. Understanding your body's natural reflexive habits can make some of this work a bit easier.

There is one more significant pitfall to the close proximity of all these articulators: tension in one area is easily passed along to another. If your jaw muscles are too tight while you sing, that hyperactivity will likely be transferred to the larynx and tongue—remember, they all are interconnected through the hyoid bone. It can be tricky to determine the primary offender in this kind of chain reaction of tension. A tight tongue could just as easily be making your jaw stiff, or an elevated, rigid larynx could make both tongue and jaw suffer.

Neurology complicates matters even further. You have sixteen muscles in your tongue, fourteen in your larynx, twenty-two in your throat and palate, and another sixteen that control your jaw. Many of these are very small and lie directly adjacent to each other, and you often are required to contract one quite strongly while its next-door neighbor must remain totally relaxed. Our brains need to develop laser-like control, sending signals at the right moment with the right intensity to the precise spot where they are needed. When we first start singing, these brain signals come more like a blast from a shotgun, spreading the neurologic impulse over a broad area to multiple muscles, not all of which are the intended target. Again, with practice and training, we learn to refine our control, enabling us to use only those muscles that will help, while disengaging those that would get in the way of our best singing.

CONCLUSION

This brief chapter has only scratched the surface of the huge field of voice science. To learn more, you might visit the websites of the National Association of Teachers of Singing, the Voice Foundation, or the National Center for Voice and Speech. You can easily locate the appropriate addresses through any Internet search engine. Remember: knowledge is power. Occasionally, people are afraid that if they know more about the science of how they sing, they will become so analytical that all spontaneity will be lost or that they will become paralyzed by too much information and thought. In my forty-plus years as a singer and teacher, I've never encountered somebody who actually suffered this fate. To the contrary, the more we know, the easier—and more joyful—singing becomes.

RESOURCES

National Association of Teachers of Singing: nats.org
National Center for Voice and Speech: ncvs.org
Voice Foundation: voicefoundation.org

3

VOCAL HEALTH AND THE COUNTRY MUSIC ARTIST

Wendy LeBorgne

GENERAL PHYSICAL WELL-BEING

All singers, regardless of genre, should consider themselves as "vocal athletes." The physical, emotional, and performance demands necessary for optimal output require that the artist consider training and maintaining their instrument as an athlete trains for an event. With increased vocal and performance demands, it is unlikely that a vocal athlete will have an entire performing career completely injury free. This may not be the fault of the singer as many injuries occur due to circumstances beyond the singer's control such as singing through an illness or being on a new medication seemingly unrelated to the voice.

Vocal injury has often been considered taboo to talk about in the performing world as it has been considered to be the result of faulty technique or poor vocal habits. In actuality, the majority of vocal injuries presenting in the elite performing population tend to be overuse and/or acute injury. From a clinical perspective over the past seventeen years, younger, less experienced singers with fewer years of training (who tend to be quite talented) generally are the ones who present with issues related to technique or phonotrauma (nodules, edema, contact ulcers), while more mature singers with professional performing careers tend to present with acute injuries (hemorrhage) or overuse and misuse injuries (muscle tension dysphonia, edema, gastroesophageal reflux disease [GERD]) or injuries following an illness. There are no current studies documenting use and training in correlation to laryngeal pathologies. However, there are studies that document that somewhere between 35 percent and 100 percent of professional vocal athletes have abnormal vocal fold findings on stroboscopic evaluation. Many times these "abnormalities" are in singers who have no vocal complaints or symptoms of vocal problems. From a performance perspective, uniqueness in vocal quality often gets hired and perhaps a slight aberration in the way a given larynx functions may become quite marketable. Regardless of what the vocal folds may look like, the most integral part of performance is that singers must maintain agility, flexibility, stamina, power, and inherent beauty (genre appropriate) for their current level of performance taking into account physical, vocal, and emotional demands.

Unlike sports medicine and the exercise physiology literature where much is known about the types and nature of given sports injuries, there is no common parallel for the vocal athlete model. However, because the vocal athlete utilizes the body systems of alignment, respiration, phonation, and resonance with some similarities to physical athletes, a parallel protocol for vocal wellness may be implemented/considered for vocal athletes to maximize injury prevention knowledge for both the singer and teacher. This chapter aims to provide information on vocal wellness and injury prevention for the vocal athlete.

CONSIDERATIONS FOR WHOLE BODY WELLNESS

Nutrition

You have no doubt heard the saying "you are what you eat." Eating is a social and psychological event. For many people, food associations and eating have an emotional basis resulting in either overeating or being malnourished. Eating disorders in performers and body image issues may have major implications and consequences for the performer on both ends of the spectrum (obesity and anorexia). Singers should be encouraged to reprogram the brain and body to consider food as fuel. You want to use high-octane gas in your engine, as pouring water in your car's gas tank won't get you very far. Eating a poor diet or a diet that lacks appropriate nutritional value will have negative physical and vocal effects on the singer. Poor dietary choices for the vocal athlete may result in physical and vocal effects ranging from fatigue to life-threatening disease over the course of a lifetime. Encouraging and engaging in healthy eating habits from a young age will potentially prevent long-term negative effects due to poor nutritional choices. It is beyond the scope of this chapter to provide a complete overview of all the dietary guidelines for pediatrics, adolescents, adults, and the mature adult; however, additional references to help guide your food and beverage choices can be found online at:

- Dietary Guidelines for Americans: www.health.gov/dietaryguide lines/.
- Nutrition.gov Guidelines from Tweens and Teens: www.nutrition .gov/life-stages/adolescents/tweens-and-teens.
- Fruits and Veggies Matter: www.fruitsandveggiesmorematters.org /myplate-and-what-is-a-serving-of-fruits-and-vegetables.

Hydration

"Sing wet, pee pale." This phrase was echoed in the studio of Van Lawrence regarding how his students would know if they were well enough hydrated. Generally, this rule of pale urine during your waking hours is a good indicator that you are well hydrated. Medications, vitamins, and certain foods may alter urine color despite adequate hydration. Due to the varying levels of physical and vocal activity of many performers, in order to maintain adequate oral hydration, the use of a hydration calculator based on activity level may be a better choice. These hydration calculators are easily accessible online and take into account the amount and level of activity the performer engages in on a daily basis. In a recent study of the vocal habits of musical theater performers, one of the findings indicated a significantly underhydrated group of performers.[1]

Laryngeal and pharyngeal dryness as well as "thick, sticky, mucus" are often complaints of singers. Combating these concerns and maintaining an adequate viscosity of mucus for performance has resulted in some research. As a reminder of laryngeal and swallowing anatomy, nothing that is swallowed (or gargled) passes over or touches the vocal folds directly (or one would choke). Therefore, nothing that a singer eats or drinks ever touches the vocal folds, and in order to adequately hydrate the mucus membranes of the vocal folds, one must consume enough fluids for the body to produce a thin mucus. Therefore, any "vocal" effects from swallowed products are limited to potential pharyngeal and oral changes, not the vocal folds themselves.

The effects of systemic hydration are well documented in the literature. There is evidence to suggest that adequate hydration will provide some protection of the laryngeal mucosal membranes when they are placed under increased collision forces as well as reducing the amount of effort (phonation threshold pressure) to produce voice. This is important for singers because it means that with adequate hydration and consistency of mucus, the effort to produce voice is less and their vocal folds are better protected from injury. Imagine the friction and heat produced when two dry hands rub together and then what happens if you put lotion on your hands. The mechanisms in the larynx to provide appropriate mucus production are not fully understood, but there is enough evidence at this time to support oral hydration as a vital component of every singer's vocal health regime to maintain appropriate mucosal viscosity.

Although very rare, overhydration (hyperhidrosis) can result in dehydration and even illness or death. An overindulgence of fluids essentially makes the kidneys work "overtime" and flushes too much water out of the body. This excessive fluid loss in a rapid manner can be detrimental to the body.

In addition to drinking water to systemically monitor hydration, there are many nonregulated products on the market for performers that lay claim to improving the laryngeal environment (e.g., Entertainer's Secret, Throat Coat Tea, Greathers Pastilles, Slippery Elm, etc.). Although there may be little detriment in using these products, quantitative research documenting change in laryngeal mucosa is sparse. One study suggests that the use of Throat Coat when compared to a placebo treatment for pharyngitis did show a significant difference in decreasing the perception of sore throat. Another study compared the use of Entertainer's Secret to two other nebulized agents and its effect on phonation threshold pressure (PTP). There was no positive benefit in decreasing PTP with Entertainer's Secret.

Many singers use personal steam inhalers and/or room humidification to supplement oral hydration and aid in combating laryngeal dryness. There are several considerations for singers who choose to use external means of adding moisture to the air they breathe. Personal steam inhalers are portable and can often be used backstage or in the hotel room for the traveling performer. Typically, water is placed in the steamer and the face is placed over the steam for inhalation. Because the mucus membranes of the larynx are composed of a saltwater solution, one study looked at the use of nebulized saline in comparison to plain water and its potential effects on effort or ease to sound production in classically trained sopranos.[2] Data suggested that perceived effort to produce voice was less in the saline group than the plain water group. This indicated that the singers who used the saltwater solution reported less effort to sing after breathing in the saltwater than singers who used plain water. The researchers hypothesized that because the body's mucus is not plain water (rather it is saltwater—think about your tears), when you use plain water for steam inhalation, it may actually draw the salt from your own saliva, resulting in a dehydrating effect.

In addition to personal steamers, other options for air humidification come in varying sizes of humidifiers from room-size to whole-house humidifiers. When choosing between a warm-air or cool-mist humidifier considerations include both personal preference and needs. One of the primary reasons warm-mist humidifiers are not recommended for young children is due to the risk of burns from the heating element. Both the warm-mist and cool-air humidifiers act similarly in adding moisture to the environmental air. External air humidification may be beneficial and provide a level of comfort for many singers. Regular cleaning of the humidifier is vital to prevent bacteria and mold buildup. Also, depending on the hardness of the water, it is important to avoid mineral buildup on the device and distilled water may be recommended for some humidifiers.

For traveling performers who often stay in hotels, fly on airplanes, or are generally exposed to other dry-air environments, there are products on the market designed to help minimize drying effects. One such device is called a Humidflyer, which is a facemask designed with a filter to recycle the moisture of a person's own breath and replenish moisture on each breath cycle.

For dry nasal passages or to clear sinuses, many singers use Neti pots. Many singers use this homeopathic flushing of the nasal passages regularly. Research supports the use of a Neti pot as a part of allergy relief and chronic rhinosinusitis control when utilized properly, sometimes in combination with medical management.[3] Conversely, long-term use of nasal irrigation (without taking intermittent breaks from daily use) may result in washing out the "good" mucus of the nasal passages, which naturally helps to rid the nose of infections. A study presented at the American College of Allergy, Asthma, and Immunology (ACAAI) 2009 annual scientific meeting reported that when a group of individuals who were using twice-daily nasal irrigation for one year discontinued using it, they had an increase in acute rhinosinusitis.[4]

Tea, Honey, and Gargle to Keep the Throat Healthy

Regarding the use of general teas (which many singers combine with honey or lemon), there is likely no harm in the use of decaffeinated tea (caffeine may cause systemic dryness). The warmth of the tea may provide a soothing sensation to the pharynx and the act of swallowing can be relaxing for the muscles of the throat. Honey has shown promising results as an effective cough suppressant in the pediatric population.[5] The dose of honey given to the children in the study was two teaspoons. Gargling with saltwater or apple cider vinegar and water are also popular home remedies for many singers with the uses being from soothing the throat to curing reflux. Gargling plain water has been shown to be effective in reducing the risk of contracting upper respiratory infections. I suggest that when gargling, the singer should only "bubble" the water with air and avoid engaging the vocal folds in sound production. Saltwater as a gargle has long been touted as a sore throat remedy and can be traced back to 2700 BCE in China for treating gum disease. The science behind a saltwater rinse for everything from oral hygiene to sore throat is that salt (sodium chloride) may act as a natural analgesic (pain killer) and may also kill bacteria. Similar to the effects that not enough salt in the water may have on drawing the salt out of the tissue during steam inhalation, if you oversaturate the water solution with excess salt and gargle it, it may act to draw water out of the oral mucosa, thus reducing inflammation.

Another popular home remedy reported by singers is the use of apple cider vinegar to help with everything from acid reflux to sore throats. Dating back to 3300 BCE, apple cider vinegar was reported as a medicinal remedy, and it became popular in the 1970s as a weight loss diet cocktail. Popular media reports apple cider vinegar can improve conditions from acne and arthritis to nosebleeds and varicose veins. Specific efficacy data regarding the beneficial nature of apple cider vinegar for the purpose of sore throat, pharyngeal inflammation, and/or reflux has not been reported in the literature at this time. Of the peer-reviewed studies found in the literature, one discussed possible esophageal erosion and inconsistency of actual product in tablet form.[6] Therefore, at this time, strong evidence supporting the use of apple cider vinegar is not published.

Medications and the Voice

Medications (over the counter, prescription, and herbal) may have resultant drying effects on the body and often the laryngeal mucosa. General classes of drugs with potential drying effects include: antidepressants, anti-hypertensives, diuretics, ADD/ADHD medications, some oral acne medications, hormones, allergy drugs, and vitamin C in high doses. The National Center for Voice and Speech (NCVS) provides a listing of some common medications with potential voice side effects including laryngeal dryness. This listing does not take into account all medications, so singers should always ask their pharmacist about the potential side effects of a given medication. Due to the significant number of drugs on the market, it is safe to say that most pharmacists will not be acutely aware of "vocal side effects," but if dryness is listed as a potential side effect of the drug, you may assume that all body systems could be affected. Under no circumstances should you stop taking a prescribed medication without consulting your physician first. Every person has a different body chemistry and reaction to medication; just because a medication lists dryness as a potential side effect, it does not necessarily mean you will experience that side effect. Conversely, if you begin a new medication and notice physical or vocal changes that are unexpected, you should consult with your physician. Ultimately, the goal of medical management for any condition is to achieve the most benefits with the least side effects. Below is a list of possible resources for the singer regarding prescription drugs and herbs:

- www.fda.gov/OHRMS/DOCKETS/98FR/06D-0480-GLD0001 .PDF
- nccam.nih.gov/health/herbsataglance.htm
- www.nlm.nih.gov/medlineplus/druginfo/herb_All.html
- www.ncvs.org

In contrast to medications that tend to dry, there are medications formulated to increase saliva production or alter the viscosity of mucus. Medically, these drugs are often used to treat patients who have had a loss of saliva production due to surgery or radiation. Mucolytic agents are used to thin secretions as needed. As a singer, if you feel that you need to use a mucolytic agent on a consistent basis, it may be worth considering getting to the root of the laryngeal dryness symptom and seeking a professional option by an otolaryngologist.

Reflux and the Voice

Gastroesophageal reflux (GERD) and/or laryngopharyngeal reflux (LPR) can have a devastating impact on the singer if not recognized and treated appropriately. Although GERD and LPR are related, they are considered slightly different diseases. GERD (Latin root meaning "flowing back") is the reflux of digestive enzymes, acids, and other stomach contents into the esophagus (food pipe). If this backflow is propelled through the upper esophagus and into the throat (larynx and pharynx), it is referred to as LPR. It is not uncommon to have both GERD and LPR, but they can occur independently.

More frequently, people with GERD have decreased esophageal clearing. Esophagitis, or inflammation of the esophagus, is also associated with GERD. People with GERD often feel heartburn. LPR symptoms are often "silent" and do not include heartburn. Specific symptoms of LPR may include some or all of the following: lump in the throat sensation, feeling of constant need to clear the throat/postnasal drip, longer vocal warm-up time, quicker vocal fatigue, loss of high frequency range, worse voice in the morning, sore throat, and bitter/raw/brackish taste in the mouth. If you experience these symptoms on a regular basis, it is advised that you consider a medical consultation for your symptoms. Prolonged, untreated GERD or LPR can lead to permanent changes in both the esophagus and/or larynx. Untreated LPR also provides a laryngeal environment that is conducive for vocal fold lesions to occur as it inhibits normal healing mechanisms.

Treatment of LPR and GERD generally includes both dietary and lifestyle modifications in addition to medical management. Some of the dietary recommendations include: elimination of caffeinated and carbonated beverages, smoking cessation, no alcohol use, and limiting tomatoes, acidic foods and drinks, and raw onions or peppers, to name a few. Also, avoidance of high-fat foods is recommended. From a lifestyle perspective, suggested changes include not eating within three hours of lying down, eating small meals frequently (instead of large meals), elevating the head of your bed, avoiding tight clothing around the belly, and not bending over or exercising too soon after you eat.

Reflux medications fall in three general categories: antacids, H2 (histamine) blockers, and proton pump inhibitors (PPI). There are now combination drugs that include both an H2 blocker and proton pump inhibitor. Every medication has both associated risks and benefits, and singers should be aware of the possible benefits and side effects of the medications they take. In general terms, antacids (e.g., Tums, Mylanta, Gaviscon) neutralize stomach acid. H2 such as Axid (nizatidine), Tagamet (cimetidine), Pepcid (famotidine), and Zantac (ranitidine) work to decrease acid production in the stomach by preventing histamine from triggering the H2 receptors to produce more acid. Then there are the PPIs: Nexium (esomeprazole), Prevacid (lansoprazole), Protonix (pantoprazole), AcipHex (rabeprazole), Prilosec (omeprazole), and Dexilant (dexlansoprazole). PPIs act as a last line of defense to decrease acid production by blocking the last step in gastric juice secretion. Some of the most recent drugs to combat GERD/LPR are combination drugs (e.g., Zegrid [sodium bicarbonate plus omeprazole]), which provide a short-acting response (sodium bicarbonate) and a long release (omeprazole). Because some singers prefer a holistic approach to reflux management, strict dietary and lifestyle compliance is recommended and consultation with both your primary care physician and naturopath are warranted in that situation. Efficacy data on nonregulated herbs, vitamins, and supplements is limited, but some data does exist.

Physical Exercise

Vocal athletes, like other physical athletes, should consider how and what they do to maintain both cardiovascular fitness and muscular strength. In today's performance culture, it is rare that a performer stands still and sings, unless in a recital or choral setting. The range of physical activity can vary from light movement to high-intensity chore-ography with acrobatics. As performers are being required to increase their onstage physical activity level from the operatic stage to the pop-star arena, overall physical fitness is imperative to avoid compromise in the vocal system. Breathlessness will result in compensation by the larynx, which will attempt to regulate the air. Compensatory vocal behaviors over time may result in a change in vocal performance. The health benefits of both cardiovascular training and strength training are well documented in the literature for physical athletes but relatively rare for vocal performers.

Mental Wellness

Vocal performers must maintain a mental focus during performance and a mental toughness during auditioning and training. Rarely during vocal performance training programs is this important aspect of perfor-mance addressed, and it is often left to individual performers to develop their own strategies or coping mechanisms. Yet, many performers are on antianxiety or antidepressant drugs (which may be the direct result of performance-related issues). If the sports world is again used as a parallel for mental toughness, there are no elite-level athletes (and few junior-level athletes) who don't utilize the services of a performance/ sports psychologist to maximize focus and performance. I recommend performers consider the potential benefits of a performance psycholo-gist to help maximize vocal performance. Several references that may be of interest to the singer include Joanna Cazden's *Visualization for*

Singers and Shirlee Emmons and Alma Thomas's *Power Performance for Singers: Transcending the Barriers*.

Unlike instrumentalists, whose performance is dependent on accurate playing of an external musical instrument, the singer's instrument is uniquely intact and subject to the emotional confines of the brain and body in which it is housed. Musical performance anxiety (MPA) can be career threatening for all musicians, but perhaps the vocal athlete is more severely impacted. The majority of literature on MPA is dedicated to instrumentalists, but the basis of definition, performance effects, and treatment options can be considered for vocal athletes. Fear is a natural reaction to a stressful situation, and there is a fine line between emotional excitation and perceived threat (real or imagined). The job of a performer is to convey to an audience through vocal production, physical gestures, and facial expression a most heightened state of emotion. Otherwise, why would audience members pay top dollar to sit for two or three hours for a mundane experience? Not only is there the emotional conveyance of the performance, but also the internal turmoil often experienced by the singers themselves in preparation for elite performance. It is well documented in the literature that even the most elite performers have experienced debilitating performance anxiety. MPA is defined on a continuum with anxiety levels ranging from low to high and has been reported to comprise four distinct components: affect, cognition, behavior, and physiology. Affect comprises feelings (e.g., doom, panic, anxiety). Effected cognition will result in altered levels of concentration, while the behavior component results in postural shifts, quivering, and trembling. Finally, physiologically the body's autonomic nervous system (ANS) will activate, resulting in the "fight or flight" response.

In recent years, researchers have been able to define two distinct neurological pathways for MPA. The first pathway happens quickly and without conscious input, resulting in the same fear stimulus as if a person were put into an emergent, life-threatening situation. In those situations, the brain releases adrenaline, resulting in physical changes of: increased heart rate, increased respiration, shaking, pale skin, dilated pupils, slowed digestion, bladder relaxation, dry mouth, and dry eyes, all of which severely affect vocal performance. The second pathway that has been identified results in a conscious identification of the fear/threat and a much slower physiologic response. With the second neuromotor response, the performer has a chance to recognize the fear, process how to deal with the fear, and respond accordingly.

Treatment modalities to address MPA include psycho-behavioral therapy (including biofeedback) and drug therapies. Elite physical performance athletes have been shown to benefit from visualization techniques and psychological readiness training, yet within the performing arts community, stage fright may be considered a weakness or character flaw precluding readiness for professional performance. On the contrary, vocal athletes, like physical athletes, should mentally prepare themselves for optimal competition (auditions) and performance. Learning to convey emotion without eliciting an internal emotional response by the vocal athlete may take the skill of an experienced psychologist to help change ingrained neural pathways. Ultimately, control and understanding of MPA will enhance performance and prepare the vocal athlete for the most intense performance demands without vocal compromise.

VOCAL WELLNESS: INJURY PREVENTION

In order to prevent vocal injury and understand vocal wellness in the singer, general knowledge of common causes of voice disorders is imperative. One common cause of voice disorders is vocally abusive behaviors or misuse of the voice to include phonotraumatic behaviors such as yelling, screaming, loud talking, talking over noise, throat clearing, coughing, harsh sneezing, and boisterous laughing. Chronic or less-than-optimal vocal properties such as poor breathing techniques, inappropriate phonatory habits during conversational speech (glottal fry, hard glottal attacks), inapt pitch, loudness, rate of speech, and/or hyperfunctional laryngeal area muscle tone may also negatively impact vocal function. Medically related etiologies, which also have the potential to impact vocal function, range from untreated chronic allergies and sinusitis to endocrine dysfunction and hormonal imbalance. Direct trauma, such as a blow to the neck or the risk of vocal fold damage during intubation, can impact optimal performance in vocal athletes depending on the nature and extent of the trauma. Finally, external irritants ranging from cigarette smoke to reflux directly impact the laryngeal mucosa and ultimately can lead to laryngeal pathology.

Vocal hygiene education and compliance may be one of the primary essential components for maintaining the voice throughout a career. This section provides the singer with information about prevention of vocal injury. However, just like a professional sports athlete, it is unlikely that a professional vocal athlete will go through an entire career without some compromise in vocal function. This may be a common upper respiratory infection that creates vocal fold swelling for a short time, or it may be a "vocal accident" that is career threatening. Regardless, the knowledge of how to take care of your voice is essential for any vocal athlete.

Train Like an Athlete for Vocal Longevity

Performers seek instant gratification in performance sometimes at the cost of gradual vocal building for a lifetime of healthy singing. Historically, voice pedagogues required their students to perform vocals exclusively for up to two years before beginning any song literature. Singers gradually built their voices by ingraining appropriate muscle memory and neuromotor patterns through development of aesthetically pleasing tones, onsets, breath management, and support. There was an intensive master-apprentice relationship and rigorous vocal guidelines to maintain a place within a given studio. Time off was taken if a vocal injury ensued or careers potentially were ended, and students were asked to leave a given singing studio if their voices were unable to withstand the rigors of training. Training vocal athletes today has evolved and appears driven to create a "product" quickly, perhaps at the expense of the longevity of the singer. Pop stars emerging well before puberty are doing international concert tours, yet many young artist programs in the classical arena do not consider singers for their programs until they are in their mid- to late twenties.

Each vocal genre presents with different standards and vocal demands. Therefore, the amount and degree of vocal training are varied. Some would argue that performing extensively without adequate vocal training and development is ill-advised, yet singers today are thrust onto the stage at very young ages. Dancers, instrumentalists, and physical athletes all spend many hours per day developing muscle strength, memory, and proper technique for their craft. The more advanced the artist or athlete, generally the more specific the training protocol becomes. Consideration of training vocal athletes in this same fashion is recommended. One would generally not begin a young, inexperienced singer without previous vocal training on a Wagner aria. Similarly, in nonclassical vocal music, there are easy, moderate, and difficult pieces to consider, pending level of vocal development and training.

Basic pedagogical training of alignment, breathing, voice production, and resonance are essential building blocks for development of good voice production. Muscle memory and development of appropriate muscle patterns happen slowly over time with appropriate repetitive practice. Doing too much, too soon for any athlete (physical or vocal) will result in an increased risk for injury. When singers are asked to do "vocal gymnastics," they must be sure to have a solid basis of strength and stamina in the appropriate muscle groups to perform consistently with minimal risk of injury.

Vocal Fitness Program

One generally does not get out of bed first thing in the morning and try to do a split. Yet many singers go directly into a practice session or audition without proper warm-up. Think of your larynx like your knee, made up of cartilages, ligaments, and muscles. Vocal health is dependent upon appropriate warm-ups (to get things moving), drills for technique, and then cool-downs (at the end of your day). Consider vocal warm-ups a "gentle stretch." Depending on the needs of the singer, warm-ups should include physical stretching; postural alignment self-checks; breathing exercises to promote rib cage, abdominal, and back expansion; vocal stretches (glides up to stretch the vocal folds and glides down to contract the vocal folds); articulatory stretches (yawning, facial stretches); and mental warm-ups (to provide focus for the task at hand). Vocalises, in my opinion, are designed as exercises to go beyond warm-ups and prepare the body and voice for the technical and vocal challenges of the music they sing. They are varied and address the technical level and genre of the singer to maximize performance and vocal growth. Cool-downs are a part of most athletes' workouts. However, singers often do not use cool-downs (physical, mental, and vocal) at the end of a performance. A recent study looked specifically at the benefits of vocal cool-downs in singers and found that singers who used a vocal cool-down had decreased effort to produce voice the next day.[7]

Systemic hydration as a means to keep the vocal folds adequately lubricated for the amount of impact and friction that they will undergo has been previously discussed in this chapter. Compliance with adequate oral hydration recommendations is important and subsequently so is the minimization of agents that could potentially dry the membranes (e.g., caffeine, medications, dry air). The body produces approximately two quarts of mucus per day. If not adequately hydrated, the mucus tends to be thick and sticky. Poor hydration is similar to not putting enough oil in the car engine. Frankly, if the gears do not work as well, there is increased friction and heat, and the engine is not efficient.

Speak Well, Sing Well

Optimize the speaking voice utilizing ideal frequency range, breath, intensity, rate, and resonance. Singers generally are vocally enthusiastic individuals who talk a lot and often talk loudly. During typical conversation, the average fundamental speaking frequency (times per second the vocal folds are impacting) for a male varies from 100 to 150Hz and 180 to 230Hz for women. Because of the delicate structure of the vocal folds and the importance of the layered microstructure vibrating efficiently and effectively to produce voice, vocal behaviors or outside factors that compromise the integrity of the vibration patterns of the vocal folds may be considered phonotrauma.

Phonotraumatic behaviors can include yelling, screaming, loud talking, harsh sneezing, and harsh laughing. Elimination of phontraumatic behaviors is essential for good vocal health. The louder one speaks, the farther apart the vocal folds move from midline, the harder they impact, and the longer they stay closed. A tangible example would be to take your hands, move them only six inches apart, and clap as hard and as loudly as you can for ten seconds. Now, move your hands two feet apart and clap as hard, loudly, and quickly as possible for ten seconds. The farther apart your hands are, the more air you move and the louder the clap, and the skin on the hands becomes red and ultimately swollen (if you do it long enough and hard enough). This is what happens to the vocal folds with repeated impact at increased vocal intensities. The vocal folds are approximately 17mm in length and vibrate at 220 times per second on A3, 440 on A4, 880 on A5, and more than 1,000 per second when singing a high C. That is a lot of impact for little muscles. Consider this fact when singing loudly or in a high tessitura for prolonged periods of time. It becomes easy to see why women are more prone than men to laryngeal impact injuries due to the frequency range of the voice alone.

In addition to the amount of cycles per second the vocal folds are impacting, singers need to be aware of their vocal intensity (volume). Check the volume of the speaking and singing voice and for conversational speech and consider using a distance of three to five feet as a gauge for how loud you need to be in general conversation (about an arm's-length distance). Speaking on cell phones and a Bluetooth device in a car generally result in louder than conversational vocal intensity, and singers are advised to minimize unnecessary use of these devices.

Singers should be encouraged to take "vocal naps" during their day. A vocal nap would be a short period of time (five minutes to an hour) of complete silence. Although the vocal folds are rarely completely still (because they move when you swallow and breathe), a vocal nap minimizes impact and vibration for a short window of time. A physical nap can also be refreshing for the singer mentally and physically.

AVOID ENVIRONMENTAL IRRITANTS: ALCOHOL, SMOKING, DRUGS

Arming singers with information about the actual effects of environmental irritants so that they can make informed choices on engaging in exposure to these potential toxins is essential. The glamour that continues to be associated with smoking, drinking, and drugs can be tempered with the deaths of popular stars such as Amy Winehouse and Cory Monteith, who engaged in life-ending choices. There is extensive documentation about the long-term effects of toxic and carcinogenic substances, but here are a few key facts to consider when choosing whether to partake.

Alcohol, although it does not pass over the vocal folds directly, does have a systemic drying effect. Due to the acidity in alcohol, it may increase the likelihood of reflux, resulting in hoarseness and other laryngeal pathologies. Consuming alcohol generally decreases one's inhibitions, and therefore you are more likely to sing and do things that you would not typically do under the influence of alcohol.

Beyond the carcinogens in nicotine and tobacco, the heat at which a cigarette burns is well above the boiling temperature of water (water boils at 212°F; cigarettes burn at over 1400°F). No one would consider pouring a pot of boiling water on their hand, and yet the burning temperature for a cigarette results in significant heat over the oral mucosa and vocal folds. The heat alone can create a deterioration in the lining, resulting in polypoid degeneration. Obviously, cigarette smoking has been well documented as a cause of laryngeal cancer.

Marijuana and other street drugs are not only addictive but can cause permanent mucosal lining changes depending on the drug used and the method of delivery. If you or one of your singer colleagues is experiencing a drug or alcohol problem, research or provide information and support on getting appropriate counseling and help.

SMART PRACTICE STRATEGIES FOR SKILL DEVELOPMENT AND VOICE CONSERVATION

Daily practice and drills for skill acquisition are an important part of any singer's training. However, overpracticing or inefficient practicing may be detrimental to the voice. Consider practice sessions of athletes: they may practice four to eight hours per day broken into one- to two-hour training sessions with a period of rest and recovery in between sessions. Although we cannot parallel the sports model without adequate evidence in the vocal athlete, the premise of short, intense, focused practice sessions is logical for the singer. Similar to physical exercise, it is suggested that practice sessions do not have to be all singing. Rather, structuring sessions so that one-third of the session is spent on warm-up; one-third on vocalise, text work, rhythms, character development, and so on; and one-third on repertoire will allow the singer to function in a more efficient vocal manner. Building the amount of time per practice session—increasing duration by five minutes per week, building to sixty to ninety minutes—may be effective (e.g., Week 1: 20 minutes 3 times per day; Week 2: 25 minutes 3 times per day, etc).

Vary the "vocal workout" during your week. For example, if you do the same physical exercise in the same way day after day with the same intensity and pattern, you will likely experience repetitive strain-type injuries. However, cross-training or varying the type and level of exercise aids in injury prevention. So when planning your practice sessions for a given week (or rehearsal process for a given role), consider varying your vocal intensity, tessitura, and exercises to maximize your training sessions, building stamina, muscle memory, and skill acquisition. For example, one day you may spend more time on learning rhythms and translation and the next day you spend thirty minutes performing coloratura exercises to prepare for a specific role. Take one day a week off from vocal training and give your voice a break. This does not mean complete vocal rest (although some singers find this beneficial), but rather a day without singing and limited talking.

Practice Your Mental Focus

Mental wellness and stress management are equally as important as vocal training for vocal athletes. Addressing any mental health issues is paramount to developing the vocal artist. This may include anything from daily mental exercises/meditation/focus to overcoming performance anxiety to more serious mental health issues/illness. Every person can benefit from improved focus and mental acuity.

SPECIFIC VOCAL WELLNESS CONCERNS FOR THE COUNTRY MUSIC ARTIST

Present-day country music is one of the top music genres listened to in America today. First emerging on the scene as a uniquely American music genre in the 1920s, country music evolved from American folk music. With significant influences from the blues, country music has evolved significantly since the 1920s in terms of vocal quality and vocal performance expectations. Unlike early country music, whose primary instrumentation included banjos, guitars, fiddles, and harmonicas, today's popular country is much more similar to pop/rock concerts, and a "crossover" vocal quality is required. Not everything about a country singer is necessarily what would be considered by other vocal standards as healthy, but most country vocal artists are unique in their sound and their ability to connect with their audience through the storytelling production (aka folk song roots) and use of their instrument (slightly twangy vocal quality). Country music has advanced through the years and includes a multitude of subgenres that are considered aesthetically acceptable. Many of the well-known country singers (both past and present) had little formal vocal training, yet they can connect with their audience through their vocal production and storytelling ability. Specific vocal stylings of country music artists that are often considered "unacceptable" in a classical singing world include vocal breaks/cracks, twangy and sometimes nasal resonance quality, intentional breathiness, rough/raspy vocal quality, and short vocal phrases, to name a few.

Literature related to the vocal health, habits, and hygiene in country singers is limited. However, there have been studies conducted on respiratory patterns, subglottic pressures, and spectral characteristics of country singers. The literature surmises that country music singers use patterns very similar to speech and heightened speech (at increased intensity levels).

Physical Fitness

Similar to contemporary pop, many country artists are required to put on high-physical-intensity shows. Both physical and vocal fitness should be foremost in the minds of anyone desiring to perform country music today. General physical health guidelines should hold true for country music vocalists as they should be both physically and vocally in shape necessary to their performance demands.

Healthy Singing

Performance of country music requires that the singer has a flexible, agile, dynamic instrument with appropriate stamina. Singers must have a good command of their instrument as well as exceptional underlying intention to what they are singing as it is much more about relaying a story to the audience with clear emotional intent than about the "beauty of the voice." It is often both the interesting voice with a unique, captivating story that will capture the country music artist's audience. The creative and performance environments for emerging country music singers can be less than optimal from a vocal health perspective (e.g., smoky bars, substance abuse during creative endeavors). Aside from the tips listed above regarding smoking, alcohol, and substance use, when having to perform in smoky environments, here are two additional considerations. First, if singers take a spray bottle (such as an empty/washed-out window cleaner bottle) and fill it with water, they can spritz the air on the stage prior to performance and in between sets to pull the dust to the floor (the water particles will weigh down the dust and pull to the floor and out of your face). Second, the use of a small fan that blows the air toward the audience will draw smoky air in from the stage and away from the singer (back toward the audience). Depending on your stage setup, this fan can either be placed at the singer's feet or on speakers. Multiple fans are fine.

Similar to other commercial music vocalists, country artists use microphones and amplification. If used correctly, amplification for the country music performer can be used to maximize vocal health by allowing the singer to produce voice in an efficient manner while the sound engineer is effectively able to mix, amplify, and add effects to the voice. Understanding both the utility and limits of a given microphone and sound system is essential for the country music artist both for live and studio performances. Using an appropriate microphone can not only enhance the country singer's performance but can reduce vocal load for the singer. Emotional extremes (intimacy and exultation) can be enhanced by appropriate microphone choice, placement, and acoustical mixing, thus saving the singer's voice.

Not everything a country music singer does is "vocally healthy," sometimes because the emotional expression may be so intense it results in vocal collision forces that are extreme. Even if the country singer does not have formal vocal training, cross-training the instrument (which can mean singing in both high and low registers with varying intensities and resonance options) before and after practice sessions is likely a vital component to minimizing vocal injury.

Ultimately, the singer must learn to provide the most output with the least "cost" to the system. Taking care of the physical instrument through daily physical exercise and adequate nutrition and hydration and maintaining focused attention on performance will provide a necessary basis for vocal health during performance. Small doses of high-intensity singing (or speaking) will limit impact stress on the vocal folds. Finally, attention to the mind, body, and voice will provide the singer with an awareness when something is wrong. This awareness and knowledge of when to rest or seek help will promote vocal well-being for singers throughout their career.

NOTES

1. W. LeBorgne, E. Donahue, S. Brehm, and B. Weinrich, "Prevalence of Vocal Pathology in Incoming Freshman Musical Theatre Majors: A Ten-Year Retrospective Study," Fall Voice Conference, New York City, October 4–6, 2012.

2. K. Tanner, N. Roy, R. Merrill, F. Muntz, D. Houtz, C. Sauder, M. Elstad, and J. Wright-Costa, "Nebulized Isotonic Saline versus Water Following a Laryngeal Desiccation Challenge in Classically Trained Sopranos," *Journal of Speech Language and Hearing Research* 53, no. 6 (2010): 1555–66.

3. C. Brown and S. Grahm, "Nasal Irrigations: Good or Bad?" *Current Opinion in Otolaryngology—Head and Neck Surgery* 12, no. 1 (2004): 9–13.

4. T. Nsouli, "Long-Term Use of Nasal Saline Irrigation: Harmful or Helpful?" American College of Allergy, Asthma and Immunology (ACAAI) 2009 Annual Scientific Meeting: Abstract 32, presented November 8, 2009.

5. M. Shadkam, H. Mozaffari-Khosravi, and M. Mozayan, "A Comparison of the Effect of Honey, Dextromethorphan, and Diphenhydramine on Nightly Cough and Sleep Quality in Children and Their Parents," *Journal of Alternative and Complementary Medicine* 16, no. 7 (2010): 787–93.

6. L. Hill, L. Woodruff, J. Foote, and M. Barreto-Alcoba, "Esophageal Injury by Apple Cider Vinegar Tablets and Subsequent Evaluation of Products," *Journal of the American Dietetic Association* 105, no. 7 (2005): 1141–44.

7. R. O. Gottliebson, "The Efficacy of Cool-Down Exercises in the Practice Regimen of Elite Singers," PhD dissertation, University of Cincinnati, 2011.

FURTHER READING

Behrman, A., J. Rutledge, A. Hembree, and S. Sheridan. "Vocal Hygiene Education, Voice Production Therapy, and the Role of Patient Adherence:

A Treatment Effectiveness Study in Women with Phonotrauma." *Journal of Speech, Language, and Hearing Research* 51 (2008): 350–66.

Brinckmann, J., H. Sigwart, and L. van Houten Taylor. (2003). "Safety and Efficacy of a Traditional Herbal Medicine (Throat Coat) in Symptomatic Temporary Relief of Pain in Patients with Acute Pharyngitis: A Multicenter, Prospective, Randomized, Double-Blinded, Placebo-Controlled Study." *Journal of Alternative and Complementary Medicine* 9, no. 2 (2003): 285–98.

Brown, C., and S. Grahm. "Nasal Irrigations: Good or Bad?" *Current Opinion in Otolaryngology—Head and Neck Surgery* 12, no. 1 (2004): 9–13.

Cleveland, T., E. Stone, J. Sundberg, and J. Iwarsson. "Estimated Subglottal Pressure in Six Professional Country Singers." *Journal of Voice* 11, no. 4 (1997): 403–9.

Cleveland, T., J. Sundberg, and E. Stone. "Long-Term-Average Spectrum Characteristics of Country Singers during Speaking and Singing." *Journal of Voice* 15, no. 1 (2001): 54–60.

Dunn, J., G. Dion, and K. McMains. "Efficacy of Nasal Symptom Relief." *Current Opinion in Otolaryngology, Head and Neck Surgery* 21, no. 3 (2013): 248–51.

Elias, M. E., R. T. Sataloff, D. C. Rosen, R. J. Heuer, and J. R. Spiegel. "Normal Strobovideolaryngoscopy: Variability in Healthy Singers." *Journal of Voice* 11, no. 1 (1997): 104–7.

Evans, R. W., R. I. Evans, and S. Carvajal. (1998). "Survey of Injuries among West End Performers." *Occupational and Environmental Medicine* 55 (1998): 585–93.

Evans, R. W., R. I. Evans, S. Carvajal, and S. Perry. "A Survey of Injuries among Broadway Performers." *American Journal of Public Health* 86 (1996): 77.

Gottliebson, R. O. "The Efficacy of Cool-Down Exercises in the Practice Regimen of Elite Singers." PhD dissertation, University of Cincinnati, 2011.

Heman-Ackah, Y., C. Dean, and R. T. Sataloff. "Strobovideolaryngoscopic Findings in Singing Teachers." *Journal of Voice* 16, no. 1 (2002): 81–86.

Hill, L., L. Woodruff, J. Foote, and M. Barreto-Alcoba. "Esophageal Injury by Apple Cider Vinegar Tablets and Subsequent Evaluation of Products." *Journal of the American Dietetics Association* 105, no. 7 (2005): 1141–44.

Hoffman-Ruddy, B., J. Lehman, C. Crandell, D. Ingram, and C. Sapienza. "Laryngostroboscopic, Acoustic, and Environmental Characteristics of High-Risk Vocal Performers." *Journal of Voice* 15, no. 4 (2001): 543–52.

Hoit, J., C. Jenks, P. Watson, and T. Cleveland. "Respiration Function during Speaking and Singing in Professional Country Singers." *Journal of Voice* 10, no. 1 (1996): 39–49.

Korovin, G., and W. LeBorgne. "A Longitudinal Examination of Potential Vocal Injury in Musical Theater Performers." The Voice Foundation's 36th Annual Symposium: Care of the Professional Voice, June 3–7, 2009, Philadelphia, PA.

Koufman, J. A., T. A. Radomski, G. M. Joharji, G. B. Russell, and D. C. Pillsbury. "Laryngeal Biomechanics of the Singing Voice." *Otolaryngology—Head and Neck Surgery* 115 (1996): 527–37.

LeBorgne, W. "Defining the Belt Voice: Perceptual Judgments and Objective Measures." PhD dissertation, University of Cincinnati, 2001.

LeBorgne, W., E. Donahue, S. Brehm, and B. Weinrich. "Prevalence of Vocal Pathology in Incoming Freshman Musical Theatre Majors: A Ten-Year Retrospective Study." Fall Voice Conference, October 4–6, 2012, New York City.

Leydon, C., M. Sivasankar, D. Falciglia, C. Atkins, and K. Fisher. "Vocal Fold Surface Hydration: A Review." *Journal of Voice* 23, no. 6 (2009): 658–65.

Leydon, C., M. Wroblewski, M. Eichorn, and M. Sivasankar. "A Meta-Analysis of Outcomes of Hydration Intervention on Phonation Threshold Pressure." *Journal of Voice* 24, no. 6 (2010): 637–43.

Lundy, D., R. Casiano, P. Sullivan, S. Roy, J. Xue, and J. Evans. "Incidence of Abnormal Laryngeal Findings in Asymptomatic Singing Students." *Otolaryngology—Head and Neck Surgery* 121 (1999): 69–77.

Nsouli, T. "Long-Term Use of Nasal Saline Irrigation: Harmful or Helpful?" American College of Allergy, Asthma and Immunology (ACAAI) 2009 Annual Scientific Meeting: Abstract 32. Presented November 8, 2009.

Phyland, D. J., J. Oates, and K. Greenwood. "Self-Reported Voice Problems among Three Groups of Professional Singers." *Journal of Voice* 13 (1999): 602–11.

Roy, N., K. Tanner, S. Gray, M. Blomgren, and K. Fisher. (2003). "An Evaluation of the Effects of Three Laryngeal Lubricants on Phonation Threshold Pressure (PTP)." *Journal of Voice* 17, no. 3 (2003): 331–42.

Satomura, K., T. Kitamura, T. Kawamura, T. Shimbo, M. Watanabe, M. Kamei, Y. Takana, and A. Tamakoshi. "Prevention of Upper Respiratory Tract Infections by Gargling: A Randomized Trial." *American Journal of Preventative Medicine* 29, no. 4 (2005): 302–7.

Shadkam, M., H. Mozaffari-Khosravi, and M. Mozayan. "A Comparison of the Effect of Honey, Dextromethorphan, and Diphenhydramine on Nightly Cough and Sleep Quality in Children and Their Parents." *Journal of Alternative and Complementary Medicine* 16, no. 7 (2010): 787–93.

Sivasankar, M. and C. Leydon. "The Role of Hydration in Vocal Fold Physiology." *Current Opinion in Otolaryngology—Head and Neck Surgery* 18, no. 3 (2010): 171–75.

Stone, R., T. Cleveland, and J. Sundberg. "Formant Frequencies in Country Singers' Speech and Singing." *Journal of Voice* 13, no. 2 (1999): 161–67.

Sundberg, J., T. Cleveland, R. Stone, and J. Iwarsson. "Voice Source Characteristics in Six Premier Country Singers." *Journal of Voice* 13, no. 2 (1999): 168–83.

Tanner, K., N. Roy, R. Merrill, F. Muntz, D. Houtz, C. Sauder, M. Elstad, and J. Wright-Costa. "Nebulized Isotonic Saline versus Water Following a Laryngeal Desiccation Challenge in Classically Trained Sopranos." *Journal of Speech Language and Hearing Research* 53, no. 6 (2010): 1555–66.

Tepe, E. S., E. S. Deutsch, Q. Sampson, S. Lawless, J. S. Reilly, and R. T. Sataloff. "A Pilot Survey of Vocal Health in Young Singers." *Journal of Voice* 16 (2002): 244–47.

Yang, J., A. Tibbetts, T. Covassin, G. Cheng, S. Nayar, and E. Heiden. "Epidemiology of Overuse and Acute Injuries among Competitive Collegiate Athletes." *Journal of Athletic Training* 47, no. 2 (2012): 198–204.

Yiu, E., and R. Chan. "Effect of Hydration and Vocal Rest on the Vocal Fatigue in Amateur Karaoke Singers." *Journal of Voice* 17 (2003): 216–27.

4

COUNTRY VOICE
PEDAGOGY AND STYLE

COMMERCIAL VERSUS CLASSICAL TRAINING

Commercial and classical vocal training share many similarities but are also somewhat different the further you advance into specific techniques. I like to think of voice training as if I were baking a cake. The basic cake layers have to first be constructed correctly before applying the filling in between the layers and the outer frosting. The filling and frosting are what make each type of cake unique in flavor and appearance. As a voice teacher, it is the same in correcting the vocal technique of a singer. The foundational concepts of breath and placement are the same in commercial singing as they are in classical singing. The main differences between commercial and classical vocal training begin with the shape of the mouth, which consequently affects the sound of the individual vowels. Commercial singing demands a flatter, more horizontal shape to the mouth while the classical approach calls for the mouth to assume a tall or vertical shape. The need for flatter or taller sound is mostly dictated by the prosody of the language and the style of each particular genre. Certain genres, especially country, call for the delivery of the lyric to be very conversational; because of this, the shape of the mouth in singing country has to sit much closer to the way in which the mouth is shaped for speech.

As a student and performer of both classical and commercial singing, I have seen firsthand the benefit in being a very good classical singer in order to become a better commercial singer. Presently, as a commercial voice teacher, I teach all the same breath mechanism and placement concepts as most of my classical colleagues. We talk about the same resonating chambers, including which ones have the ability to be manipulated or reshaped. The difference between classical and commercial can be thought of in terms of a difference in style. Granted, we will discuss some commercial techniques that are not usually talked about in classical training, but I like to think of it as if classical is the foundation and commercial voice pedagogy is simply a layer of technique beyond fundamental classical concepts. We will now take a look at each mechanistic component involved in the act of singing and discuss how each is used when producing a commercial tone—particularly the various vocal sounds that are most often used in country music.

BREATH

Breath is the lifeblood of every good singer! Not only is it one of the essential components to keeping the human body alive, it is the powerhouse mechanism that enables the human body and vocal tract to vibrate and achieve phonation. In simple lay terms, it allows the vocal folds—or vocal cords—to produce a "sung" or sustained tone in the voice. The act of breathing for a singer can be boiled down to the simple motion of inhalation and exhalation. When one stands on a beach and watches the waves, the waves do not come in and stop, wait for a second or two, and then return to the ocean. The moment the waves roll in as far as they can on the beach, they instantly go back from whence they came. There is no stop motion; the waves have an ebb-and-flow motion to them. In the same way, a singer's breath should not contain any stoppage, but should be an ebb-and-flow motion like waves on a beach. I have found that the stoppage of breath in a singer can sometimes lead to problems with subglottal back pressure beneath the vocal folds. One of the biggest challenges of young singers is to learn to use the breath: breathing in, filling up the mechanism, and instantly using it.

Good breathing is good breathing regardless of the style. The *appoggio* technique advocated in classical singing is an approach that will allow the singer to support or suspend each breath and get a lot more mileage out of it, especially, if simultaneously, they can keep the rib cage lifted. The rib cage lifts automatically every time we breathe, but if the singer can learn to keep the cage lifted, a natural vacuum will set up every single time at the end of exhalation. This vacuum aids in the efficiency of how quickly a singer can replenish the breath and instantly recharge the breath support mechanism. This technique of thoracic-abdominal breathing is widely used among most voice teachers, commercial or classical alike, but let us now discuss the importance of using this approach for the country music singer.

Understanding the Breath Mechanism for Singing Country

The importance of managing the breath for singing country is closely connected to the fact that most artists in country will eventually use what we call a "belt" technique. Whereas some may only associate this technique with musical theater singers, it is also used frequently in popular and country singing to achieve the big "shout-style" projected sound. In either genre, most teachers simply refer to it as "belting." Singing in a country style is usually done with a spoken approach; some people refer to this as "speech-level" singing. This is a technique and term that was coined by vocal coach and technician Seth Riggs. Part of this stylistic "spoken" approach comes from a rich history of country, folk, or Americana singers delivering the lyric in a "down-home" or grassroots style. The emphasis of country music has always been on the story of the songs, so the artist almost certainly has to be a storyteller. Because of this, the lyric has to be delivered in a conversational and more "speech-like" manner. Again, this "shout-style" method is a popular approach in country because it lends itself to the style of telling the "story" of the song. However, producing a belted vocal tone cannot be achieved without a consistent suspension of the breath mechanism. The belt technique is an advanced technique that is layered on top of or in addition to the general breath suspension previously mentioned.

Advanced Breath Techniques Used in Belting

Good healthy belt technique is completely dependent upon whether or not the student uses good breath suspension. If the student does not have a comprehensive understanding of general breath suspension, then the student can possibly injure the vocal folds if belting is attempted. In addition to general breath suspension, there is an advanced technique that is associated with belting that will allow the singer to belt healthily without injury. When the general suspension is engaged, the abdomen will expand, the ribs will be lifted, and the oblique abdominal muscles will engage to essentially "hold out" or "hold open" the abdomen so as to not squeeze upon the breath in any way. Advance belt technique is then a push outward or a "kick" outward in the area of the belt, in the belly button area of the abdomen. The kick outward sends an extra surge of breath through the mechanism but not in a tight manner or with any amount of back pressure to the vocal folds. Even though it is widely held among voice professionals that cricothyroid (CT) and thyroarytenoid (TA) function and breath are completely independent of one another, this breath technique is imperative in order to get that big "belt" sound correctly and without injury.

PLACEMENT

Placement of the voice is a controversial subject in some circles of educators. Some voice teachers maintain that one cannot "place" the voice in one particular spot. Even though I understand this argument, I tend to believe that the "placement" of the voice that many teachers speak of religiously is more of a sensation than literal "placement." Placement of a particular word can also be affected by the color of the vowel. Correct placement of the voice usually refers to sitting or "placing" the voice in the "mask" area of the face. The lower side of this area of the face is just below the nose, across the breadth of the cheeks, and upward to the eyes. For years, I have had students who were initially afraid that this would make their voices sound nasal. A nasal or "pinched" sound is not what we are trying to achieve. A nasal sound would be produced if the voice were placed in a more narrow area around the nose. The kind of "mask" placement taught in voice study is a much broader surface area going across both cheeks that will not produce a "pinched" sound if executed properly. When the voice is placed in the mask area of the face, singers will usually initially feel a buzzing sensation that they might not have felt before. This is usually a method of getting the singer to find the correct placement.

Another term that I often use in association with placement is the term "mix." Mixing is talked about in conjunction with placement because the two concepts are so closely related. When I teach "mixing," I discuss using the components of producing "head tone" in conjunction with the components that produce chest voice. Essentially, it is a mixing of the different ways in which the vocal mechanism produces a tone. Directionally, with the cricothyroid (CT) and thyroarytenoid (TA) musculature, instead of only lengthening or shortening to thicken the vocal folds, the mechanism begins to work in conjunction or collectively in more of a diagonal motion. This is essentially the basic idea of mixing. Being able to achieve this concept is contingent on placing the sensation of the voice into the mask area of the face and relaxation of the vocal tract.

General Placement Options for Singing Country

The most desirable sound for a vocal in country music has also been to place the voice forward in the mask of the face. Although some feel this creates a nasal "twang," it can also be perceived as a brighter, more vibrant tone, sometimes thought to have more edge or drive to the voice. A forward placement lends itself to support the conversational approach that country has demanded for decades. From Patsy Cline and Buck Owens to Tammy Wynette, Loretta Lynn, and George Jones, bright forward placement of the vocal has been one of the primary distinguishing factors of a genuine country vocal for almost a century.

THE VOCAL "COLOR PALETTE"

Just beyond the concepts of breath and placement lies another component necessary for authentic country style: the concept of vocal color. Just as a visual artist needs to have every color imaginable on his artist palette, a singer needs to have every possible vocal color at her disposal on her vocal color palette. Developing these colors takes a lot of experimentation with reshaping and manipulating the resonating chambers. We are talking about the singer simply developing more tools that can be used to deliver the tone or color that might be asked of him or her at any moment. This is particularly useful for background vocalists or demo singers who work with a variety of producers. Producers in this type of setting normally already have the sound they want to hear in their heads. It is the studio singer's job to deliver whatever color he or she is asked to produce. Usually the singers who are versatile and incredibly good at this will be asked back and rehired time and time again. Let us now explore several different ways that singers can develop a broader color palette in their voice.

Reshaping Resonating Chambers to Affect Sound/Color

The vocal mechanism contains four major resonating chambers, two of which can be reshaped or altered to affect the color or tone of the vocal sound. The sinus cavity is the first or highest resonator in the body. The bone structure surrounding the sinus cavity greatly determines one's sound but cannot be altered short of a singer having their adenoids removed, which usually only produces a slight difference in sound.

The mouth is the highest resonating chamber that can actually be reshaped by altering the space inside the mouth cavity and the position of the tongue and jaw. The voice community often identifies this reshaping technique as vowel modification. "Vowel modification" is the technique of changing the shape of the vowel slightly to relax tension in the jaw and tongue, freeing up the position of the vocal tract/mechanism.

The throat is the next lowest resonating chamber and also has the ability to be reshaped. The shape of the throat can vary from constricted and tight to open and relaxed. I can usually always get a student to open their throat by using a "football player" or "New Yorker" vocal exercise. Football players tend to use a deep, low-larynx, open throat when they speak. New York males have a tendency to speak to each other in the same way. For instance, if you bump into a New Yorker on the street, he might say, "Hey, what are you doing?" with a very low, dark, even "hooty" sound. Getting that rich, dark sound is all about opening up the throat and allowing the larynx to "sit down." To clarify, I am not saying the larynx should be forced down in any way but allowed to sit down in a relaxed position. This technique will help the singer achieve an open throat.

The fourth resonating chamber is the chest or upper bronchial area of the chest. This chamber cannot be altered, but in the lower range of both males and females, one is able to hear the chest "resonate." This resonation is usually also perceived by the singer as a "buzz" or vibration in the upper chest area.

THE USE OF DYNAMICS IN COUNTRY MUSIC

The use of dynamics is a very important part of country singing. A singer has to have some amount of control in the voice to transition from loud to soft in an instant. The country belt voice, by nature of how it is produced, is normally louder than other singing. The placement of the tone in a frontal or forward position also contributes greatly to this loud dynamic. On the flip side, the country singer has to have the ability to sing quietly and thoughtfully in most opening verses of a country ballad. The country ballad is usually designed to be a story song. Without the ability to sing the beginning of the story-song ballad quietly, the country singer will have a more difficult time drawing the audience in. We call this "hooking" the audience. When telling a story, you want your audience to "lean in" in the beginning in order to hear exactly what you are saying, captivating them, essentially having them sit on the edge of their seats. Some up-tempo country songs in today's market are a little louder on the verses but still have a spoken and dynamically "down" quality to them.

The Dynamic Range Effect on Audience Perception

Loud dynamics with a sustained amplitude over a prolonged amount of time usually has a wearing effect on the audience. No one wants to be screamed at continuously without a break. In the same way, no one wants to be sung to softly for an extended period of time. That would begin to get boring and uninteresting for the audience. A dynamic range, or ebb and flow, of a song is part of what gives the singer a storytelling quality. It is very closely related to patterns of speech and the rise and fall we use in the voice while speaking. When speaking and telling a story, we do not speak everything on the same dynamic level. We use different loudness to emphasize different words and phrases. Audiences also tend to stay more engaged if there is fluctuation in the dynamic range.

COMMERCIAL VOCALIZATION

Commercial vocalizations are ways to not only wake up the voice but also to wake up the placement and style. Think of it as if you are reminding yourself and the mechanism how certain placements and techniques should feel. One commercial vocalization that I like to use with my students is what I call a "siren" sound, similar to what an ambulance produces but of course not nearly as loud. This vocalization technique normally starts on a low pitch in the voice and then the singer slides the voice upward in pitch/frequency to a comfortable high place in the vocal range. The singer then allows the voice to slide or fall in pitch/frequency back into the lower range where it began.

Another commercial vocalization that I use as a stylistic warm-up is what I like to call "cycling." This is the process of taking a vocal run, sometimes called a trick, and cycling it over and over repeatedly in the same spot in the voice (see appendix B). This exercise is one that I also use to teach flexibility in the voice.

The concept of delineation is used in vocal embellishments or in what some refer to as "runs," "vocal licks," or "tricks." Delineation is the concept of putting a small amount of space between the notes in order to clean up the execution. The notes can then be linked more closely together later after the execution is more precise. There is a pop culture reference I use to help with this concept. I refer to it as my "Elmer Fudd" exercise. Many of you who might remember Bugs Bunny cartoons will recall that Elmer Fudd would say, "We are huntin' wabbits!" and he would do it with a popping sound in his voice. This technique is achieved by using the diaphragm. Classical voice teachers often have their students do this popping sound as a breath exercise. In commercial vocalization, it can be used in the same way while singing a particular melodic embellishment. For instance, the singer can begin by singing a

D minor 7 chord starting on the five, singing the pitches five-four-three-one-seven. The singer ends the "lick" on the seven of the chord. This is a very common lick that pop and country artists use frequently (see appendix B). This "Elmer Fudd" technique can essentially be used on any run or embellishment that needs greater precision in the execution.

Basic Warm-Up Vocalization Exercises

Basic warm-ups are essential to keeping the voice healthy. I like to begin my warm-up with students on a simple one-two-three-two-one pattern going up the keyboard in half-step intervals. I like to begin this exercise in their lower range and not take it too terribly high the first time around. The middle section of the voice should essentially "wake up" first, and then we can test the outer limits while keeping the student relaxed and within the realm of healthy vocal production. Many classical teachers I know use this same exercise, but I eventually like to have students do the exercise while singing straight tone. I have found that this is a good way to monitor their straight tone usage to make sure they are still producing a healthy unpressed tone.

Basic Warm-Up Exercises While Changing Vowel Shape

Once a student has found a way to produce a healthy tone on one particular vowel (let's say an "ah"), we then need to begin to change the vowels she uses during her exercises. This could be something as simple as AY-EE-OH-EE-AH. The intent of this concept is to begin to get her production of the exercise back more closely to the prosody of the language. Realistically, the songs that the students will be singing contain a constant change of vowel, so getting the students to warm up in this way will only help them associate their healthy commercial vocalization with good healthy singing in their songs.

Using Unassociated Spoken Phrases As Vocalization

Taking an unassociated, random phrase and using it as a vocalise is a way to connect vocal exercises more closely to the prosody of the language that the artist is singing in his or her songs. Two phrases I have used as exercises with students are "Where are you going?" and "What are you doing?" I ask the student to speak the phrase on a relatively high pitch and then slide the phrase down in pitch to the lower area of the range while chewing and overemphasizing the words. This type of exercise is an attempt to use almost the entire range while the vowel and shape of the mouth is changing dramatically. Getting the student to speak the phrase while sliding the pitch from top to bottom is the key to this exercise. I have found this to be particularly helpful with students who seem to speak in a relaxed manner but tighten up the minute they think "sing." This exercise helps to disconnect their incorrect association of "singing" and "tension."

Connecting the Vocalization with the Song Lyric

The next step is to get the singer to connect the same exercise with the lyric of their songs. The best approach is to get them to just speak the lyric. Try to get them to speak it on a single monotone pitch while trying to connect each word. Sustaining the voice while speaking the lyrical phrase is the main concept that we are trying to achieve with this exercise.

Speaking the Song Lyric with a Rise and Fall

Even though it may seem elementary, being able to speak the song lyric with a sustained rise and fall in the voice is actually something of a vocalise. Have students begin to speak the lyric and raise the voice to different pitches and lower the voice to different pitches at will. They can take the pitch all over the place as long as they move the pitch around while speaking the lyric. With an exercise of this type, the singer will begin to understand how to control the voice while connecting it to the prosody of the language.

Speaking the Song Lyric on Pitch

One of the final stages in this connectivity process is to speak the song lyric on pitch. Many people refer to this as speech-level singing—to get the singing voice on the same level as speech. I have found that as soon as I can get students to relate their singing voice to their speaking voice, the vocal mechanism begins to achieve a more relaxed state. I have even used the concept of what I like to call a "controlled shout." Some teachers might not agree with this concept, but getting students to act as if they are trying to get someone's attention on the other side of the street has been just short of magical when it comes to freeing up the voice and getting them to understand projection and connecting the voice to the breath.

Speaking the Song Lyric on Pitch While Sustaining

Speaking the song lyric on pitch while sustaining the tone is just shy of singing. This technique is a good one to use with students who carry a lot of tension in the jaw, neck, and face. I try to get them to just speak the lyric and, as I like to say, "elongate" the tones. When done in a nonchalant manner, it begins to show them that sustaining a tone in singing does not have to be tense. Sustaining the tones, even though it is only speech at this point, is getting them to understand how to have consistency in the breath and how to connect the breath to phonation. For them to be able to produce a smooth, consistent tone in singing country, they need to be able to produce a smooth, consistent line of breath without "bumps in the road" or inconsistencies in the tone quality. A breath exercise mentioned earlier that uses a very consistent breathy hiss would also be a good exercise to remind the students of this concept.

Belt Technique Exercises and Phrases

The concept of belt technique is one that demands some very specific exercises to help keep the voice healthy. When warming up a student's "belt" voice, it might be a good idea to first make sure she is warmed up with a basic traditional vocalise of some kind. Once the voice is warmed up, proceed with having her speak the words, "Oh, yeah" on a pitch somewhere in the middle of her range. This exercise is a good one to use because of the way the "Y" springs the voice open on the second half of the short phrase. Taking this exercise up in half-steps through her upper belt range, but not stretching the mechanism too much, will give the student's voice a good workout. Another word that is helpful to use as a vocalise is the word "run." This word is particularly helpful because of the way the "R" is closed and then opens up into an "Ah" vowel. It is similar to the concept of the "springing the vowel open" action that was used with the "Oh, yeah" vocalise. When working on the student's belt voice and trying to get her to achieve complete freedom and openness in the upper belt register, it is imperative for the exercises to first have some kind of action from the tongue and to second, have a springing action into a vowel that is open and relaxed. The action of the tongue from the "Y" to the "eah" gives the student a moment where the tongue releases and sits down, which allows her to experience the "free" sensation associated with healthy belting.

STYLE TECHNIQUES FOR SINGING COUNTRY

Beyond the technical aspects of singing country lies the ability to style a phrase and to be able to do so in a way that sounds authentically country. There is a broad range of what some would consider a "country" sound. For instance, someone with a thick Northeast accent who doesn't sound country at all when speaking could sing in a country style perfectly well. He might not have as much of a drawl in the voice as someone from the Deep South, but nonetheless, it could still be country. The main thing to remember with country style is that it is a very conversational style. It needs to be an authentic sound for whoever is singing it. Let us take a look at some specific style techniques that are used frequently in producing a country vocal.

Vocal Flip

The vocal flip is a concept that most teachers and singers understand as flipping across the register break from chest to head voice. This vocal flip is what allows a student to be able to yodel. Think of it as a gymnast who is doing backflips all the way across the gymnasium. He bounces on his hands, then feet, then hands, and so on. Yodeling is similar in that the singer is continuously flipping back and forth across the upper register break. As a note, some people also call this upper register break the upper bridge. Yodeling is predominantly about the execution of the vocal flip, but it is not the only subgenre that incorporates the use of vocal flip. If you listen to a broad spectrum of country singers and songs, you will hear them frequently flip across the break into their head voice (females) and falsetto (males). Stylistically, it is also a nice shift in dynamics from a loud chest quality to a quiet upper head/falsetto tone.

The Country "Hitch"

The country "hitch" is actually the opposite direction of what we just discussed with the vocal flip. It also involves flipping across the register break but from the high voice down into the lower voice. I like to say it sounds like a "cry" in the voice. I suppose I use that term because usually when someone starts to cry, you will hear his or her voice break. With this technique the singer thinks head voice and starts there but immediately lets the voice break across the register and land in the chest voice.

Dip and Push

The term "dip and push" is just a description we have begun to use of a technique that is as old as country music itself. Patsy Cline was probably one of the artists who was best at this technique. It is really as simple as "dipping" below the note, immediately rising to the correct pitch, and then pushing the tone slightly. You will hear this used more in the traditional country singers, but even in pop country the "dip" or "scoop" up to the note is used frequently.

The "Fall Off"

The "fall off" in country style is just the technique of letting the pitch fall at the ends of phrases. Most country singers try to use this technique sparingly or it could get annoying. You wouldn't want to hear the end of every phrase contain a "fall off," right? But used in the right place, this technique can be very effective. Just to clarify, sometimes the "fall off" might not be a slide but could be just a one-note "step down" or "step off."

Rich Lower Voice

Another quality that is quite useful in country style is the rich lower voice. This type of sound is achieved with some of the open-throat techniques that we discussed earlier. To get that warm open sound, the throat has to remain open and relaxed. The "football player" concept or "New Yorker" way of speaking might help the student understand how to open up his throat and get a much richer sound in the lower part of his range.

Light, Wispy Upper Voice

A wispy, light quality in the upper voice is also a necessary sound to have in a singer's so-called bag of tricks. I sometimes like to call these "hooty" embellishments. Saying the word "Who" or "Hoo" in the upper voice with a very light, wispy quality is something that could be used toward the end of a big ballad where a little improvisation might be in order. Some of the pop stars of the past, like Whitney Houston, have made this "hooty" voice one of their signature licks. Even in country style, there will most definitely be moments where this little nugget will be exactly what the end of the recorded track needs.

THE POWER OF A HEALTHY "BELT" VOICE

We are going to end our discussion about country vocal pedagogy and style by talking a little about the healthy "belt" voice. If there is one technique in country that is a "must-have," it is the belt voice. The sheer power of a healthy belt voice will carry a big ballad and essentially "sell" it to the audience. Coupled with some "hitch" or "cry" in the voice, it will often evoke great emotion in the performance. I believe the sensation that is achieved here is of the singer being in a desperate and emotional place, "shouting it out" from the very depths of her soul and "telling it like it is." When used correctly, a big, healthy belt voice can be quite powerful in the moment during a singer's performance.

5

THE COUNTRY SONG

SONG TYPES

For decades, country music has been a genre that has gleaned much of
its popularity from the "story" of the country song and the delivery of
its "storytellers." Within the genre, there are a variety of different song
types including the ballad, story song, up-tempo "barnburner," mid-
tempo "feel good" song, and the regional country song forms of blues,
Cajun, and zydeco. The artistic album cut and radio single are types of
album cuts that largely depend on the record label's estimation of their
general market popularity. All these different types and uses of songs
are things that need to be considered by the aspiring country singer who
is attempting to build a career from the ground up.

The Ballad

Historically, the country ballad has been the vehicle for telling the
sad love song or thought-provoking slow song. These are the songs that
typically pull at the emotions of the listener, making them cry or get sentimental, remembering what was or what could have been. The tempo
of a ballad is slow, and the harmony usually changes at a fairly slow rate,
usually no more that two chords per bar or less. The usual characteristic

of a ballad is to have verses that set up a story of some kind with a pay-off or a high point in the song somewhere around two-thirds of the way through. There is normally a slight distinction in rhythm from the verse to the chorus, just to give the song some variety. The rhythm on the chorus is more drawn out and the melody is typically higher on the country ballad so that the singer has the ability to make the chorus "soar." ♪

The Story Song

The "story song" is just what it sounds like, a song that tells a story. Often a story song is also a ballad, but it can also be up-tempo. The verses on a story song are intended to set up the chorus. The chorus is the answer to the question that is posed by the verses. As an artist considers story songs for albums or live shows, she needs to consider what she wants to sing about. It is all well and good for an artist to say that she sings story songs, but if the country singer cannot relate to the story, then the singer will have a difficult time convincing her audience and making the story believable. Choosing or writing the right material, and more specifically the correct story song, is quite important to building the artist's career and in finding a way to genuinely relate to their audience. ♪

The Up-Tempo "Barnburner"

The up-tempo "barnburner" is a fast song that is often a good choice to open or close live concert appearances. These songs can include a story but generally are a little bit less serious or "lighter" in tone and message. The harmony is usually a little more simple, but the rhythm of a barnburner can be quite complex but repetitive. Often the message of this type of song is a "good love gone bad," or "I told you so" type of lyric. Some people would call these types of songs "sassy" or "spicy" with a little intentional "tongue-in-cheek" attitude to them. Nonetheless, these songs are audience pleasers that will bring a smile to the face of almost any die-hard country music fan. Although the up-tempo barnburner can be a little more basic in harmony, the rhythmic complexity calls for more attention to detail in execution from the band. These songs usually require a little more rehearsal. The rhythmic hits and transitions from one section of the song to another need to be incredibly precise. The rhythmic pocket in which the band all plays together is what will take the most time to get correct. ♪

The Mid-Tempo "Feel Good" Song

The mid-tempo "feel good" song is sometimes used as a second song in a live set or an inside cut on an album to change the pace or the flow. These songs can also sometimes be story songs but are often just songs about everyday life. The harmony of these songs is usually rather simple and quite repetitive with a clear distinction between the different verse-chorus-bridge sections of the song. The lyrics of these songs are usually topics that reflect positive ideals, an attempt to make the audience "feel good." ♪

Regional Country Forms: Blues, Cajun, Zydeco

Regional country song forms come out of different sections of the country because they are connected to the people of that area. The regional country form of blues has been found in many areas of North America, but probably none more popular than the Memphis, Tennessee, area. The blues have influenced country music since the very beginnings of the style itself, but country blues (also folk blues, rural blues, backwoods blues, or downhome blues) is mainly known to be an acoustic, guitar-driven form of the blues that mixes blues elements with characteristics of folk. When African American musical tastes began to change in the early 1960s, moving toward soul and rhythm and blues music, country blues found renewed popularity as "folk blues" and was sold to a primarily white, college-age audience. ♪

Cajun country songs are usually associated with the French/Louisiana area. Cajun music is relatively harsh with an infectious beat and a lot of forward drive, placing the accordion at the center. Besides the voices, only two melodic instruments are usually heard, the accordion and fiddle, but usually in the background can also be heard the high, clear tones of a metal triangle. The harmonies of Cajun music are simple, basically I, IV, and V (tonic, subdominant, and dominant) with many tunes just using I and V. The melodic range is fairly limited, usually spanning just one octave. ♪

Zydeco is a musical genre that evolved in southwest Louisiana among French Creole speakers. It blends blues, rhythm and blues, and music indigenous to the Louisiana Creoles and the native people of Louisiana. Usually fast tempo and dominated by the button or piano accordion and a form of a washboard known as a "rub-board," "scrub-board," or "wash-board," zydeco music was originally created at house dances, where families and friends gathered for socializing. In the past, zydeco music typically integrated waltz, shuffles, two-steps, blues, rock and roll, and other dance music forms of the era. Today, zydeco integrates genres such as R&B, soul, brass band, reggae, hip-hop, ska, rock, Afro-Caribbean, and other styles, in addition to the traditional forms. ♪

The Radio Single

The radio single is a particularly notable song recorded on an artist's album (usually no more than 3:30 in length) that has been processed with an extra amount of compression by the mastering engineer and promoted or sent to radio stations seeking airplay. The compression is done so that all the frequencies are at a more even level, making the recording more suitable for radio broadcast. The artist's first radio single is usually an up-tempo song unless one of the ballads on the album seems to have an unusual "hit" factor, and even then sometimes the ballad is still saved for the "second single" spot instead of the first. Radio singles are a significant revenue stream for artists and songwriters since they get paid for every time the song plays on the air. The performance rights organizations—ASCAP, BMI, and SESAC—are the institutions that collect these monies from the performance halls, venues, and radio stations and pay out the revenue for each song to the artist/writer.

The Artistic Album Cut

Even though some artists and producers might like for every song on an album to be a single, realistically it's not usually possible and maybe should not even be designed in such a way. There are cuts (songs recorded) on an artist's album that are generally known in the industry as "inside" cuts. These are songs that probably would not translate well to radio play but have a particular artistic value to the artist and to the artist's audience. Sometimes these songs are much longer than the usual length for radio singles and often have a harmonic progression or melody that is just a little off the beaten path, thus the description of "artistic" album cut.

SONG STRUCTURE

A country song is generally structured into one of three forms: verse chorus verse chorus chorus (ABABB), verse chorus verse chorus bridge chorus (ABABCB), or verse verse chorus verse (AABA). There are a few songs that have just a repeated verse format, but those are not very common. The verse material is usually always a setup for the chorus and is usually less active rhythmically and less complex harmonically than the chorus. The general rule for putting a bridge into a song is to give the song a bit of a lift or perhaps say something that hasn't already been said. It can sometimes illuminate the meaning of the rest of the song or give the song a twist lyrically into the last chorus. It is common for publishers to discourage young artists/writers from writing a bridge unless they have something new to say or want to give the song a musical break or lift.

Crafting the Hook/Title

From the songwriter's perspective, the hook or title of the song is of utmost importance! The hook is what the grassroots American music lovers remember as they are riding around in their cars or as they are parking their Chevy trucks and walking into Walmart. You want that title to be so singable and memorable that it sticks with them. You want them to not be able to stop humming the song when they get out of their car. This is what some people refer to as the "hit" factor. Some also call it the "it" factor, because they think a song that captivates the general public in such a way definitely has "*it!*" The hook is the part of the song that we as songwriters think the public will be able to "hold on to" or "grab on to" as listeners. The hook is usually the title but occasionally is not. If the hook *is* the title, it will only help the artist or company with the ability to promote and market the song to the highest degree. Additionally, the melody must be crafted in a way that is easily singable for people who are not as musically inclined. The lyrics of the hook also need to be words that are easy to remember and somewhat meaningful to the listener, or at least something they can relate to.

Developing the Idea

As a songwriter begins to develop the idea for a song, many times he will write a paragraph about what he is trying to say before he begins writing the lyric itself. Think about a speech you might give. The first thing you would do is write down some of your ideas for the speech, correct? It is the same concept in songwriting. When developing the idea, the songwriter should think about what the payoff will be. The verses are certainly going to set up or ask the question while the chorus is the answer to the question. The bridge is sometimes the payoff that either illuminates the chorus in a whole new way or makes the chorus suddenly mean something completely different. This is what we usually mean by "payoff." What is going to be that "gotcha" moment in the chorus or bridge that draws the listener in and makes them cry or maybe just makes them really happy? It might also be a moment that makes them remember a very happy time in their life. Then after the idea has been considered and discussed (if co-writers are involved), the lyric will begin to be crafted by the writer or writer(s) line by line.

Setting up the "Hook"

Setting up the "hook" in the song is sometimes the greatest trick of all in songwriting. As discussed previously, the verse poses the question and then the chorus answers the question. However, the way in which the hook hits, whether it be the top of the chorus or somewhere else, usually takes quite a bit of crafting from the songwriters. You want the hook to be set with a line just ahead of it that makes it feel completely natural, as if it just came spontaneously out of a conversation between two people. This is what will make the listener connect to the song and be captivated by the "hook" of the song.

Concept Twist

A concept twist in a song is not a technique that is used frequently but occasionally is exactly what is needed. This concept twist usually happens on the bridge or last chorus and takes the general idea of the song and turns it into something that means a little more or that might mean something a little different to the listener.

To Bridge or Not to Bridge

Whether or not a songwriter writes a bridge into a song should mostly be a question of whether or not he or she anything else to say. Sometimes an artist can create a bridge with a musical or instrumental break of some kind. This is a technique that will just give the song a lift or a break before going into the last chorus and finishing off the song.

Arrangement Considerations

After writing a country song, the country artist/writer has myriad options to explore when it comes to the arrangement of the song. Normally country songs contain an intro, the body of the song, and then what is called an "outro." This outro is very similar to the intro but finds a nice, easy way to musically draw the song to a close. The chords that are used throughout the verse, chorus, and bridge are usually always the same, but the arranger usually decides what those are prior to preparing charts for the performances or the recording session. In country, most of the harmony is pretty basic: I, IV, and V (tonic, subdominant, and dominant) chords with an occasional ii or vi minor chord included to create a musical lift. There are very few seventh chords in country music harmony except on songs that have more of a blues, gospel, or soulful edge to them.

Payoff/Selling Point

Anyone who wants to be successful singing country music needs to consider the payoff or "selling point" in the performance of any particular song he or she chooses to sing. This payoff moment is a high point or pinnacle spot in the song that audiences have grown to expect. It is a bit like taking a journey up a mountainside only to be able to say "Eureka!" once you hit the summit and then start back down the other side. The journey that a performer takes us on into a song is quite similar. The beginning of the song should be a gentle slope, easing us into the song in order to set up the audience for the big payoff. This is also true on fast songs because the intro of the fast song is the ramp just before takeoff. There are exceptions to this rule in that occasionally a song starts off with a "bang," but, if you will notice, after the big or loud beginning of a song of that type, the dynamics come back down once the song proceeds into the verse.

The way a country singer sings these payoff moments is just as important as the "story" or the lyric itself. The payoff moment or selling point in the song has to be sung well or it could be a massive letdown for the audience. Especially on ballads and the choruses of fast songs, country singers will usually engage the "belt" technique that was mentioned in a previous chapter. If their belt technique is not healthy and open or suddenly sounds strangely different from the rest of the voice, then the payoff moment might be lost. The belt technique that is used in a payoff moment of this kind should sound open and free, not strained and tight. This healthy belt technique will only make more out of the payoff or selling point of the song.

Closing the Sale

From the moment that the selling point or payoff of the song is over, it is the country singer's responsibility to "close the sale" on the song. The end of the song, or downward slope, so to speak, is the part of the song where the singer has to have a tremendous amount of control. The quiet, controlled sound that still has a beautiful tone quality and keeps the listener engaged is the most difficult sound to maintain. The breath support and breath suspension that were discussed previously is what will make or break the singer's ability to "close the sale" and beautifully negotiate the final few notes and lyrics of the song.

DICTION MATTERS

A singer's diction is what makes a country song sound country or a rock song sound rock. It is the way in which the singer delivers the lyric, or the words of a song. Most country singers deliver the words of their songs with a little bit of a southern drawl or southern dialect in the voice. In other words, they sound like they are from the country. Even Shania Twain, who is from Canada and does not speak with a southern drawl, sounds a little bit like a southerner when she sings. Singers who want a career in country music need to pay attention to their diction because believe it or not, diction really does matter. ♪

Diction Options in Country Music

There are several different options for a singer's diction in country music, but they all take a trip through the land of "southern drawl." Previously mentioned techniques like the "dip and push" help make a contribution to the voice sounding more southern. If you will notice when someone is simply speaking with a southern accent, they are dipping and slurring many of their words. Sometimes I like to call this "chewing" their vowels, but certainly the "dip up" into a word is quite prominent in the southern dialect.

INSTRUMENTATION ISSUES

Instrumentation is a big piece of the puzzle when one begins to consider what makes country "country." For decades, the moment a mandolin, banjo, or fiddle took the stage, especially altogether, audiences have instantly known what type of music they were about to hear. The instrumentation somewhat defines the style even within the country genre. If an artist wants to make her song more bluegrass, she will employ the use of a fiddle, mandolin, banjo, and dolbro. If the artist wants to make his song sound more country pop, he might not use any of those instruments and might instead use piano, keyboard, and electric guitar.

Instrumentation According to Style

One other thing that an artist might want to consider is that the song will sometimes dictate the instrumentation. Songs can certainly be pushed or forced into a certain style, but many times the type of melody and the way in which the song is written will have a lot to do with what style is actually the best option for the song. This is one reason an artist needs to be very careful when picking out material. Also, if the artist is a writer, she does not need to try to sing the song just because she wrote it. Maybe that particular song is not the best material for her and might be better if a different type of artist recorded that particular song.

Touring Considerations

When it comes to an artist's instrumentation, it might be wise to consider the type of musicians and instrumentation you want to be touring with for a very long time. The style that an artist chooses needs to be something she is absolutely crazy about or she will get sick of it after a while. There will probably be times he grows sick of it anyway, but if the artist really loves the style he is performing, he will make it through the rough times when nothing seems fun. The kinds of people and bandmates that an artist might want to spend a lot of time with are an important consideration that has to be discussed. An artist's manager or agent will probably be a good resource to help make some of these tough decisions along the way.

Developing an Instrumentation Concept

The aspiring artist needs to begin developing a concept for her very specific style and instrumentation early on in her career. This will only come with experimentation or trial and error. If the artist is a writer, some of this will come from the type of songs she is writing, but it does not have to. It is, however, a little easier to find material if the artist is generating her own songs, and usually an artist/writer will write to the material that she enjoys the most.

6

PERFORMING COUNTRY MUSIC

THE STAGE SHOW

Being onstage is the performer's opportunity to connect with the audience in a very personal way. With that being said, it is also the place where the performer will either gain lifelong fans or lose members of his or her fan base depending on the quality of the performance. There are aspects such as show concept, instrumentation, sound reinforcement, lighting, personnel, transportation, management, and business considerations that cannot be overlooked as important components of the artist's show. Much of the success of the artist's career will depend on how well the artist or the artist's manager is managing all aspects of the live stage show.

Show Concept Programming

One of the first things an artist needs to decide is: What is the message? What do you want to say? These questions will help artists begin to come up with a concept for their stage show. Some artists might just want the audience to have fun the whole time. Others might have a particular message that they want the audience members to walk away with when the show is over. Whatever the message is, the artists themselves need to come up with some kind of concept for the live show. Another possibility is the first half of the show being one concept and the second half being another. Maybe the first half is "high energy" while the second half is "thought provoking" until a certain point toward the end of the show. Maybe the artist wants the second half of the show to make people think or be sentimental and then wants to do a few up-tempo, high-energy songs toward the end to "take it home," so to speak. Most artists do end up closing their live shows with several up-tempo songs in order to leave the audience on a high note.

Instrumentation

The instrumentation that the artist uses for the live show should coincide with the artist's recording. The fan base that the artist has worked so hard to gain will want to hear the songs the way they hear them on the recordings. So, with that in mind, the artist needs to hire the same instrumentation that is on the record. It does not have to be the same players who played on the recording, but it certainly needs to be the same instruments. Sometimes the recording will contain some programming. In this case, the artist needs to make sure to hire a programmer who can replicate the tracks. Another option would be to have a digital audio workstation (DAW) onstage with them where the original tracks can be imported and used as a part of the stage performance. The artist will need to be prepared to either personally rehearse the band or hire a musical director who can rehearse the band, whatever the instrumentation, prior to the tour.

Sound Reinforcement: Plugged or Unplugged?

Sound reinforcement in a concert is something an artist cannot do without. Sometimes the artist will be doing a small house concert and will not need much amplification, but if there is just a guitar or piano playing along with the singer, the artist will at the very least need a microphone in order for the audience to hear the voice. In the case of the artist performing in a very large venue, the sound reinforcement is of paramount importance to the success of the show. Without sound reinforcement in a large hall, no one will ever be heard. When a large venue is booked for the artist, the artist's management usually employs a company to take care of setting up, operating, and tearing down the sound reinforcement system. Some artists who do more medium-sized concerts either travel with their own gear and sound engineer or use the equipment and engineer that is associated with the venue.

Framing the Show: Lighting Concepts

There are many different possibilities when it comes to lighting up the artist's performance. Many smaller venues will have their own lights, while some artists are busy enough that they like to own their own lights and design their own lighting concept. Other artists who are performing in large performance venues will require a lighting director and crew. Wherever an aspiring artist might be on this lighting spectrum, he or she just needs to understand that the lighting concept is a big part of the overall look of the live stage show. For a large show, lighting trusses are typically used and literally frame the show on the stage between the trusses with an assortment of colored moving lights that the lighting director utilizes throughout the show.

Personnel Considerations and Transportation

Hiring the right people might be one of the biggest decisions an artist has to make. These are the people who will be shaping the music and essentially all of the artist's creativity. There is quite a lot at stake when it comes to personnel. These are also people that you are going to have to spend a lot of time with in a bus, van, or car, so you better be able to get along with them really well. Band issues have been notorious for splitting up artist groups. The people you hire to be in your band should also respect you as an artist and at least appreciate your music. The main thing for you to remember is to hire band members that you get along with and with whom you think you would be able to spend a lot of time.

If the artist is transporting a large show, management will probably employ a bus and/or trucking company to get the artist's entourage and equipment to each performance venue. If the artist is transporting a medium to small show, it might be that the artist rents a van, a bus, or a couple of trucks whenever they are needed. Some medium-sized artists own their own buses, but remember that these transports can be very expensive to purchase and maintain.

Business Considerations and Management

Aspiring country music singers need to realize that eventually they will need to think of themselves as the CEO of their "company." The artist will be the only one who is ultimately responsible for what happens in his or her career. For this reason, aspiring artists need to be very careful of the kind of people they have around them. These people need to be individuals who are honest and trustworthy with a strong moral fiber. They need to be people who have the artist's best interest at heart, not their own. Sometimes these people can be family or friends in the beginning of the artist's career as long as they don't get greedy. It would probably be a good idea for artists to have some kind of an escape clause with anyone they employ as a part of their company. Artists should most definitely have a good accountant who knows something about the music business. This will especially help when preparing taxes every year.

Young artists should not worry about getting a manager until they are too busy to do it themselves. Sometimes a family member or friend can begin to help when things get crazy, but management can be expensive, so there is no need to rush into it. As an artist's career grows, so will the need for management. I've heard many managers and artists say that when you really need a manager, you will know it clearly because you will not feel as though you have any time for creativity anymore. When an artist's time to write songs starts to get eaten up by managing affairs, then it is time for the artist to start working with a manager of some kind.

THE RECORDING STUDIO

The recording studio is an environment that is unavoidable for the aspiring country singer. Whether doing demonstration recordings or master recordings, the artist will spend a good amount of time in the recording studio. At first, this environment will be a place that most likely will cause some amount of stress for the artist, but with time the artist will gain confidence and get more acclimated to the scene, finding ways to capture their very best musical offerings.

Deciding on an Album/Project Concept

Much like the stage show, before artists go into the recording studio, they need to decide on a concept for the album or project. What stylistic "camp" is the music going to sit in? What kind of message is the artist wanting to put out with this recording? Defining the concept and coming to a consensus with the rest of the artist's team is a very important step in the recording process.

Choosing Songs

Two scenarios exist when it comes to choosing songs. Either the artist wrote the songs or she is looking for songs that other people wrote. If the artist is a songwriter and plans to write all the material for her artist recording, the artist needs to make sure the songs she chooses are perfectly suited for them. Some artist/writers write certain songs that are better suited for others, and if they are wise, they usually let other artists record those. If the artist does not write and will be looking elsewhere for songs, the artist needs to put out feelers to every publisher and songwriter she knows to make sure people are aware that she is looking for material. The artist's process of looking for material usually takes a few months (or longer). When she has found a good thirty to forty songs, she starts listening and trying to narrow them down. Finding the right songs is imperative to the project going forward. If the artist and team do not feel good about the songs they have, then they need to keep looking or keep writing.

Hiring a Producer

The producer that the artist decides to work with is going to greatly affect the direction of the project and how it is executed. Whoever the artist chooses to produce usually takes the reins and hires the musicians, gets the charts prepared and directs the musicians during the recording session, not to mention producing the artist's vocals, mixing the project, and choosing a tracking and mastering engineer. So because much is determined by the producer, artists need to make sure they choose wisely. Choose someone who is experienced and trustworthy. Remember, this producer will also be handling your money.

Hiring an Arranger

The arranger on the artist's project is the person who is going to decide every chord that the band plays prior to the recording session. During the recording session, occasionally a chord will be changed, but the arranger is the one who prepares everything prior to the session. He is also the one who usually prepares all the charts for the musicians who play the session or else he gets a music copyist to do some of the preparation. If there are any full band hits (where the whole band hits together), then he is the one who will write those into the charts. Tempo is usually determined by the producer and artist, but the arranger has been known to weigh in on tempo for each chart/song.

Chart Preparation

Chart preparation has to be done by someone prior to the recording session. The arranger is sometimes the one who generates the charts; however, occasionally he will give the arrangements to a music copyist and have her prepare the charts. The charts need to look clean and be easy to read in order for the studio musicians to work as quickly as possible. The charts for the recording session include the tempo, meter markings, band hits, all the chords from the intro all the way to the outro, lyrics, and any holds or ritards that might happen somewhere in the chart.

Choosing an Engineer and Studio

Choosing a good engineer can end up being one of the best decisions an artist will make. This is the guy who will more or less be "flying the plane" in the cockpit. He will choose all the microphones, place the microphones, correct phasing problems on stereo mics if any occur, hit the record button, create the tracks to record on, clean up the tracks, and more importantly always be giving his opinion to the producer who sits by his side in the control room. The recording engineer can make or break a recording.

A big part of choosing a studio for a recording project is deciding how much space you need and if a particular studio has the kind of gear that will help you get your project finished. The engineer you choose will be able to help you decide if you are choosing the perfect studio for your project. Chances are the engineers you are considering have all worked in many of the studios that might be possibilities, so basically they will be able to tell you quite clearly which studio is going to be the best place to record your project.

Deciding on Studio Musicians

The studio musicians you use for your recording are critical to getting exactly what you want as an artist. The producer you choose will probably have a lengthy discussion with you regarding this decision. As an artist, you want to make sure you choose musicians that you believe will capture the spirit and the essence of the music you are trying to create.

Setting a Recording Date

Finding a recording date is sometimes a tricky thing to do. Whoever is setting up the session (whether that be the producer or the artist) needs to make sure that everyone involved can do it and the studio is completely free on that particular date. It is better if there is not another session going on down the hall in the same studio. This type of scenario can lead to distraction, not only for the artist but for the guest musicians. The artist's team should be the only ones there, completely free from distraction. The date should also be set far enough in advance that if the arranger or copyist gets a little behind, it still will not affect the recording date.

Preparing for the Session

Preparation for the recording session begins with the recording engineer making some decisions about how to record everything. This includes how instruments will be positioned, how microphones will be positioned, and what type of template to create in the DAW, whether it be ProTools, Logic, or another DAW. Preparation will also include charting and copying out enough parts for all the players by the arranger or music copyist. The artist will need to have lyric sheets in order to sing scratch vocals for the session. The producer will also want a set of charts early in order to make some notes as to the sound to look for from the studio musicians.

Studio Etiquette

There are a few big rules of thumb to remember in the studio. Never set a drink of any kind on the recording console. This is a good way to ruin a very expensive piece of gear and shut down a recording studio for a few days. The second thing to remember is to try to keep the talking to a minimum in the control room. The artist can certainly ask questions since it is her project, but always remember that any talking in the control room has the potential to distract someone from a very important task. This is a good rule for the artist to remember if she has guests come in to observe the session. She needs to make it very clear to the guests beforehand to keep their talking to a bare minimum.

The Safety of Multiple Hard Drives

Everything that is recorded in the modern digital studio on a DAW is recorded onto external hard drives. External hard drives are generally ticking time bombs. They will all blow up eventually. Because of this, a good engineer will want to back up the recording to multiple hard drives after every session—that is right, every session! After every three hours of recording, it would be in the best interest of the artist for the engineer to take time to do a backup. As one engineer once told me, if the project does not exist in at least three places, then it does not exist. I later understood firsthand what he meant by this when I had two hard drives fail while I was doing a backup. Thankfully, I had already backed everything up to another (fourth) hard drive, so I was saved. You cannot be too careful when you have just recorded some great music—you must back it up if you want to make sure not to lose it.

7

CAREER OPTIONS
IN COUNTRY MUSIC

WORKING AS A RECORDING/PERFORMING ARTIST

Becoming a recording artist/stage performer in country music might sound like a "pie-in-the-sky" pipe dream, but for some it has become a reality. Two things are imperative to making this dream come true for the aspiring artist: trying to make good career decisions and learning from mistakes. Working as a performer in the country music industry means getting out and beating the bushes for gigs on a daily basis. A career in country music is a very long road of hard work for the aspiring artist, but it certainly can be done. The opportunities to perform, however, will not just present themselves unless the artist already has some amount of name recognition. New start-up artists have no name recognition and have to somehow get the ball "rolling down the hill," so to speak. They have to get out and try to find venues that will allow them opportunities to perform. This is a difficult task without name recognition, but one way to get started is to do "open-mic" nights at various venues. "Open-mic nights" is a term used by venues that advertise for aspiring artists to show up at the venue on a particular night and do one song. When the artist arrives at the venue, he or she gets a number and in so doing signs up to do one song during the evening's performance. Depending on the venue, this can be a very good way for a young artist to be discovered by a producer or record executive who might be attending the venue to look for local talent. For example, the Bluebird Café in Nashville is a famous venue in the Green Hills community that does open-mic nights every Monday evening. It is a small venue but is frequented by many industry professionals and broadcasts a live stream over the web of every single performance.

The aspiring performer/recording artist also needs to think about recording from the moment she steps onstage. If she is not recording, then she is certainly not yet an actual recording artist. Part of being a performing artist in the modern-day marketplace is doing recordings that can be sold at the artist's live performances or downloaded digitally online.

Another way for an aspiring artist to build a career is with regional promotional events such as National Association for Campus Activities (NACA). This is an organization that hosts regional events where young aspiring artists can showcase their musical talents to a variety of college agents and talent buyers. These talent buyers are always looking for young new artists to bring in to student events on their particular campuses all over the United States. The artist can sign up to be invited to regional showcases in different parts of the country, which introduces him or her to college talent agents. This is only one example of an organization that does this kind of thing, but nonetheless one very good resource for getting an unknown artist in front of a lot of college students who might be potential fans. Building the fan base for the aspiring artist has to be a priority from the very beginning of his or her career. Collecting the attendees' e-mail addresses at the merchandise table at gigs is a way to stay in touch with a fan base. The artist should also try to send out a newsletter to the fan base at least three to four times a year.

Building the Company from Recording Up

The aspiring artist is building a company from the ground up. This means that the artist needs to begin to think of herself as a CEO, or chief executive officer. The CEO is generally responsible for everything that happens in a company, and in the same way, the artist is responsible for every aspect of her career. A good way to think of this is the "artist in 360." This phrase refers to everything affecting and surrounding the artist in 360 degrees. With this in mind, as has been mentioned before, there is not much of a career to build upon until the artist has done some recording. In our modern-day marketplace, the recorded material is the demonstration of what exactly that artist can do. The recording is also one of the commodities, along with the live performance, that is consumed by the public, so the artist needs to make recorded material a priority.

Looking for and finding viable material that the artist can record is a big part of the recording process. Most artists take a good amount of time for this process, anywhere from six months to a year. Once material is chosen, the artist will then move into the arranging stage. If the artist is working with a producer, then the producer will have some hand in helping choose the material, getting it arranged, and making sure that the artist is more than happy with the direction of the recording project. While the songs are in the arranging stage, the producer will begin to choose the recording studio and set up what is called "tracking" dates. "Tracking" is the recording session where the artist is present with the band but is only doing a scratch vocal so that the producer can concentrate on the band tracks. "Tracking" is basically the process of laying down or recording the basic tracks played by the main players in the band, otherwise known as the rhythm section. The singer does what is called a "scratch" vocal just so that the band has an idea of what the singer is going to do. Sometimes this vocal is not even recorded on a vocal condenser mic but can be if available. This vocal is just a template for the final vocals that will be recorded later on a high-quality condenser microphone.

After the band completes the tracking session, usually they will begin to do what is called overdubs. Overdubs are extra guitar parts, perhaps an organ track, extra percussion, or extra keyboard parts. These tracks are usually just extra tracks that are added to the recording to "sweeten" the other tracks or complement the arrangement, adding texture or a thickening sensation to the tracks. Once tracking and overdubs are done, it is time to start recording lead vocals. Lead vocals are normally always recorded before background vocals so that the backgrounds vocals can match every word, vowel shape, and nuance that the lead vocalist is doing.

The lead vocal is often doubled by the artist. In doing so, the artist would record one vocal and then record a second vocal that identically matches the first vocal. He does this by singing along with himself and trying to match every nuance perfectly. This is a technique many producers use that tends to add dimension to the sound of the lead vocal and will set it apart from any other vocal in the recording. A specified amount, depending on the artist, of vocal tuning and editing work usually begins to take place after lead vocals have been recorded. This will include everything from tuning the lead vocal to cleaning up all the instrumental tracks. After vocal tuning and editing takes place, the next phase is the background vocal sessions. The producer and artist will hire the best singers to make the most out of the project, but sometimes the artist is a good choice to be one of those singers. Depending on the artist's level of ability, sometimes the artist's tone and "blendability" is the best choice for background vocals or even as a member of the background vocal group of singers. Another round of vocal tuning and editing is done with the background vocal tracks. Because of the number of background vocal tracks, this process of tuning can be lengthy and time consuming but is usually necessary. With this in mind, it is usually best to try to get the background vocalists to execute the vocals as in tune as possible. This will cut down on time in the vocal-tuning process.

After all the recording is completed, the producer will move the recording project into the mix stage. Usually a separate mix engineer is chosen and a fee is paid for each track that is going to be mixed. The mix stage is a process of getting all the components at the best level so that everything can be heard and nothing is overpowering the lead vocal. After the mix stage, the project will need to be mastered by a mastering engineer. This is more a surgical procedure where if any of the mix is off or if there is a pop or frequency that should be present, the mastering engineer might be able to correct it. It is also the stage where compression is added to each track depending on its use. If a song is going to radio, it is normally compressed a little more than it is for the master recording. After the project has been mastered, the recording is then ready to be duplicated or uploaded to the marketplace. It is then a matter of the producer, artist, or powers that be to get it out to the public through whatever means possible.

WORKING AS A SESSION SINGER,
BACKUP VOCALIST, OR SIDEMAN MUSICIAN

Building a career as a session singer, backup vocalist, or sideman musician is a little different than being an artist but still requires a great amount of planning and effort. For instance, if one of my students in my voice studio begins to talk about wanting to become a session singer, I immediately respond with "Who are you singing for?" or "What demos are you singing on now?" If singers want to do session work, they need to begin by doing as many free demos for their friends as possible until they build up a demand for their work and their voice. Eventually when the phone starts ringing and they start getting calls from people they don't know, they will begin to get paid for what they love doing. Doing free demos might sound like singers are allowing themselves to be taken advantage of, but it is really about the singers being able to get some good samples of their work and their singing. When a singer does a free demo, it is completely appropriate for the singer to ask for a copy of the final recording. This helps singers build up a collection of samples of their work. This is called a demo reel. Once word gets around and people start to appreciate their vocals, they will start having people call and want to hire them to do a vocal. When a singer moves into this stage of being hired, it is always a really good feeling. If a singer does good work and it is heard by the right people, this type of scenario is eventually inevitable. It is all about the artist building a demand for his or her voice.

Being a backup singer for a traveling artist is a little more about letting people know what you are looking for, doing some good singing for those who hire you, and then a whole lot of luck and being in the right place at the right time. There are a few audition opportunities for backup vocalists, but those are not as popular as in years past. Most of the time these days, backup singers get hired because someone referred them to the artist, producer, label, or management company.

Being a musician or sideman in the music industry is similar to being a session singer. If an instrumentalist is interested in doing session work, he needs to do as many free demos for his friends as absolutely possible. Again, when the phone starts ringing, he will start getting paid. It is all about doing good work and playing well, in hopes that other people start to hear some of his good work and want to hire him. In doing this, the artist is creating a demand for his work as a creative artist. In the same way, if instrumentalists are aspiring to play live gigs for other artists, they need to take any and every invitation they get to play. And on every one of these gigs, they need to try to give their very best performance every single time. Each time they play a live gig, it is likely that someone else will hear them and approach them about playing an additional gig.

How to Make a Living Working behind the Scenes

If you love music, even love to sing, and would love to find some kind of job in the music industry, chances are you probably will. The possibilities are limitless when it comes to doing work behind the scenes in the music industry. Just about every kind of job you can imagine is available in the music industry—from receptionist, to road/touring workers, to publishing assistants, to studio managers. Some of these positions require very little skill and some require a certain amount of skill.

Often I have students who decide that being some kind of performing artist might not be for them, but they would still like to work in the music industry. My best advice to them is to figure out what area or aspect of the music industry interests them, then do whatever it takes to get an entry-level job in that area and work their way up through the ranks. The music industry is really just like any other industry—get plugged in with a job on the "ground floor" and work your way up.

There are also jobs such as personal assistants for artists, publicists, accountants, and attorneys for record labels. Most labels have these positions in house. In other words, they provide an office space and salary is paid by the company. Artist management companies and booking agencies also have every level of job available from receptionists to principal artist managers and agents.

8

BUSINESS CONSIDERATIONS

ARTIST MANAGEMENT

Every serious aspiring artist will eventually need to utilize someone to help her manage her career. It is the same as managing a business or even managing a household. There are so many things to take care of, it usually requires the efforts of more than one person to get everything done. When the artist is young and just starting out, this "artist manager" might be a family member or a close friend. This person just needs to be someone who is invested enough in the artist's life and career to help out even though he might not be able to be compensated. The artist manager is someone who usually helps to make the decisions for every aspect of the artist's career, from photo shoots to publicity to recordings and performance venues. The artist needs to be extremely careful in choosing an artist manager because it takes a certain personality type to take control and lead the team yet be willing to yield to the artist's wishes. Many a family has split up or ended up with bad blood because a "manager dad" or "manager mom" has overstepped his or her bounds and caused a rift with the artist, who happens to also be his or her child. This is not the only danger in using a family member for management. If things go bad, it is hard to get out of the relationship. If you hire an outside person to be the artist manager, then you can always fire him if he heads off in a direction that is contrary to the artist's wishes. An artist manager should be the kind of person who is looking out for the artist and trying to take care of the artist's career in 360 degrees. At some point down the road, when the artist starts to make some money, the artist will most likely pay an industry artist manager anywhere from 10 to 20 percent of his annual income.

BOOKING AGENTS

In the early years of a career, most young artists will act as their own booking agents. They will try to get gigs anywhere and everywhere, singing or playing for anyone who will let them sing or play. This is doable in the beginning but will become increasingly hard to manage and maintain and will eat into the aspiring artist's creative time. As the years roll on, most artists will secure the services of a family member or friend to help them book different venues. Many times young artists have several people helping with this process. However, this situation can only work when one central person is managing the calendar; otherwise, the artist might become double booked, which would just make them look bad to the performance venue, concert promoter, and even to their fan base.

Once the artist either gets a record deal or begins to achieve some amount of acclaim, the artist will usually hire an industry professional to be her booking agent. Some of the popular ones in the industry are the William Morris Endeavors Entertainment agency or the Creative Artist Agency. It is common for these agencies to get between 10 and 20 percent of the artist's income. When a record label signs an artist, sometimes they will not even sign the contract until they know that the artist has secured a representative booking agent. The label wants to make sure that if they spend the money on the recording, the artist is set up to support the record and tour. These agencies also often have a team or at least a couple of people who work with the same artist, booking anything from fair dates to large performance hall venues. The more the artist is able to perform, especially early in her career, the quicker she will build a fan base.

CONCERT PROMOTIONS

The concert promoter is the person who takes all the risk bringing an artist into a city. The concert promoter hopes that tickets will sell out and fans will buy lots of food and merchandise. If this is the case, then the concert promoter makes back the earnest money put up as a deposit to secure the date with the artist, plus hopefully the promoter will make some extra from concessions and merchandise specific to that concert date. The artist himself also has to be concerned about concert promotions in order for his fan base to know about performances. One thing the artist will sometimes do is to call in to the local radio station in the city of the venue a few weeks prior to the concert to try and sell more tickets and promote the concert. Sometimes the radio DJs will do a free ticket or T-shirt giveaway. The artist also needs to promote his full itinerary on his website so that loyal fans will know where to catch the next performance.

BUILDING THE FAN BASE

Building the fan base is one of the most important things an artist can begin doing from the very beginning of his or her career. There are many different ways to do this, one being the simple discipline of collecting e-mail addresses at the artist merchandise table every night at every single concert appearance. The artist can also create a website that allows guest to sign in on the site. This will also collect some contact information that will be invaluable for the artist to keep in touch with loyal fans. Once the artist has begun to collect fan-base contact information, he needs to seriously consider publishing a newsletter at least three or four times a year, maybe more. Some artists publish a newsletter once a month, which includes interesting articles about the artist's life and the artist's monthly itinerary. This will allow the loyal fan to feel connected to the artist and will help populate the artist's concerts by letting the fans know where he will be performing each night. Some artists do giveaways on their website for loyal fans, keeping fans coming back to their websites on a regular basis.

BRANDING

In the same way that a store like Home Depot has made it very clear what their brand is, aspiring artists have to succinctly define their brand and their style of music. This is one of the hardest things for a young artist to do. Many of them like to say that they sing a little of everything or that they sing all styles. The problem is that no one then knows what that artist does best and no one knows how to market that artist. When you go in Walmart and go to the area of the store where they have CDs sitting in racks, they are labeled according to category: gospel, country, country-rock, country-pop, R&B, pop, alternative, and so on. There are almost as many categories as there are CDs. A distribution site like Walmart has to know what "pigeonhole" to put that artist in, or else they don't know what to do with her and she will be put into the "other" category, which is usually harder for the consumer to find. Early on, the artist needs to think very carefully about what she wants her image and brand to be. When someone thinks about Home Depot, they know very clearly what one can buy at Home Depot. In the same way, the public needs to be able to look at the artist's CD or digital download cover photo and know pretty clearly what flavor of music will probably be available on that recording. For instance, a hard-edge "rocker" look would probably not be appropriate for a sweet inspirational gospel recording. That is what we would call a mixed message. The look of the artist needs to match the music and vice versa. Many artists secure the services of an image consultant early in their careers to help them put this brand together and formulate some ideas that will help them hit upon the right look as they try to brand themselves into an artist that is recognizable.

THE "SELF-MADE" CORPORATION

The artist who thinks he can just perform, sing, or play and never have to deal with business issues better run the other way. A big part of the artist's career is that of managing the artist's corporation. This is a corporation that is "self-made" by the artist from the beginning of the artist's career. Hopefully the artist has built it in such a way that it is solid and includes a reliable team of people who will not let him down. The artist needs time to be creative and think about his stage show. The more good business management people the artist has on his team, the more time the artist will have to be "the artist." The things that are said onstage, the songs that are chosen, the way the artist moves on stage and relates to the audience are all creative things that the artist needs to have plenty of time to put together himself without extraneous distractions.

OFFICE MANAGEMENT

Every good artist corporation needs a good office location and office manager. This might only be a part-time position in the early years of an artist's career, but eventually the office manager will be someone who is involved in everyday operations. Young artists should be on the lookout to recruit a friend or family member who would be willing to help them manage their office affairs. This kind of volunteer help in the early years of the artist's career can be invaluable.

DOCUMENTING MUSICAL WORKS

Documenting your original works is an important step if you are beginning to play your original songs at public performances. A song is a "copyright" from the moment it is created; however, it is not protected legally until it is registered with the Library of Congress. "Song Form PA" registers songs on the Library of Congress website. Likewise, "Song Form SR" registers sound recordings. If a songwriter is singing his or her songs at a public venue and the songs are not yet registered, there is nothing stopping someone from going home and using part of that artist's melody or lyric. In a court of law, there would be no registration to prove which song was created first. Registering a songwriter's original works is a very necessary part of the artist's career.

9

USING AUDIO ENHANCEMENT TECHNOLOGY

Matthew Edwards

In the early days of popular music, musicians performed without electronic amplification. Singers learned to project their voices in the tradition of vaudeville performers with a technique similar to operatic and operetta performers who had been singing unamplified for centuries. When microphones began appearing on stage in the 1930s, vocal performance changed forever since the loudness of a voice was no longer a factor in the success of a performer. In order to be successful, all a singer needed was an interesting vocal quality and an emotional connection to what he or she was singing; the microphone would take care of projection.[1]

Vocal qualities that may sound weak without a microphone can sound strong and projected when sung with one. At the same time, a singer with a voice that is acoustically beautiful and powerful can sound harsh and pushed if he or she lacks microphone technique. Understanding how to use audio equipment to get the sounds a singer desires without harming the voice is crucial. The information in this chapter will help the reader gain a basic knowledge of terminology and equipment commonly used when amplifying or recording a vocalist as well as provide tips for singing with a microphone.

THE FUNDAMENTALS OF SOUND

In order to understand how to manipulate an audio signal, you must first understand a few basics of sound including frequency, amplitude, and resonance.

Frequency

Sound travels in waves of compression and rarefaction within a medium, which for our purposes is air (see figure 9.1). These waves travel through the air and into our inner ears via the ear canal. There they are converted, via the eardrums, into nerve impulses that are transmitted to the brain and interpreted as sound. The number of waves per second is measured in Hertz (Hz), which gives us the frequency of the sound that we have learned to perceive as pitch. For example, we hear 440Hz (440 cycles of compression and rarefaction per second) as the pitch A above middle C.

Amplitude

The magnitude of the waves of compression and rarefaction determines the amplitude of the sound, which we call its "volume." The larger the waves of compression and rarefaction, the louder we perceive the sound to be. Measured in decibels (dB), amplitude represents changes in air pressure from the baseline. Decibel measurements range

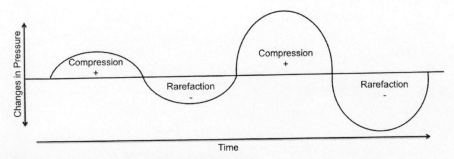

Figure 9.1.   Compression and rarefaction
Creative Commons

from zero decibels (0dB), the threshold of human hearing, to 130dB, the upper edge of the threshold of pain.

Harmonics

The vibrating mechanism of an instrument produces the vibrations necessary to establish pitch (the fundamental frequency). The vibrating mechanism for a singer is the vocal folds. If an acoustic instrument, such as the voice, were to produce a note with the fundamental frequency alone, the sound would be strident and mechanical like the emergency alert signal used on television. Pitches played on acoustic instruments consist of multiple frequencies, called overtones, which are emitted from the vibrator along with the fundamental frequency. For the purposes of this chapter, the overtones that we are interested in are called harmonics. Harmonics are whole number multiples of the fundamental frequency. For example, if the fundamental is 220Hz, the harmonic overtone series would be 220Hz, 440Hz (fundamental frequency times two), 660Hz (fundamental frequency times three), 880Hz (fundamental frequency times four), and so on. Every musical note contains both the fundamental frequency and a predictable series of harmonics, each of which can be measured and identified as a specific frequency. This series of frequencies then travel through a hollow cavity (the vocal tract) where they are attenuated or amplified by the resonating frequencies of the cavity, which is how resonance occurs.

Resonance

The complex waveform created by the vocal folds travels through the vocal tract where it is enhanced by the tract's unique resonance characteristics. Depending on the resonator's shape, some harmonics are amplified and some are attenuated. Each singer has a unique vocal tract shape with unique resonance characteristics. This is why two singers of the same voice type can sing the same pitch and yet sound very different. We can analyze these changes with a tool called a spectral analyzer as seen in figure 9.2. The slope from left to right is called the spectral slope. The peaks and valleys along the slope indicate amplitude variations of the corresponding overtones. The difference in spectral slope

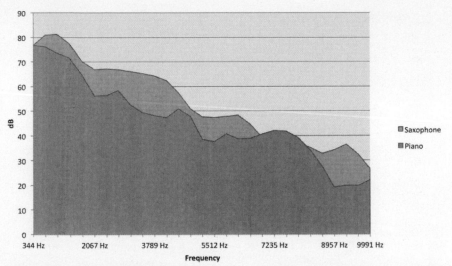

Figure 9.2.   Two instruments playing the same pitch. The peak at the far left is the fundamental frequency and the peaks to the right are harmonics that have been amplified and attenuated by the instrument's resonator resulting in a specific timbre.
Matthew Edwards

between instruments (or voices) is what enables a listener to aurally distinguish the difference between two instruments playing or singing the same note.

Because the throat and mouth act as the resonating tube in acoustic singing, changing their size and shape is the only option for making adjustments to timbre for those who perform without microphones. In electronically amplified singing, the sound engineer can make adjustments to boost or attenuate specific frequency ranges, thus changing the singer's timbre. For this and many other reasons discussed in this chapter, it is vitally important for singers to know how audio technology can affect the quality of their voice.

SIGNAL CHAIN

The signal chain is the path an audio signal travels from the input to the output of a sound system. A voice enters the signal chain through a microphone, which transforms acoustic energy into electrical impulses.

The electrical pulses generated by the microphone are transmitted through a series of components that modify the signal before the speakers transform it back into acoustic energy. Audio engineers and producers understand the intricacies of these systems and are able to make an infinite variety of alterations to the vocal signal. While some engineers strive to replicate the original sound source as accurately as possible, others use the capabilities of the system to alter the sound for artistic effect. Since more components and variations exist than can be discussed in just a few pages, this chapter will discuss only basic components and variations found in most systems.

Microphones

Microphones transform the acoustic sound waves of the voice into electrical impulses. The component of the microphone that is responsible for receiving the acoustic information is the diaphragm. The two most common diaphragm types that singers will encounter are dynamic and condenser. Each offers advantages and disadvantages depending on how the microphone is to be used.

Dynamic Dynamic microphones consist of a dome-shaped Mylar diaphragm attached to a free-moving copper wire coil that is positioned

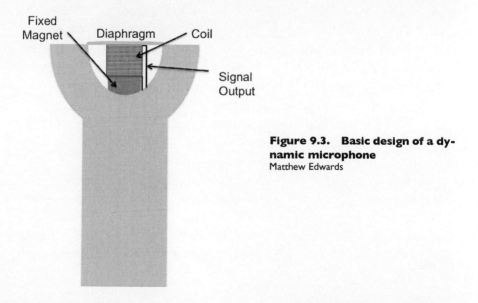

Figure 9.3. Basic design of a dynamic microphone
Matthew Edwards

between the two poles of a magnet. The Mylar diaphragm moves in response to air pressure changes caused by sound waves. When the diaphragm moves, the magnetic coil that is attached to it also moves. As the magnetic coil moves up and down between the magnetic poles, it produces an electrical current that corresponds to the sound waves produced by the singer's voice. That signal is then sent to the soundboard via the microphone cable.

The Shure SM58 dynamic microphone is the industry standard for live performance because it is affordable, nearly indestructible, and easy to use. Dynamic microphones such as the Shure SM58 have a lower sensitivity than condenser microphones, which makes them more successful at avoiding feedback. Because of their reduced tendency to feedback, dynamic microphones are the best choice for artists who use handheld microphones when performing.

Condenser   Condenser microphones are constructed with two parallel plates: a rigid posterior plate and a thin flexible anterior plate. The anterior plate is constructed of either a thin sheet of metal or a piece of Mylar that is coated with a conductive metal. The plates are separated by air, which acts as a layer of insulation. In order to use a condenser microphone, it must be connected to a soundboard that supplies "phantom power." A component of the soundboard, phantom power sends a 48-volt power supply through the microphone cable to the microphone's plates. When the plates are charged by phantom power, they form a capacitor. As acoustic vibrations send the anterior plate into motion, the distance between the two plates varies, which causes the capacitor to release a small electric current. This current, which corresponds with the acoustic signal of the voice, travels through the microphone cable to the soundboard where it can be enhanced and amplified.

Electret condenser microphones are similar to condenser microphones, but they are designed to work without phantom power. The anterior plate of an electret microphone is made of a plastic film coated with a conductive metal that is electrically charged before being set into place opposite the posterior plate. The charge applied to the anterior plate will last for ten or more years and therefore eliminates the need for an exterior power source. Electret condenser microphones are often used in head-mounted and lapel microphones, laptop computers, and smartphones.

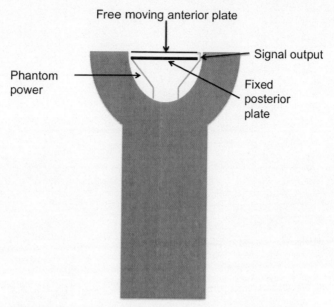

Figure 9.4. Basic design of a condenser microphone.
Matthew Edwards

Recording engineers prefer condenser microphones for recording applications due to their high level of sensitivity. Using a condenser microphone, performers can sing at nearly inaudible acoustic levels and obtain a final recording that is intimate and earthy. While the same vocal effects can be recorded with a dynamic microphone, they will not have the same clarity as those produced with a condenser microphone.

Frequency Response Frequency response is a term used to define how accurately a microphone captures the tone quality of the signal. A "flat response" microphone captures the original signal with little to no signal alteration. Microphones that are not designated as "flat" have some type of amplification or attenuation of specific frequencies, also known as cut or boost, within the audio spectrum. For instance, the Shure SM58 microphone drastically attenuates the signal below 300Hz and amplifies the signal in the 3kHz range by 6dB, the 5kHz range by nearly 8dB, and the 10kHz range by approximately 6dB. The Oktava 319 microphone cuts the frequencies below 200Hz while boosting everything above 300Hz with nearly 5dB between 7kHz and 10kHz (see

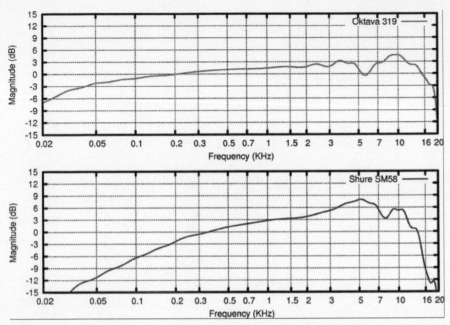

Figure 9.5. Example of frequency response graphs for the Oktava 319 and the Shure SM58
Wikimedia Commons

figure 9.5). In practical terms, recording a bass singer with the Shure SM58 would drastically reduce the amplitude of the fundamental frequency while the Oktava 319 would produce a slightly more consistent boost in the range of the singer's formant. Either of these options could be acceptable depending on the situation, but the frequency response must be considered before making a recording or performing live.

Amplitude Response   The amplitude response of a microphone varies depending on the angle at which the singer is positioned in relation to the axis of the microphone. In order to visualize the amplitude response of a microphone at various angles, microphone manufacturers publish polar pattern diagrams (also sometimes called a directional pattern or a pickup pattern). Polar pattern diagrams usually consist of six concentric circles divided into twelve equal sections. The center point of the microphone's diaphragm is labeled "0°" and is referred to as "on-axis" while the opposite side of the diagram is labeled "180°" and is described as "off-axis."

Although polar pattern diagrams appear in two dimensions, they actually represent a three-dimensional response to acoustic energy. You can use a round balloon as a physical example to help you visualize a three-dimensional polar pattern diagram. Position the tied end of the balloon away from your mouth and the inflated end directly in front of your lips. In this position, you are singing on-axis at 0° with the tied end of the balloon being 180°, or off-axis. If you were to split the balloon in half vertically and horizontally (in relationship to your lips), the point at which those lines intersect would be the center point of the balloon. That imaginary center represents the diaphragm of the microphone. If you were to extend a 45° angle in any direction from the imaginary

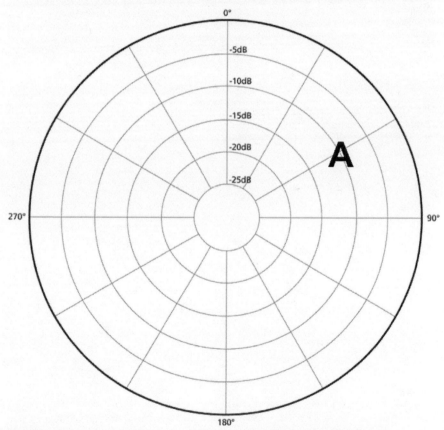

Figure 9.6.   An example of a microphone polar pattern diagram
Wikimedia Commons

center and then drew a circle around the inside of the balloon following that angle, you would have a visualization of the three-dimensional application of the two-dimensional polar pattern drawing.

The outermost circle of the diagram indicates that the sound pressure level (SPL) of the signal is transferred without any amplitude reduction, indicated in decibels (dB). Each of the inner circles represents a -5dB reduction in the amplitude of the signal up to -25dB. For example, look at figure 9.7 below.

The examples that follow (figures 9.8, 9.9, and 9.10) show the most commonly encountered polar patterns.

When you are using a microphone with a polar pattern other than omnidirectional (a pattern that responds to sound equally from all directions), you may encounter frequency response fluctuations in addition to amplitude fluctuations. Cardioid microphones in particular are

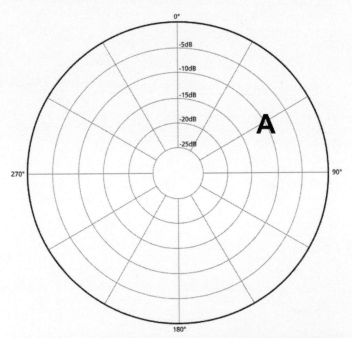

Figure 9.7. If the amplitude response curve intersected with point A, there would be a -10dB reduction in the amplitude of frequencies received by the microphone's diaphragm at that angle
Wikimedia Commons

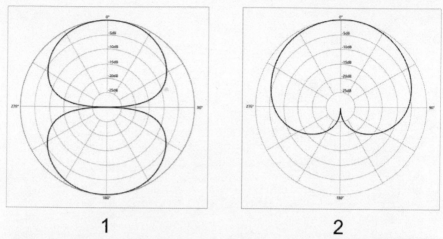

Figure 9.8. Diagram one represents a bi-directional pattern; diagram two represents a cardioid pattern
Creative Commons

known for their tendency to boost lower frequencies at close proximity to the sound source while attenuating those same frequencies as the distance between the sound source and the microphone increases. This is known as the "proximity effect." Some manufacturers will notate these frequency response changes on their polar pattern diagrams by

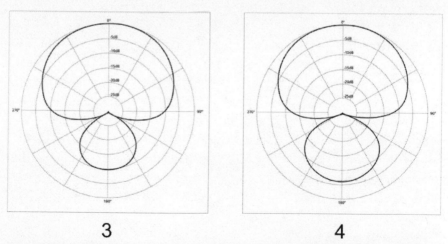

Figure 9.9. Diagram three represents a super-cardioid pattern; diagram four represents a hyper-cardioid pattern
Creative Commons

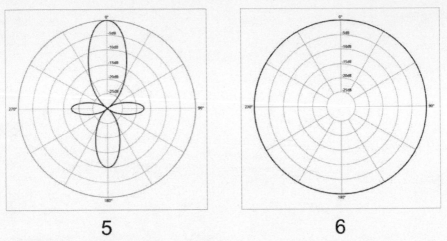

5   6

Figure 9.10. Diagram five represents a shotgun pattern; diagram six represents an omnidirectional pattern
Creative Commons

using a combination of various lines and dashes alongside the amplitude response curve.

Sensitivity While sensitivity can be difficult to explain in technical terms without going into an in-depth discussion of electricity and electrical terminology, a simplified explanation should suffice for most readers. Manufacturers test microphones with a standardized 1kHz tone at 94dB in order to determine how sensitive the microphone's diaphragm will be to acoustic energy. Microphones with greater sensitivity can be placed farther from the sound source without adding excessive noise to the signal. Microphones with lower sensitivity will need to be placed closer to the sound source in order to keep excess noise at a minimum. When shopping for a microphone, the performer should audition several next to each other, plugged into the same soundboard, with the same volume level for each. When singing on each microphone, at the same distance, the performer will notice that some models replicate the voice louder than others. This change in output level is due to differences in each microphone's sensitivity. If a performer has a loud voice, he or she may prefer a microphone with lower sensitivity (one that requires more acoustic energy to respond). If a performer has a lighter voice, he or she may prefer a microphone with higher sensitivity (one that responds well to softer signals).

Equalization (EQ)

Equalizers enable the audio engineer to alter the audio spectrum of the sound source and make tone adjustments with a simple electronic interface. Equalizers come in three main types: shelf, parametric, and graphic.

Shelf   Shelf equalizers cut or boost the uppermost and lowermost frequencies of an audio signal in a straight line (see figure 9.11). While this style of equalization is not very useful for fine-tuning a singer's tone quality, it can be very effective in removing room noise. For example, if an air conditioner creates a 60Hz hum in the recording studio, the shelf can be set at 65Hz, with a steep slope. This setting eliminates frequencies below 65Hz and effectively removes the hum from the microphone signal.

Parametric   Parametric units simultaneously adjust multiple frequencies of the audio spectrum that fall within a defined parameter. The engineer selects a center frequency and adjusts the width of the bell curve surrounding that frequency by adjusting the "Q" (see figure 9.12). He or she then boosts or cuts the frequencies within the bell curve to alter the audio spectrum. Parametric controls take up minimal

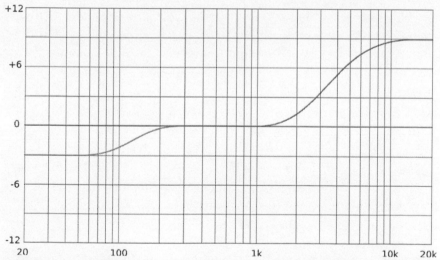

Figure 9.11.   The frequency amplitude curves show the affect of applying a shelf EQ to an audio signal
Wikimedia Commons

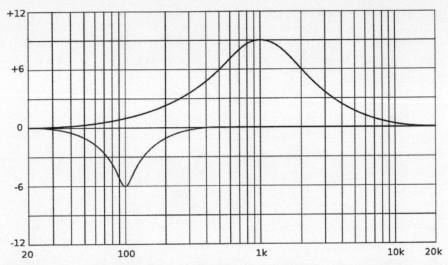

Figure 9.12. The frequency amplitude curves display two parametric EQ settings. The top curve represents a boost of +8dB set at 1kHz with a relatively large bell curve—a low Q. The lower curve represents a high Q set at 100Hz with a cut of -6dB.
Wikimedia Commons

space on a soundboard and offer sufficient control for most situations. Therefore most live performance soundboards have parametric EQs on each individual channel. With the advent of digital workstations, engineers can now use computer software to fine-tune the audio quality of each individual channel using a more complex graphic equalizer in both live and recording studio settings without taking up any additional physical space on the board. However, many engineers still prefer to use parametric controls during a live performance since they are usually sufficient and are easier to adjust mid-performance.

Parametric adjustments on a soundboard are made with rotary knobs similar to those in figure 9.13. In some cases you will find a button labeled "low cut" or "high pass" that will automatically apply a shelf filter to the bottom of the audio spectrum at a specified frequency. On higher-end boards, you may also find a knob that enables you to select the high pass frequency.

Graphic   Graphic equalizers enable engineers to identify a specific frequency for boost or cut with a fixed frequency bandwidth. For example, a ten-band equalizer enables the audio engineer to adjust ten

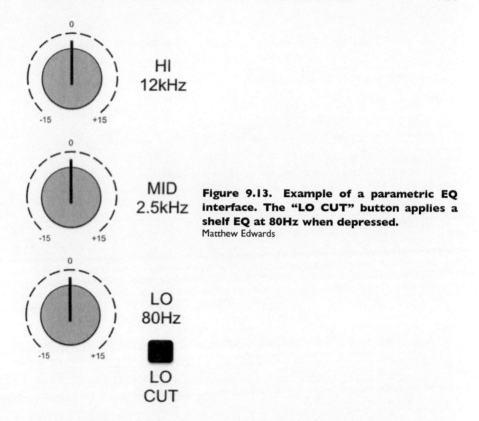

Figure 9.13. Example of a parametric EQ interface. The "LO CUT" button applies a shelf EQ at 80Hz when depressed.
Matthew Edwards

specific frequencies (in Hz): 31, 63, 125, 250, 500, 1k, 2k, 4k, 8k, and 16k. Graphic equalizers are often one of the final elements of the signal chain, preceding only the amplifier and speakers. In this position, they can be used to adjust the overall tonal quality of the entire mix.

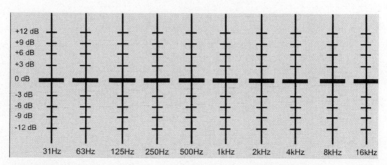

Figure 9.14. Example of a graphic equalizer interface
Matthew Edwards

Utilizing Equalization   Opinions on the usage of equalization vary among engineers. Some prefer to only use equalization to remove or reduce frequencies that were not a part of the original sound signal. Others will use EQ if adjusting microphone placement fails to yield acceptable results. Some engineers prefer a more processed sound and may use equalization liberally to intentionally change the vocal quality of the singer. For instance, if the singer's voice sounds dull, the engineer could add "ring" or "presence" to the voice by boosting the equalizer in the 2kHz to 10kHz range.

Compression

Many singers are capable of producing vocal extremes in both frequency and amplitude levels that can prove problematic for the sound team. To help solve this problem, engineers often use compression. Compressors limit the output of a sound source by a specified ratio. The user sets the maximum acceptable amplitude level for the output, called the "threshold," and then sets a ratio to reduce the output once it surpasses the threshold. The typical ratio for a singer is usually between 3:1 and 5:1. A 4:1 ratio indicates that for every 4dB beyond the threshold level, the output will only increase by 1dB. For example, if the singer went 24dB beyond the threshold with a 4:1 ratio, the output would only be 6dB beyond the threshold level (see figure 9.15).

Adjusting the sound via microphone technique can provide some of the same results as compression and is preferable for the experienced artist. However, compression tends to be more consistent and also gives the singer freedom to focus on performing and telling a story. The additional artistic freedom provided by compression is especially beneficial to singers who use head-mounted microphones, performers who switch between vocal extremes such as falsetto and chest voice, and those who are new to performing with a microphone. Compression can also be helpful for classical singers whose dynamic abilities, while impressive live, are often difficult to record in a manner that allows for consistent listening levels through a stereo system.

Multiband Compression   If a standard compressor causes unacceptable alterations to the tone quality, engineers can turn to a multiband compressor. Rather than affecting the entire spectrum of

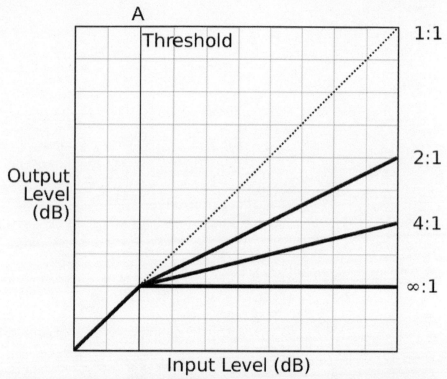

Figure 9.15. This graph represents the effects of various compression ratios applied to a signal. The 1:1 angle represents no compression. The other ratios represent the effect of compression on an input signal with the threshold set at line A.
Wikimedia Commons

sound, multiband compressors allow the engineer to isolate a specific frequency range within the audio signal and then set an individual compression setting for that frequency range. For example, if a singer creates a dramatic boost in the 4kHz range every time he sings above an A4, a multiband compressor can be used to limit the amplitude of the signal in only that part of the voice. By setting a 3:1 ratio in the 4kHz range at a threshold that corresponds to the amplitude peaks that appear when the performer sings above A4, the engineer can eliminate vocal "ring" from the sound on only the offending notes while leaving the rest of the signal untouched. These units are available for both live and studio use and can be a great alternative to compressing the entire signal.

Reverb

Reverb is one of the easier effects for singers to identify; it is the effect you experience when singing in a cathedral. Audiences experience natural reverberation when they hear the direct signal from the singer and then, milliseconds later, they hear multiple reflections as the acoustical waves of the voice bounce off the side walls, floor, and ceiling of the performance hall.

Many performance venues and recording studios are designed to inhibit natural reverb. Without at least a little reverb added to the sound, even the best singer can sound harsh and even amateurish. Early reverb units transmitted the audio signal through a metal spring, which added supplementary vibrations to the signal. While some engineers still use spring reverb to obtain a specific effect, most now use digital units. Common settings on digital reverb units include wet/dry, bright/dark, and options for delay time. The wet/dry control adjusts the amount of direct signal (dry) and the amount of reverberated signal (wet). The bright/dark control helps simulate the effects of various surfaces within a natural space. For instance, harder surfaces such as stone reflect high frequencies and create a brighter tone quality while softer surfaces such as wood reflect lower frequencies and create a darker tone quality. The

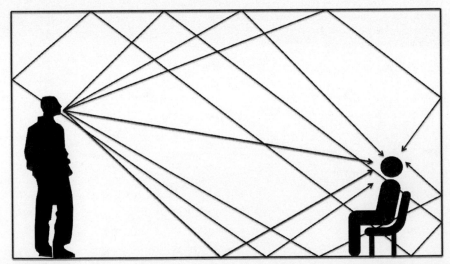

Figure 9.16. This diagram illustrates the multiple lines of reflection that create reverb
Matthew Edwards

delay time, which is usually adjustable from milliseconds to seconds, adjusts the amount of time between when the dry signal and wet signals reach the ear. Engineers can transform almost any room into a chamber music hall or concert stadium simply by adjusting these settings.

Delay

Whereas reverb blends multiple wet signals with the dry signal to replicate a natural space, delay purposefully separates a single wet signal from the dry signal to create repetitions of the voice. With delay, you will hear the original note first and then a digitally produced repeat of the note several milliseconds to seconds later. The delayed note may be heard one time or multiple times and the timing of those repeats can be adjusted to match the tempo of the song.

Auto-Tune

Auto-Tune was first used in studios as a useful way to clean up minor imperfections in otherwise perfect performances. Auto-Tune is now an industry standard that many artists use, even if they are not willing to

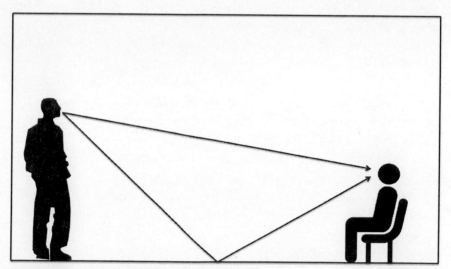

Figure 9.17.   This diagram illustrates how a direct line of sound followed by a reflected line of sound creates delay
Matthew Edwards

admit it. Auto-Tune has gained a bad reputation in the past few years, and whether or not you agree with its use, it is a reality in today's market. If you do not understand how to use it properly, you could end up sounding like T-Pain.[2]

Both Antares and Melodyne have developed Auto-Tune technology in both "auto" and "graphical" formats. "Auto" Auto-Tune allows the engineer to set specific parameters for pitch correction that are then computer controlled. "Graphical" Auto-Tune tracks the pitch in the selected area of a recording and plots the fundamental frequency on a linear graph. The engineer can then select specific notes for pitch correction. They can also drag selected pitches to a different frequency, add or reduce vibrato, and change formant frequencies above the fundamental. To simplify, the "auto" function makes general corrections while the "graphic" function makes specific corrections. The "auto" setting is usually used to achieve a specific effect (for instance, "I Believe" by Cher), while the "graphic" setting is used to correct small imperfections in a recorded performance.

Digital Voice Processors

Digital voice processors are still relatively new to the market and have yet to gain widespread usage among singers. While there are several brands of vocal effects processors available, the industry leader as of this printing is a company called TC-Helicon. TC-Helicon manufactures several different units that span from consumer to professional grade. TC-Helicon's premier performer-controlled unit is called the VoiceLive 3. The VoiceLive 3 incorporates more than twelve vocal effects, eleven guitar effects, and a multi-track looper with 250 factory presets and 250 memory slots for user presets. The VoiceLive 3 puts the effects at the singer's feet in a programmable stomp box that also includes phantom power, MIDI in/out, a USB connection, guitar input, and monitor out. Onboard vocal effects include equalization, compression, reverb, and "auto" Auto-Tune. The unit also offers μMod (an adjustable voice modulator), a doubler (for thickening the lead vocal), echo, delay, reverb, and several other specialized effects.[3]

One of the most impressive features of digital voice processors is the ability to add computer-generated harmonies to the lead vocal. After the user sets the musical key, the processor identifies the fundamental frequency of each sung note. The computer then adds digitized voices at designated intervals above and below the lead singer. The unit also offers the option to program each individual song, with multiple settings for every verse, chorus, and bridge.

THE BASICS OF LIVE SOUND SYSTEMS

Live sound systems come in a variety of sizes from small practice units to state-of-the-art stadium rigs. Most singers only need a basic knowledge of the components commonly found in systems that have one to eight inputs. Units beyond that size usually require an independent sound engineer and are beyond the scope of this chapter.

Following the microphone, the first element in the live signal chain is usually the mixer. Basic portable mixers provide controls for equalization, volume level, auxiliary (usually used for effects such as reverb and compression), and, on some units, controls for built-in digital effects processors. Powered mixers combine an amplifier with a basic mixer, providing a compact solution for those who do not need a complex system. Since unpowered mixers do not provide amplification, you will need to add a separate amplifier to power this system.

The powered mixer or amplifier connects to speaker cabinets, which contain a "woofer" and a "tweeter." The "woofer" is a large round speaker that handles the bass frequencies while the "tweeter" is a horn-shaped speaker that handles the treble frequencies. The crossover, a component built into the speaker cabinet, separates high and low frequencies and sends them to the appropriate speaker (woofer or tweeter). Speaker cabinets can be either active or passive. Passive cabinets require a powered mixer or an amplifier in order to operate. Active cabinets have an amplifier built in and do not require an external amplifier.

If you do not already own a microphone and amplification system, you can purchase a simple setup at relatively low cost through online vendors such as Sweetwater.com and MusiciansFriend.com. A dynamic microphone and a powered monitor are enough to get started. If you would like to add a digital voice processor, Digitech and TC-Helicon both sell entry-level models that will significantly improve the tonal quality of a sound system.

Monitors

Monitors are arguably the most important element in a live sound system. The monitor is a speaker that faces the performers and allows them to hear themselves and/or the other instruments onstage. Onstage volume levels can vary considerably, with drummers often producing sound levels as high as 120dB. Those volume levels make it nearly impossible for singers to receive natural acoustic feedback while performing. Monitors can improve aural feedback and help reduce the temptation to oversing. Powered monitors offer the same advantages as powered speaker cabinets and can be a great option for amplification when practicing. They are also good to have around as a backup plan in case you arrive at a venue and discover they do not supply monitors. In-ear monitors offer another option for performers and are especially useful for those who frequently move around the stage.

MICROPHONE TECHNIQUE

The microphone is an inseparable part of the CCM singer's instrument. Just as there are techniques that improve singing, there are also techniques that will improve microphone use. Understanding what a microphone does is only the first step to using it successfully. Once you understand how a microphone works, you need hands-on experience.

Practicing with a Microphone

The best way to learn microphone technique is to experiment. Try the following exercises to gain a better understanding of how to use a microphone when singing.

- Hold a dynamic microphone with a cardioid pattern directly in front of your mouth, no farther than one centimeter away. Sustain a comfortable pitch and slowly move the microphone away from your lips. Listen to how the vocal quality changes. When the microphone is close to the lips, you should notice that the sound is louder and has more bass response. As you move the microphone away from your mouth, there will be a noticeable loss in volume and the tone will become brighter.

- Next sustain a pitch while rotating the handle down. The sound quality will change in a similar fashion as when you moved the microphone away from your lips.
- Now try singing breathy with the microphone close to your lips. How little effort can you get away with while producing a marketable sound?
- Try singing bright vowels and dark vowels and notice how the microphone affects the tone quality.
- Also experiment with adapting your diction to the microphone. Because the microphone amplifies everything, you may need to underpronounce certain consonants when singing. You will especially want to reduce the power of the consonants t, s, p, and b.

CONCLUSION

Since this is primarily an overview, you can greatly improve your comprehension of the material by seeking other resources to deepen your knowledge. There are many great resources available online, in addition to those found in the bibliography, that may help clarify some of these difficult concepts. Most importantly, you must experiment. The more you play around with sound equipment on your own, the better you will understand it and the more comfortable you will feel when performing or recording with audio technology.

NOTES

1. Paula Lockheart, "A History of Early Microphone Singing, 1925–1939: American Mainstream Popular Singing at the Advent of Electronic Amplification," *Popular Music and Society* 26, no. 3 (2003): 367–85.

2. For example, listen to T-Pain's track "Buy You a Drank (Shawty Snappin')."

3. "VoiceLive 3," TC-Helicon, www.tc-helicon.com/products/voicelive-3/ (accessed May 2, 2016).

10

CONCLUSION

The history of country music is vast and varied, spanning many decades and a myriad of different artists. From Jimmie Rodgers and the Carter Family to Patsy Cline, Loretta Lynn, and Garth Brooks, these artists have shaped the country vocal style that so many young aspiring singers listen to and try to imitate today. The vocal techniques these historical artists used during their careers have been studied and have become the textbook of what is taught presently in so many of the commercial music schools and artist development companies within the music industry. The life experiences these artists had along the way shaped everything about how they approached singing and how they communicated a story to their audience. Country vocal style has certainly evolved through countless legendary artists through the years and will continue to evolve.

As young singers work on their craft, they need to be in tune with vocal health and techniques that will set them up for success many years down the road. Breath, placement, vocal color, and style are four very important areas that need to be considered in order to maintain good vocal health. Vocalization and warm-up exercises will give young singers tools to work on their voices and find a greater amount of consistency in their singing. There are style techniques for singing country that differ from other styles—from the vocal flip and country hitch to the "dip and push" and the "fall off." Many aspiring country singers also have various other vocal qualities in their toolbox such as the "belt" voice, a rich lower register, or a light, wispy upper register.

The art and craft of writing a good country song or even being able to recognize a good country song is a big part of the country artist's career. Artists who write will spend their lives trying to write their next hit song, and artists who do not write will spend their lives looking for their next hit. Either way, the successful country artist's career begins with a good song. In country, if the song is not a quality song, no amount of good singing will make the artist successful. Country music is about storytelling, and if aspiring artists can figure out how to tell a good story, they just might be on to something meaningful and inspiring.

Instrumentation is important to defining country style. We took a look several chapters ago at different instruments that make country music sound "country." Some of these include banjo, dolbro, and fiddle—especially in bluegrass—and more electric instruments like guitar, piano, and B3 organ on pop country. The instruments that are a part of each artist's "sound" will quickly define what genre or "bin" they are placed in on the consumer shelves. These are considerations that cannot be overlooked as the artist is plotting the direction of her music and sound.

As performers, country singers have to work on both the stage show and their recordings. The stage show is a production that has to have every move and every detail seamlessly planned from point A to point B. An artist's studio recording is an exercise in detailed preparation and precise execution from the studio musicians. Both of these processes will begin to take up a large portion of the artist's time. When the artist's business affairs start to interfere with time to do these creative tasks, that is when the artist needs to hire more members to the team.

The artist's team will grow as the artist's career grows. Eventually artists should be able to think only about their creative areas like the show, writing, or recording and allow other team members to help with other things. Managers, booking agents, concert promoters, producers, publishers, and office managers will eventually come into play with the artist. This growth will be a natural progression over time and should not be rushed. Artists will most likely do many of these things themselves until these areas start to crowd out and take over their creative time.

Bottom line, if aspiring artists want to work in the music industry, then they probably will. Even if they do not end up being front and center on a stage, they might decide along the way that being the lead artist is not for them. If that is the case, then they will probably land in another supporting role position somewhere that ends up being quite fulfilling for them. However, it just might be that lightning strikes and the aspiring artist ends up signing a recording contract to be the next big hit in country music! Crazier things have happened, but they usually do not happen without a lot of hard work and elbow grease. Here is to rolling up your sleeves as a young aspiring artist and chasing the dream. If you are not careful, you just might find it!

APPENDIX A:
SUGGESTED REPERTOIRE/SONGS

EARLY YEARS/CLASSIC COUNTRY

Female Artists

Patsy Montana	"I Want to Be a Cowboy's Sweetheart" (1935)
Kitty Wells	"It Wasn't God Who Made Honky Tonk Angels" (1952)
Patsy Cline	"Walking after Midnight" (1956)
	"I Fall to Pieces" (1961)
	"Crazy" (1961)
	"She's Got You" (1962)
	"Sweet Dreams" (1963)
Tammy Wynette	"Apartment No. 9" (1966)
	"D-I-V-O-R-C-E" (1968)
	"Stand by Your Man" (1968)
	"Till I Can Make It on My Own" (1976)
Loretta Lynn	"Don't Come Home A-Drinking" (1967)
	"Coal Miner's Daughter" (1970)
	"You're Looking at Country" (1971)
	"She's Got You" (1977)
Lynn Anderson	"I Never Promised You a Rose Garden" (1970)
Dolly Parton	"Jolene" (1973)
Crystal Gayle	"Don't It Make My Brown Eyes Blue" (1977)

Tanya Tucker   "Delta Dawn" (1972)
Jeanne Pruett   "Satin Sheets" (1973)
Reba McEntire   "Whoever's in New England" (1986)

Male Artists

Jimmie Rodgers   "Blue Yodel" (1930)
Gene Autry   "That Silver-Haired Daddy of Mine" (1932)
                      "Tumbling Tumbleweeds" (1935)
                      "Back in the Saddle Again" (1939)
                      "South of the Border" (1939)
Hank Williams   "Lovesick Blues" (1949)
                      "Cold Cold Heart" (1951)
                      "Your Cheatin' Heart" (1952)
Hank Snow   "I'm Moving On" (1950)
Eddy Arnold   "Make the World Go Away" (1965)
Jim Reeves   "He'll Have to Go" (1959)
Sonny James   "Young Love" (1956)
Johnny Cash   "Folsom Prison Blues" (1955)
                      "I Walk the Line" (1956)
                      "Ring of Fire" (1963)
Buck Owens   "I've Got a Tiger by the Tail" (1964)
                      "Act Naturally" (1966)

BLUEGRASS

Female Artists

Alison Krauss and   "Every Time You Say Goodbye" (1992)
   Union Station
Rhonda Vincent   "If Heartaches Had Wings" (2004)
Dolly Parton   "The Grass Is Blue" (1999)
Gillian Welch   "Revival" (1996)
Patty Loveless   "Bluegrass and White Snow" (1979)
Sara Watkins   "Anthony" (2005)
Claire Lynch   "New Day" (2006)
Kathy Boyd and   "Twelve More Miles to Clatskanie" (2010)
   Phoenix Rising
Penny Nichols   "All Life Is One" (1990)
Missy Raines   "Inside Out" (2009)

Hazel Dickens   "Won't You Come and Sing for Me" (1973)
Kathy Chiavola   "Somehow" (2007)
Mandolin Orange   "Old Ties and Companions" (2015)

Male Artists

Doyle Lawson   "Rock My Soul" (1981)
  and Quicksilver
Lonesome River   "Still Learning" (2010)
  Band
Ricky Skaggs   "Brand New Strings" (2004)
  and Kentucky
  Thunder
Del McCoury Band   "It's Just the Night" (2004)
Jim Van Cleve and   "Force of Nature" (2004)
  Mountain Heart
Lester Flatt and   "Foggy Mountain Breakdown" (1949)
  Earl Scruggs
J. D. Crowe and   "You Can Share My Blanket" (1977)
  the New South
Dan Paisley and   "The Room over Mine" (2008)
  Southern Grass
The Dillards   "Roots and Branches" (1972)
Infamous   "Fork in the Road" (2007)
  Stringdusters
Bill Monroe   "Uncle Pen" (1950)
The Country   "Hootenanny" (1963)
  Gentlemen
Ralph and Carter   "I'm a Man of Constant Sorrow" (1950)
  Stanley (Stanley
  Brothers)
The Nashville   "My Native Home" (1985)
  Bluegrass Band
Nitty Gritty   "Will the Circle Be Unbroken" (1972)
  Dirt Band
The Seldom Scene   "Baptizing" (1978)
Jerry Douglas   "Traveler" (2012)
Bela Fleck   "Crossing the Tracks" (1979)
Sam Bush   "Late As Usual" (1984)
Tim O'Brien   "The Battle Hymn of Love" (1990)

Tony Rice   "Cold on the Shoulder" (1984)
Mark O'Connor   "An Appalachian Christmas" (2011)
Dailey and Vincent   "Brothers from Different Mothers" (2009)
Keith Whitley   "I'm No Stranger to the Rain" (1988)
The Grascals   "Me and John and Paul" (2005)
Osbourne Brothers   "Rocky Top" (1967)
Chris Thile   "Little Cowpoke" (1994)
Larry Sparks   "40" (2004)
Steel Drivers   "The Muscle Shoals Recordings" (2015)

MODERN COUNTRY

Female Artists

Carrie Underwood   "Jesus, Take the Wheel" (2005)
Miranda Lambert   "Kerosene" (2005)
Trick Pony   "Pour Me" (2000)
Little Big Town   "The Road to Here" (2005)
Lady Antebellum   "Need You Now" (2010)
Martina McBride   "Independence Day" (1993)
Trisha Yearwood   "She's in Love with the Boy" (1991)
Jennifer Nettles   "That Girl" (2014)
   (and Sugarland)
LeAnn Rimes   "Blue" (1996)
The Band Perry   "If I Die Young" (2010)
Faith Hill   "The Way You Love Me" (1999)
Sara Evans   "No Place That Far" (1999)
Dixie Chicks   "Wide Open Spaces" (1998)

Male Artists

Brad Paisley   "Letter to Me" (2009)
Luke Bryan   "Rain Is a Good Thing" (2007)
George Strait   "Unwound" (1981)
Keith Urban   "Somebody Like You" (2002)
Dierks Bentley   "What Was I Thinkin'" (2003)
Blake Shelton   "Austin" (2001)
Garth Brooks   "Friends in Low Places" (1990)
Tim McGraw   "It's Your Love" (1997)
Alan Jackson   "Don't Rock the Jukebox" (1991)

Florida Georgia   "Cruise" (2013)
   Line
Chris Young   "The Man I Want to Be" (2009)
Bret Eldredge   "Mean to Me" (2014)
Chris Stapleton   "Tennessee Whiskey" (2015)
Kenny Chesney   "All I Need to Know" (1995)
Toby Keith   "How Do You Like Me Now?!" (1998)
Trace Adkins   "(This Ain't) No Thinkin' Thing" (1997)
Zac Brown Band   "Chicken Fried" (2008)
Hunter Hayes   "Wanted" (2011)
Jason Aldean   "Why" (2005)
Brooks & Dunn   "Red Dirt Road" (2003)
Brantley Gilbert   "You Don't Know Her Like I Do" (2011)
Josh Turner   "Long Black Train" (2003)
Rascal Flatts   "Bless the Broken Road" (2005)

APPENDIX B:
SINGING/WARM-UP EXERCISES

Appendix B

Singing/Warm-up Exercises

APPENDIX C:
BIOGRAPHIES

Alabama was signed to RCA Records in 1980 and had a number-one hit with the song "Tennessee River." It was the first of twenty consecutive number-one hits, a record that has yet to be equaled. Alabama was not only the first band to win the Country Music Association's (CMA) Entertainer of the Year Award; they won it three years in a row from 1982 to 1984. The band was composed of three cousins, Jeff Cook, Teddy Gentry, and Randy Owen (all from Fort Payne, Alabama), and a drummer friend, Mark Herndon. They were also unique in that they played for themselves; Cook plays lead guitar and occasionally fiddle, while Gentry and Owen play bass and rhythm guitar. Some of their biggest hits include "Feel So Right," "Old Flame," "Mountain Music," and "Tennessee River." ♪

Jason Aldine (Williams) was born in Macon, Georgia, on February 28, 1977, and is known professionally as **Jason Aldean**. Since 2005, Jason Aldean has recorded for Broken Bow Records, a record label for which he has released six albums and twenty-two singles. His 2010 album, *My Kinda Party*, is certified triple platinum by the Recording Industry Association of America (RIAA). His 2012 album, *Night Train*, is certified double platinum, while his 2005 self-titled debut, 2007 album *Relentless*, 2009 album *Wide Open*, and 2014 album *Old Boots, New Dirt* are all certified platinum. Of his singles, thirteen have reached number one on the Hot Country Songs or Country Airplay charts: "Why," "She's Country," "Big Green Tractor," "The Truth," "Don't You Wanna Stay" (a duet with Kelly Clarkson), "Dirt Road Anthem," "Fly over States," "Take a Little Ride," "The Only Way I Know" (a collaboration with Luke Bryan and Eric Church), "Night Train," "When She Says Baby," "Burnin' It Down," and "Just Gettin' Started." Nine more of his singles have reached the top ten on the same charts. ♪

Lynn Anderson's recording of "I Never Promised You a Rose Garden" was an epic mega-hit during the Countrypolitan era. Anderson's crossover appeal and regular exposure on national television helped her to become one of the most popular and successful country singers of the 1970s with a string of hits well into the 1980s. ♪

Eddy Arnold accumulated eighteen number-one songs between 1946 and 1955. His band consisted of fiddle, steel guitar, guitar, and upright bass with occasional piano and mandolin. He was known as a "crooner" with silky-smooth vocals that won him a large female following. He sang an unusual number of romantic songs like "I'll Hold You in My Heart," but even his heartbreak songs were without bitterness, like "Bouquet of Roses." Fans were drawn to his boyish good looks and sincere performances. In 1948, starting with his hit "Anytime," he held the number-one spot on *Billboard*'s country chart for sixty consecutive weeks with a total of four songs. He occasionally did a yodeling song like "Cattle Call," which he recorded in 1944, but beyond that he was certainly a pop star in the making. ♪

Gene Autry, born in Texas, the son of a horse trader and livestock dealer, grew up on an Oklahoma ranch. Interestingly enough, he bought his first guitar from a Sears mail-order catalog for twelve dollars when he was twelve years old. Later in life, Autry could be heard on several Christmas song classics including the popular "Here Comes Santa Claus," which he wrote himself, and the original recordings of "Frosty the Snowman" and "Rudolph the Red-Nosed Reindeer." Some of Gene Autry's biggest cowboy hits were "That Silver-Haired Daddy of Mine" and "Back in the Saddle Again." When Gene Autry first auditioned for record companies in New York in 1928, he was told to "go back home and cultivate his yodeling and his cowboy songs." He was heavily influenced by Jimmie Rodgers, and like other performers of his time, he learned to imitate Rodgers quite well. In 1932, Autry was performing regularly on WLS's *National Barn Dance* in Chicago. Later that year, Autry signed a recording contract with producer Art Satherley of the American Record Corporation. Autry collaborated regularly with a group of musicians called Sons of the Pioneers. They supplied songs for his films and significantly contributed to his commercial success. They would make appearances onscreen, even singing as a part of the film's plot. One of the biggest career hits for Sons of the Pioneers was the title song for *Tumbling Tumbleweeds*, a movie in which Autry was the star. ♪

Deford Bailey was introduced by George D. Hay on the Opry in 1927 as an African American harmonica player, who played a train song, "Pan American Blues." This was a song that had been inspired by the famous southern train that ran near Bailey's home. For years on the Opry, George D. Hay would start the show with a steamboat whistle, say, "Let her go, boys," and then Deford Bailey would play his country harmonica blues. Bailey, diminutive and partially crippled, would be one of the most popular and frequently scheduled performers on the Grand Ole Opry from 1925 to 1941. ♪

Clint Black built a following playing the clubs of the Houston-Galveston circuit with his songwriting partner, Hayden Nichols, but didn't gain national recognition until he started working with manager Bill Ham. Ham was the former manager of ZZ Top and signed Black to a contract with RCA in 1988. Shortly thereafter, Black recorded one of the most successful debut albums of all time, *Killin' Time*, which sold more than three million copies and produced four number-one singles. His next album, *Put Yourself in My Shoes*, was released in 1990 and pigeonholed Black as a traditionalist in the honky-tonk vein. This was a label that he quickly overcame with his next two albums. ♪

Troyal Garth Brooks, known in the industry as "Garth Brooks," was born in Luba, Oklahoma, on February 7, 1962, and was known for his remarkable ability to fuse the dynamics of rock culture with the traditional ways of country music. This uncanny ability to blur the lines between rock and country earned him his popularity with the public. His first album was released in 1989 and peaked at number two on the U.S. country album chart while climbing to number thirteen on the *Billboard 200* album chart. His progressive approach allowed him to dominate the country single and album charts while crossing over into the mainstream pop arena. Garth's first song to appear on the country charts was "Much Too Young to Feel This Damn Old." It rose to number eight in May 1989, but over the next three years, Brooks would produce a string of number-one songs and the best-selling country albums of all time: *No Fences, Ropin' the Wind*, and *The Garth Brooks Collection*. By 1996, Brooks's accomplishment of selling sixty million albums had only been surpassed by the Beatles and Billy Joel, but he had done it quicker than anyone in history in any field of music. During the 1990s, he ushered contemporary country music into the arena age by filling twenty-thousand-seat venues and eventually selling one hundred million albums. Brooks broke records for both sales and concert attendance throughout the 1990s. His recordings continue to sell well, and according to Nielsen Soundscan, his albums sales up to May 2013 were 68,630,000, which makes him the best-selling albums artist in the United States in the Soundscan era (since 1991), a title held since 1991. This is more than five million ahead of his nearest rival, the Beatles. According to the RIAA, he is the second best-selling solo albums artist in the United States of all time (ahead of Elvis Presley) with 135 million units sold. Brooks is one of the world's best-selling artists of all time, having sold more than 150 million records. Brooks has released six albums that achieved diamond status in the United States, those being: *Garth Brooks* (10x platinum), *No Fences* (17x platinum), *Ropin' the Wind* (14x platinum), *The Hits* (10x platinum), *Sevens* (10x platinum), and *Double Live* (21x platinum). Since 1989, Brooks has released twenty records in all, which include ten studio albums, one live album, three compilation albums, three Christmas albums, and three box sets, along with seventy-seven singles. He won several important awards in his career, including two Grammy Awards, seventeen American Music Awards (including the "Artist of the '90s") and the RIAA Award as Best-Selling Solo Albums Artist of the Century in the United States. Troubled by conflicts between career and family, Brooks officially retired from recording and performing from 2001 until 2009. During this time, he sold millions of albums through an exclusive distribution deal with Walmart and sporadically released new singles. In 2005, Brooks started a partial comeback and has since given several performances and released two compilation albums. On October 15, 2009, Garth Brooks announced the end of his retirement. In December 2009, he began a five-year concert deal with the Encore Hotel and Casino on the Las Vegas Strip. Following the conclusion of his residency in Las Vegas, Brooks announced his signing with Sony Music Nashville in July 2014. In September 2014, he began his comeback world tour. His most recent album, *Man against Machine*, was released on November 11, 2014, via his new online music store, Ghost Tunes. Brooks was inducted into the Country Music Hall of Fame on October 21, 2012. Country music became a worldwide phenomenon thanks to Garth Brooks, who enjoyed one of the most successful careers in popular music history, breaking records for both sales and concert attendance throughout the decade. Garth Brooks is now married to country music artist and author Trisha Yearwood. ♪

Brooks & Dunn is a country music duo consisting of Kix Brooks and Ronnie Dunn and was founded in 1990 through the suggestion of Tim DuBois. Prior to this, both members were solo recording artists. Brooks wrote number-one singles for John Conlee, Nitty Gritty Dirt Band, and Highway 101; both he and Dunn also charted two solo singles apiece in the 1980s, with Brooks also releasing an album for Capitol Records in 1989. In 1992, they began to be identified with the line dance craze with their hit "Boot Scootin' Boogie." Signed to Arista Nashville in 1991, the duo has recorded ten studio albums, one Christmas album, and three compilation albums for the label. They have also released fifty singles, of which twenty went to number-one on the Hot Country Songs charts and nineteen more reached the top ten. Two of these number one songs, "My Maria" (a cover of the B. W. Stevenson song) and "Ain't Nothing 'bout You," were the top country songs of 1996 and 2001, respectively, according to the *Billboard* year-end charts. The latter is also the duo's longest-lasting number one, at six weeks. Brooks and Dunn also won the Country Music Association Vocal Duo of the Year Award every year between 1992 and 2006, except for 2000. Two of their songs won the Grammy Award for Best Country Performance by a Duo or Group with Vocal: "Hard Workin' Man" in 1994 and "My Maria" in 1996. All but two of the duo's studio albums are certified platinum or higher by RIAA. Their highest-certified is their 1991 debut, *Brand New Man*, which is certified sextuple platinum for shipments of six million copies. Their 2001 hit "Only in America" was used by both George W. Bush and Barack Obama in their respective presidential campaigns. Brooks and Dunn have collaborated with several artists, including Reba McEntire, Vince Gill, Sheryl Crow, Mac Powell, Billy Gibbons, and Jerry Jeff Walker, among others. After announcing their retirement in August 2009, they performed their final concert on September 2, 2010, at the Bridgestone Arena in Nashville, Tennessee. Both Brooks and Dunn have continued to record for Arista Nashville as solo artists. Dunn released a self-titled album in 2011, which included the top ten country hit "Bleed Red," while Brooks released *New to This Town* in September 2012. The duo reunited in 2015 for a series of concerts with McEntire in Las Vegas, Nevada. ♪

Thomas Luther "Luke" Bryan was born in Leesburg, Georgia, on July 17, 1976, and began his musical career in the mid-2000s, writing songs for Travis Tritt and Billy Currington. After signing with Capital Records in Nashville, Tennessee, in 2007 with his cousin, Chad Christopher Boyd, he released the album *I'll Stay Me*, which included the singles "All My Friends Say," "We Rode in Trucks," and "Country Man." The follow-up album, *Doin' My Thing*, included "Do I," which Bryan co-wrote with Charles Kelley and Dave Haywood of Lady Antebellum, and the number-one singles "Rain Is a Good Thing" and "Someone Else Calling You Baby." *Tailgates and Tanlines*, released in 2011, includes "Country Girl (Shake It for Me)," and the number-one singles "I Don't Want This Night to End," "Drunk on You," and "Kiss Tomorrow Goodbye." Bryan's fourth album, *Crash My Party*, was released in August 2013 and includes the number-one singles "Crash My Party," "That's My Kind of Night," "Drink a Beer," "Play It Again," "Roller Coaster," and "I See You." Bryan co-wrote all of his singles with the exception of "Drunk on You," "Crash My Party," "That's My Kind of Night," "Drink a Beer," "Play It Again," and "Roller Coaster" and co-produced all four albums and one compilation album with Jeff Stevens. Bryan was the recipient of both the Academy of Country Music and Country Music Association Entertainer of the Year Awards. ♪

The Carter Family, from Poor Valley, Virginia, began recording in 1927 and continued recording for the next seventeen years. Maybelle would usually be playing stella guitar, Sara would be on lead vocals/auto-harp, and Sara's husband A. P. would chime in on vocal harmonies with Maybelle. They would go on to record some three hundred old-time ballads, traditional tunes, country songs, and gospel hymns representing America's southeastern folklore and Appalachian heritage. One of their most popular recordings was a song called "Wildwood Flower." They also recorded a gospel tune, "Will the Circle Be Unbroken," as late as 1935. ♪

Kenneth Eric Church, singer-songwriter, was born in Granite Falls, North Carolina, on May 3, 1977, and is known professionally as Eric Church. Signed to Capitol Records since 2005, he has since released a to-tal of four studio albums for that label. His debut album in 2006, *Sinners Like Me*, produced four singles on the *Billboard* country charts including the top twenty hits "How 'bout You," "Two Pink Lines," and "Guys Like Me." His second album in 2009, *Carolina*, produced three more singles: "Smoke a Little Smoke" and his first top-ten hits, "Love Your Love the Most" and "Hell on the Heart." *Chief* (2011), his first number one al-bum, gave him his first two number-one singles, "Drink in my Hand" and "Springsteen," and the hits "Homeboy," "Creepin'," and "Like Jesus Does." His third number-one single was "The Only Way I Know," which he, Jason Aldean, and Luke Bryan recorded for Aldean's album *Night Train*. A fourth album, *The Outsiders*, was released in February 2014. It produced four new singles between 2013 and 2015 with the title track, "Give Me Back My Hometown," "Cold One," and "Talledega." "Talla-dega" and "Give Me Back My Hometown" each reached number one on the Country Airplay chart. Eric Church got his sixth number-one hit with Keith Urban in May 2015 with the single "Raise 'Em Up." ♪

Patsy Cline was born in Winchester, Virginia, as Virginia Patterson Hensley. She grew up in a working-class white family in a small town with sharp divisions of race and class. Being from the "poor" side of town, her taste for country music, her colorful clothes, and her brazen personality made all the society ladies in town look down on her. This was a slight that Patsy never forgot. She married Gerald Cline in 1953 and took a modified version of her middle name and his last name as her stage name. She got her big break in 1954 when she appeared in Washington, D.C., on the television show of country music promoter Connie B. Gay. From there, she signed a recording contract with a company from California, 4 Star Records, but the label's owner, Bill McCall, would only let her record songs for which he owned the copyright. Many believe this limitation in her choice of songs is what might have hampered her early career. In 1956, she had a hit single, "Walking after Midnight," that was more or less a honky-tonk rendition of a pop song. With no other hits following, her career floundered within a few years. But McCall agreed for her to start working with Owen Bradley through a collaboration deal with Decca Records. By 1960, her deal with 4 Star had ended and Decca picked her up. She began to be able to record songs by the top songwriters in Nashville and was soon inducted into the Grand Ole Opry. Over the next few years, her career soared as she and Owen Bradley cultivated her Nashville Sound into a full-scale crossover phenomenon. Bradley encouraged her to abandon the brash vocal style she had used in live performances to a more expressive, nuanced vocal style. The result of her new vocal stylings were recordings such as "I Fall to Pieces" and "She's Got You," songs that crossed over into pop radio. Cline became the poster child for a new brand of country, a style that was more widely accepted and embraced by a much wider audience. Her producers began to ask her to wear elegant evening gowns and cultivate a more sophisticated image. Patsy wanted to wear cowgirl fringe and sing covers of Hank Williams and Bill Monroe songs. This caused some tension between Cline and producer Bradley, but the result was an appeal to a much broader audience. On March 5, 1963, Cline sang a benefit concert in Kansas City and then boarded a plane for Nashville with band members Hawkshaw Hawkins, Cowboy Copas, and manager/pilot Randy Hughes. The plane crashed just ninety miles outside of Nashville, killing everyone on board. Her music stayed in the public spotlight for a few more years as her label released several posthumous records. Her music drifted out of the spotlight in the 1970s when the industry started to shift away from the Nashville Sound. Several high-profile artists brought her music back a few years later. Loretta Lynn, one of Patsy's dearest female friends in the music industry, recorded an album of her songs called *I Remember Patsy*. Three years later, writer and entertainment executive Ellis Nassour published a biography of her, k.d. lang eventually covered several of her songs, and in 1985, a Hollywood film starring Jessica Lange entitled *Sweet Dreams* was released. The film chronicled her career and troubled relationships, including her marriage to second husband Charlie Dick. ♪

John Denver, singer/guitarist, released a series of hugely successful songs between 1972 and 1975 blending country and folk-rock musical styles ("Rocky Mountain High," "Sunshine on My Shoulders," "Annie's Song," "Thank God I'm a Country Boy," and "I'm Sorry") and was named Country Music Entertainer of the Year in 1975 ♪

The Dixie Chicks became one of the most popular country bands in the 1990s and early 2000s. Their 1998 debut album, *Wide Open Spaces*, went on to become certified 12x platinum while their 1999 album, *Fly*, went on to become 10x platinum. After their third album, *Home*, was released in 2003, the band made political news in part because of lead singer Natalie Maines's comments disparaging then-president George W. Bush while the band was overseas. Maines stated that she and her bandmates were ashamed to be from the same state as Bush, who had just commenced the Iraq War a few days prior. The comments caused a rift between the band and the country music scene, and the band's fourth (and, to date, final) album, 2006's *Taking the Long Way*, took a more rock-oriented direction. This album was commercially successful overall but was largely ignored by country audiences. The band is currently on hiatus as Maines pursues a solo career; in the meantime, the two other members are continuing with their side project, the Court Yard Hounds. The "Chicks," as they are called by loyal fans, were also known to sing songs about social injustices. The song "Goodbye Earl" made a statement in a humorous way about an abused wife and her best friend who take the law into their own hands to deal with an abusive husband. ♪

Vince Gill is one of a few country music superstars who has accepted membership into the Grand Ole Opry and still makes periodic appearances on the Saturday night shows. Originally from Oklahoma, Gill has accumulated more awards than any other country entertainer, including two CMAs for Entertainer of the Year and at least eighteen Grammys.

These Grammys have not only been for singing but also for instrumental composition and songwriting. Between 1989 and 1997, Gill monopolized the Grammy Award category for Best Male Country Vocal. Ironically, when he was first starting out, he initially received recognition as a guitar player in the industry and then slowly began to get attention as a singer. ♪

Faith Hill was born in Ridgeland, Mississippi, as Audrey Faith Perry on September 21, 1967. She grew up as an adopted child, just south of Jackson, in the tiny town of Star, Mississippi, and first sang publicly at age three in church. She relocated to Nashville when she was nineteen and worked at Opryland as a hostess and T-shirt salesperson until 1993 when her "big break" came in the industry. She is a country-pop singer and occasional actress who became one of the most successful country artists of all time, selling more than forty million records worldwide. Hill is married to country singer Tim McGraw, with whom she has recorded several successful duets. *Take Me As I Am* (1993) and *It Matters to Me* (1995) placed a combined three number ones on *Billboard*'s country charts and were major successes in North America. Hill later rose to mainstream, crossover, and international fame with the release of her next two albums, *Faith* (1998) and *Breathe* (1999). *Faith* spawned her first international hit, "This Kiss," and went multi-platinum in various countries. *Breathe* became her best-selling album to date and one of the best-selling country albums of all time, with the huge crossover success of her signature songs, "Breathe" and "The Way You Love Me." It had massive sales worldwide and earned Hill three Grammy Awards, including Best Country Album. In 2001, she recorded "There You'll Be" for the *Pearl Harbor* soundtrack, and it became an international hit and her best-selling single in Europe. Hill's next two albums, *Cry* (2002) and *Fireflies* (2005), were both commercial successes and kept her mainstream popularity; the former spawned another crossover single, "Cry," which won Hill a Grammy Award, and the latter produced the hit singles "Mississippi Girl" and "Like We Never Loved at All," which earned her another Grammy Award. Hill has won five Grammy Awards, fifteen Academy of Country Music Awards, six American Music Awards, and several other awards. Her Soul2Soul II Tour 2006 with McGraw became the highest-grossing country tour of all time. In 2001, she was named one of the "30 Most Powerful Women in America" by *Ladies Home Journal*. In 2009, *Billboard* named her as the number-one Adult Contemporary Artist of the 2000 decade and also as the thirty-ninth best artist. From 2007 to 2012, Hill was the voice of *NBC Sunday Night Football*'s intro song. ♪

Alan Eugene Jackson was born the youngest child with four older sisters on October 17, 1958, and grew up in the small town of Newnan, Georgia. He is known for blending traditional honky-tonk and main-stream country sounds and penning many of his own hits. He has re-corded fifteen studio albums, three greatest hits albums, two Christmas albums, two gospel albums, and several compilations. ♪

Jackson has sold more than eighty million records worldwide, with more than fifty of his singles appearing on *Billboard*'s list of the top thirty country songs. Of Jackson's entries, thirty-five were number one hits, with fifty in the top ten. He is the recipient of two Grammys, six-teen CMA Awards, and seventeen Academy of Country Music (ACM) Awards and nominee of multiple other awards. He is a member of the Grand Ole Opry and was inducted into the Georgia Music Hall of Fame in 2001. Also in 2001, Jackson recorded "Where Were You When the World Stopped Turning?"—a sensitive and heartfelt song written about the 9/11 disasters in New York. It was a masterpiece of compassion and became an enormous hit and commercial success for Jackson. In August 2014, the Country Music Hall of Fame opened an exhibit celebrating Jackson's twenty-five years in the music industry. It was also announced that he was an artist in residency as well, performing shows on October 8 and 22. The exhibit highlights the different milestones in his career with memorabilia collected over the years. His twenty-fifth anniversary "Keeping It Country" tour began January 8, 2015, in Estero, Florida. ♪

Sonny James, after serving in the Korean War, followed the same ca-reer path as many other country musicians, appearing on the *Louisiana Hayride* and then on television's *Ozark Jubilee*. His biggest hit came in 1957 with the song "Young Love." It went number one on both the pop and country charts. James joined the Grand Ole Opry in the early 1960s and a decade later scored sixteen number-one hits in a row. ♪

Waylon Arnold Jennings was born in Littlefield, Texas, just north of Lubbock, in 1937. He began playing guitar at eight and began performing on KVOW radio at the age of twelve. His first band was called the Texas Longhorns. His father drove a truck for a living and "picked" Jimmie Rodgers tunes on guitar for fun. From then on, Waylon turned to music every chance he got, trying to imitate his favorite singer, Ernest Tubb. He once even broke off a broomstick to use to play air guitar. In 1958, Buddy Holly arranged Jennings's first recording session and then hired him to play bass. In Clear Lake, Iowa, Jennings gave up his seat on the ill-fated flight that crashed and killed Buddy Holly, J. P. Richardson, and others. The day of the flight was later known as "the Day the Music Died." Jennings formed a rockabilly club band called the Waylors and recorded for independent Trend Records and A&M Record but then achieved creative control with RCA Victor. During the 1970s, Jennings joined the outlaw country movement. He released critically acclaimed albums *Lonesome, On'ry and Mean*, and *Honky Tonk Heroes*, followed by hit albums *Dreaming My Dreams* and *Are You Ready for the Country*. In 1976, he released the album *Wanted! The Outlaws* with Willie Nelson, Tompall Glaser, and Jessi Colter. This was the first platinum country music album of all time. That success was followed by the album *Ol' Waylon* and the hit single "Luckenbach, Texas." From 1980 until 1984, Jennings struggled with a cocaine addiction. Later he joined the super group The Highwaymen with Willie Nelson, Kris Kristofferson, and Johnny Cash. During that period, he released *Will the Wolf Survive*. He toured less in 1997 to spend more time with his family. Between 1999 and 2001, his appearances were limited because of health problems. On February 13, 2002, Jennings died from complications associated with diabetes. Jennings composed and sang the theme song for hit television show *The Dukes of Hazzard*. In 2001, he was inducted into the Country Music Hall of Fame, and in 2007, he was posthumously awarded the Cliffie Stone Pioneer Award by the Academy of Country Music. ♪

George Glenn Jones, born in Saratoga, Texas, on September 12, 1931, first heard country music when he was seven and was given a guitar at the age of nine. Jones learned how to sing country music by imitating his idols, Roy Acuff, Hank Williams, and Lefty Frizzell. He was destined to sing sad songs one way or another because when he was born his doctor dropped him and broke his arm. Jones achieved international fame for his long list of hit records, including "White Lightning," which, in 1959, launched his career as a singer. Jones was also known for his distinct voice and phrasing but received his inspiration from Hank Williams. For the last twenty years of his life, Jones was frequently referred to as the greatest living singer in country music. He married his first wife, Dorothy Bonvillion, in 1950 and was divorced in 1951. He served in the United States Marine Corps until his discharge in 1953 and a year later married Shirley Ann Corley. When his second marriage ended in divorce in 1968, he married fellow country music singer Tammy Wynette one year later. Many years of alcoholism caused his health to deteriorate severely and led to his missing many performances, earning him the nickname "No Show Jones." After his divorce from Wynette in 1975, Jones married his fourth wife, Nancy Sepulvado, in 1983 and became mostly sober. Jones died in 2013, aged eighty-one, from hypoxic respiratory failure. He was buried in Woodlawn Cemetery. During his career, Jones had more than 150 hits, both as a solo artist and in duets with other artists. ♪

Naomi Judd was born Diana Ellen Judd on January 11, 1946, in Ashland, Kentucky. She played piano at her local church. At age seventeen, she married Michael Ciminella, with whom she had Christina Ciminella, who would later be renamed **Wynonna Judd**. After Diana's parents divorced, she and her daughter moved to Los Angeles, California, in 1968 and lived on welfare after she and Michael divorced in 1972. By 1979, Diana and her daughter moved back to Tennessee. Diana renamed herself Naomi and began playing music with her daughter, who sang lead and played guitar. At the same time, Naomi began studying to be a nurse. But the success they had finally achieved did not happen overnight. Prior to 1984, they had put in several years of hard work, sacrifice, and preparation, not to mention a stint in Hollywood attempting movie careers. Signed to RCA Records in 1983, the Judds released six studio albums between then and 1991. As one of the most successful acts in country music history, they are known for having won five Grammy Awards for Best Country Performance by a Duo or Group with Vocals and eight Country Music Association Awards. The duo also charted twenty-five singles on the country music charts between 1983 and 2000, fourteen of which went to number one and six more of which made top ten on the same chart. The Judds ended their performance careers as a duo in 1991 after Naomi was diagnosed with hepatitis C. Shortly after, Wynonna began her solo career. The two have occasionally reunited for special tours, the most recent of which began in late 2010. In 2011, the duo starred in the reality television series *The Judds* during their Last Encore Tour. ♪

Alison Maria Krauss was born in Champaign, Illinois, on July 23, 1971. She was the real groundbreaker and one of the first true superstars to emerge in the bluegrass idiom. She entered the music industry at an early age, winning local talent contests by the age of ten. Krauss began experimenting with bluegrass music around 1983, when she was only twelve years old, playing fiddle in and around her hometown. By 1986, she had formed her own band, Union Station; recorded her first album, *Too Late to Cry*, for Rounder Records; and was beginning to realize that she could sing as well as she could play. Despite her instrumental abilities, her voice became her claim to fame. She later released her first album with Union Station as a group in 1989. Krauss has released fourteen albums, appeared on numerous soundtracks, and helped renew interest in bluegrass music in the United States. Her soundtrack performances have led to further popularity, including the *O Brother, Where Art Thou?* soundtrack, an album also credited with raising American interest in bluegrass, and the *Cold Mountain* soundtrack, which led to her performance at the 2004 Academy Awards. As of 2012, she had won twenty-seven Grammy Awards from forty-one nominations, tying her with Quincy Jones as the most awarded living recipient, second only to the late classical conductor Sir Georg Solti, who holds the record for most wins of all time with thirty-one. She is the most awarded singer and the most awarded female artist in Grammy history. At the time of her first, the 1991 Grammy Awards, she was the second-youngest winner (currently tied as the ninth youngest). Krauss was inducted into the Grand Ole Opry in 1993 as the youngest member ever chosen and the first bluegrass performer since 1964. She still makes occasional appearances on the Opry stage. ♪

Lady Antebellum made its debut in 2007 as guest vocalists on Jim Brickman's single "Never Alone," before signing to Capitol Records Nashville. Lady Antebellum has released five albums for Capitol: *Lady Antebellum, Need You Now, Own the Night, Golden*, and *747*, plus one Christmas album (*On This Winter's Night*). Their first three albums are certified platinum or higher by the RIAA. The albums have produced sixteen singles on the Hot Country Songs and Country Airplay charts, of which nine have reached number one. Their longest-lasting number-one single is "Need You Now," which spent five weeks at that position in 2009; both that song and 2011's "Just a Kiss" also reached number one on the Adult Contemporary charts. Lady Antebellum was awarded Top New Duo or Group by the Academy of Country Music and New Artist of the Year by the Country Music Association in 2008. They were nominated for two Grammys at the fifty-first Grammy Awards and two more at the fifty-second Grammy Awards. Of these nominations, they took home the award for Best Country Performance by Duo or Group with Vocals for "I Run to You." They were awarded Top Vocal Group, Song of the Year ("Need You Now"), and Single of the Year ("Need You Now") at the forty-fourth ACM Awards on April 18, 2010. They won five awards at the fifty-third Grammy Awards, including Song of the Year and Record of the Year for "Need You Now." Lady Antebellum also scored Best Country Album at the fifty-fourth Grammy Awards. By August 2013, the group had sold more than 12.5 million digital singles and 10 million albums in the United States. ♪

Miranda Lambert made her debut with the release of "Me and Charlie Talking," the first single from her 2005 debut album, *Kerosene*. This album, which was certified platinum in the United States, also produced the singles "Bring Me Down," "Kerosene," and "New Strings." All four singles were top 40 hits on *Billboard* Hot Country Songs. Whereas some country females carried a sweet, good-girl sentiment, Lambert's song-writing tended to be more strident. Her songs "Gunpowder and Lead" and "Kerosene" are every bit as harsh and incendiary as their titles imply. After Epic's Nashville division closed, Lambert was transferred to Columbia Records Nashville for her second album, *Crazy Ex-Girlfriend*, which was released in early 2007. Although the title track failed to make top 40, the next three singles ("Famous in a Smalltown," "Gunpowder and Lead," and "More Like Her") were top-twenty hits, with "Gunpowder and Lead" becoming her first top-ten country hit in July 2008. Her third album, *Revolution*, was released in September 2009. Five singles were released from the album, including two number-one hits: "The House That Built Me," which spent four weeks at the top, and "Heart Like Mine." In 2011, Lambert married fellow country singer Blake Shelton (divorced 2015). She also released her fourth album, *Four the Record*, which includes the singles "Baggage Claim," "Over You," "Fastest Girl in Town," "Mama's Broken Heart," and "All Kinds of Kinds." Lambert also collaborated with Ashley Monroe and Angeleena Presley in the side project *Pistol Annies*. Lambert released her fifth album, "Platinum," in June 2014. The album was preceded by the lead single, "Automatic," which hit number four on the country charts and won the Grammy Award for Best Country Album. The album's second single, "Somethin' Bad," featured Carrie Underwood. It was premiered at the *Billboard* Music Awards. ♪

Loretta Lynn, born Loretta Webb, in Butcher Hollow, Kentucky, is a multiple-gold-album American country music singer-songwriter whose work spans more than fifty years. As the daughter of a coal miner, she has sold more than forty-five million albums worldwide. In January 1946, before she turned fourteen, she married Oliver "Doolittle" Lynn, and their life together inspired much of the music she wrote. In 1953, Doolittle bought her a Harmony guitar for seventeen dollars. After teaching herself to play and improving over the next three years, she started her own band, Loretta and the Trailblazers. Her brother, Jay Lee, played lead guitar. She would frequently play at taverns in Washington state where they lived at the time. She cut her first record, *Honky Tonk Girl*, in February 1960. Shortly thereafter, she and Doolittle moved to Tennessee and she became a part of Nashville's country music scene. In 1967, Loretta charted her first of sixteen number-one hits, some of which include: "Don't Come Home a Drinkin' (With Lovin' on Your Mind)," "You Ain't Woman Enough," "Fist City," and "Coal Miner's Daughter." She has had more than seventy charted songs as a solo artist or a duet partner. Her most recent album, *Van Lear Rose*, released in 2004, was produced by friend and fellow musician Jack White. Lynn and White were nominated for five Grammys and won two of them. She was the opening act for Jack White's world tour in 2014. Lynn was inducted into the Nashville Songwriter's Hall of Fame in 1983, the Country Music Hall of Fame in 1988, and the Songwriters Hall of Fame in 2008. In 2010, she was honored at the Country Music Awards, and her most recent honor is the Presidential Medal of Freedom from President Barack Obama in 2013. She has been a member of the Grand Ole Opry since joining on September 25, 1962. Loretta Lynn has recorded seventy albums, including fifty-four studio albums, fifty compilation albums, and one tribute album to Patsy Cline. ♪

Barbara Ann Mandrell, a 2009 Country Music Hall of Fame inductee, was born in Houston, Texas, on December 25, 1948. She is known for a series of top-ten hits and TV shows in the 1970s and 1980s that helped her become one of country's most successful female vocalists during that era. Mandrell's proficiency with the steel guitar is what led her into a professional performing career. Joe Maphis and Chet Atkins heard twelve-year-old Barbara play the steel guitar at an annual trade show in Chicago in 1960. Since Barbara was living in California at the time, Maphis recommended her to start playing on the *Town Hall Party* in Los Angeles. By the time she hit Nashville in 1969, her versatility as a musician was taking priority over her ambition to become a lead vocalist. Recording for Columbia and producer Billy Sherrill, she began to create a sound that was closer to the Motown and Memphis sound than it was to country. Nonetheless, whatever style she chose to record, she became one of the superstars of country music. Like Johnny Cash, she was brilliant at self-promotion and was extraordinarily skilled at getting her name before the widest possible audience. Her weekly television show in the early 1980s presented her and her sisters to a large audience that enjoyed all styles of music, including country. It was said that her show looked more like Las Vegas than Nashville, but she would include tunes that showcased the full range of her abilities. The songs ranged from sexy to religious, and she would include dance routines as well as her ability to play one instrument after another. She was the first performer to win the Country Music Association's Entertainer of the Year Award twice. She was the only female to have done so until Taylor Swift equaled her. She also won twice the Country Music Association's Female Vocalist of the Year in 1979 and 1981. Mandrell's first *Billboard* number-one hit was 1978's "Sleeping Single in a Double Bed," immediately followed by "(If Loving You Is Wrong) I Don't Want to Be Right" in early 1979. In 1980, "Years" also reached number-one. She added one more chart-topper in each of the next three years. "I Was Country When Country Wasn't Cool" (her signature song), then "Till You're Gone" and "One of a Kind, Pair of Fools" all hit number one between 1981 and 1983, a period during which Mandrell also received numerous industry awards and accolades. ♪

Martina McBride born as Martina Maria Schiff, in Sharon, Kansas, on July 29, 1966, began her career in the early 1990s. She is known for her extensive vocal range and country-pop material. When McBride recorded her biggest hit, "Independence Day," in 1993, she had no idea that it would emerge as a career-defining song or that it would become a validating anthem for women triumphing over domestic abuse. She just knew that she really loved the song. It was a controversial song in which the singer recalls a Fourth of July celebration when she was eight years old. As an adult looking back on the event, the singer realizes that her mother was a victim of a violently abusive alcoholic husband. The lyric of the song describes a scene where, in desperation, the mother burns down the family's home around him. The song and video's graphic portrayal of domestic abuse produced a firestorm of controversy across the music community, as did Garth Brooks's video for "Thunder Rolls," in which an abused wife shoots her cheating husband. The song "Independence Day" established McBride with her powerful voice as a major star and became her signature hit. She continues to take a stand for social justice, to speak out against domestic abuse, and to choose songs that represent strong-minded, middle-aged females. Martina's recording of "Concrete Angel" is also a song that condemns child abuse. McBride has recorded a total of twelve studio albums, two greatest hit compilations, one live album, as well as two additional compilation albums. Eight of her studio albums and two of her compilations have received an RIAA Gold Certification or higher. In the United States she has sold more than fourteen million albums. In addition, McBride has won the Country Music Association's Female Vocalist of the Year Award four times (tied with **Reba McEntire** and **Miranda Lambert** for the most wins) and the Academy of Country Music's Top Female Vocalist Award three times. She is also a fourteen-time Grammy Award nominee. ♪

Reba Nell McEntire was born in McAlester, Oklahoma, on March 28, 1955, who came from a genuine roping and riding background. She grew up the third of four children on an eight-thousand-acre cattle ranch near Chockie in southeastern Oklahoma. Every summer of her childhood, Reba and her family would pile into an old green Ford for a tour of the southwestern rodeo circuit. It was on those long drives that Reba's mother, who had once had ambitions of being a singer, led her children in sing-alongs to pass the time. McEntire's second MCA album, *My Kind of Country* (1984), brought her breakthrough success, bringing her a series of successful albums and number-one singles in the 1980s and 1990s. McEntire has since released twenty-six studio albums, acquired forty number-one singles, fourteen number-one albums, and twenty-eight albums that have been certified gold, platinum, or multi-platinum in sales by the RIAA. She has sometimes been referred to as the "queen of country," and she is one of the best-selling artists of all time, having sold more than eighty-five million records worldwide. In the early 1990s, McEntire branched into film starting with 1990's *Tremors*. She has since starred in the Broadway revival of *Annie Get Your Gun* and in her television sitcom, *Reba* (2001–2007), for which she was nominated for the Golden Globe Award for Best Performance by an Actress in a Television Series—Musical or Comedy. ♪

Samuel Timothy "Tim" McGraw, singer and actor, was born in Delhi, Louisiana, on May 1, 1967. He has been married to fellow singer Faith Hill since 1996 and is the son of the late baseball player Tug McGraw. McGraw has released thirteen studio albums: eleven for Curb Records and two for Big Machine Records. Ten of his albums have reached number one on the Top Country Albums charts, with his 1994 breakthrough album, *Not a Moment Too Soon*, being the top country album of 1994. These albums have produced more than fifty singles, of which twenty-five have reached number one on the Hot Country Songs or Country Airplay charts. His album *Set This Circus Down* leaped to the number one position the same week it was released in May 2001. Three of his singles—"It's Your Love," "Just to See You Smile," and "Live Like You

Were Dying"—were the top country songs of 1997, 1998, and 2004 respectively, according to *Billboard* year end. McGraw has won his share of awards with three Grammy Awards, fourteen Academy of Country Music Awards, eleven Country Music Association (CMA) Awards, ten American Music Awards, and three People's Choice Awards. His Soul-2Soul II Tour with Faith Hill is the highest-grossing tour in country music history and one of the top five among all genres of music. McGraw has ventured into acting, with supporting roles in *The Blind Side* (with Sandra Bullock), *Friday Night Lights*, *The Kingdom*, *Four Christmases* (with Vince Vaughn and Reese Witherspoon), and *Tomorrowland* (with George Clooney), and lead roles in *Flicka* (2006) and *Country Strong* (2010). He was a minority owner of the Arena Football League's Nashville Kats. Taylor Swift's debut single, "Tim McGraw," refers to him and his song "Can't Tell Me Nothin'." ♪

Ronnie Lee Milsap, a country music singer and pianist, was born in Robbinsville, North Carolina, on January 16, 1943. He was one of country music's most popular and influential performers of the 1970s and 1980s. He became country music's first successful blind singer and was one of the most successful and versatile country "crossover" singers of his time. Milsap appealed to both country and pop music markets with hit songs that incorporated pop, R&B, and rock-and-roll elements. He began his career with roots in the honky-tonk style with the hit "I Hate You," but then quickly moved into more popular forms. His biggest crossover hits include "It Was Almost Like a Song," "Smoky Mountain Rain," "(There's) No Gettin' over Me," "I Wouldn't Have Missed It for the World," "Any Day Now," and "Stranger in My House." He is credited with six Grammy Awards and forty number-one country hits, third to George Strait and Conway Twitty. He was selected for induction into the Country Music Hall of Fame in 2014. ♪

Willie Hugh Nelson, one of the main figures of outlaw country, otherwise known as "Willie Nelson," was born in Abbott, Texas, in 1933. The success of the albums *Shotgun Willie* (1973), *Red Headed Stranger* (1975), and *Stardust* (1978) made Nelson one of the most recognized artists in country music. He has acted in thirty films, has co-authored several books, and has been involved as an activist for social causes that he finds to be important. Nelson was born during the Great Depression and was raised by his grandparents. He wrote his first song at the age of seven and joined his first band at ten. During his high school years, he played guitar and sang lead vocals for a band called Bohemian Polka. After graduation in 1950, he joined the Air Force but was later discharged because of problems with his back. After his return, he attended Baylor University for two years, but then withdrew because his music career was beginning to take off. After dropping out of college, he worked as a disc jockey for Texas radio stations and as a singer in honky-tonks. Nelson moved to Vancouver, Washington, where he wrote *Family Bible* and recorded the song "Lumberjack" in 1956. In 1958, he moved to Houston, Texas, after signing a contract with D Records. During this time, he wrote songs that would be country standards, including "Funny How Time Slips Away," "Hello Walls," "Pretty Paper," and "Crazy." In 1960, he moved to Nashville and later signed a publishing contract with Pamper Music, which allowed him to join Ray Price's band as a bassist. In 1962, he recorded his first album, . . . *And Then I Wrote*. Due to the success of the album, he signed with RCA Victor in 1964 and joined the Grand Ole Opry the following year. After many chart hits in the late 1960s and early 1970s, Nelson retired to Austin, Texas, in 1972. Nelson came out of retirement when the hippie movement started to rise, performing frequently at the Armadillo World Headquarters. In 1973, after signing with Atlantic Records, Nelson turned to outlaw country, including albums such as *Shotgun Willie* and *Phases and Stages*. He switched to Columbia Records in 1975, where he recorded the critically acclaimed album *Red Headed Stranger*. About this time, he also recorded another outlaw country album, *Wanted! The Outlaws*, along with Waylon Jennings, Jessi Colter, and Tompall Glaser. During the mid-1980s, while recording hit albums like *Honeysuckle Rose* and hit singles like "On the Road Again," "To All the Girls I've Loved Before," and "Pancho and Lefty," he joined the supergroup the Highwaymen, along with singers Johnny Cash, Waylon Jennings, and Kris Kristofferson. In 1990, Nelson's assets were seized by the Internal Revenue Service, which claimed that he owed $32,000,000. It was later discovered that his accountants, Price Waterhouse, did not pay Nelson's taxes for years. The difficulty of paying his outstanding debt was aggravated by weak investments he had made during the 1980s. In 1991, Nelson released *The IRS Tapes: Who'll*

Buy My Memories? In 1992, the profits of the double album, destined for the IRS, and the auction of Nelson's assets finally cleared his debt. During the 1990s and 2000s, Nelson continued touring extensively and released albums every year. Reviews ranged from positive to mixed. He explored genres such as reggae, blues, jazz, and folk. Nelson made his first movie appearance in the 1979 film *The Electric Horseman*, followed by other appearances in movies and television. Nelson is a major liberal activist and the co-chair of the advisory board of the National Organization for the Reform of Marijuana Laws, which is in favor of marijuana legalization. On the environmental front, Nelson owns the biodiesel brand Willie Nelson Biodiesel, which is made from vegetable oil. Nelson is also the honorary chairman of the Advisory Board of the Texas Music Project, the official music charity of the state of Texas. ♪

Olivia Newton-John, an Australian pop singer, won the Best Female Country Vocal Performance as well as the Country Music Association's most coveted award for females, Female Vocalist of the Year in 1974. In response, George Jones, Tammy Wynette, and other traditional Nashville country artists, dissatisfied with the new trend, formed the short-lived Association of Country Entertainers the same year. ♪

The Nitty Gritty Dirt Band had the biggest hit of their careers in 1970 with the song "Mr. Bojangles," but their blend of youth and country music came together came in 1972 when they recorded the album *Will the Circle Be Unbroken*. They had started out as a jug band in Orange County, California, in the mid-1960s, but like other young bands, they were ultra-eclectic, playing everything from mountain music and bluegrass to hard rock. Largely through the encouragement of their manager and producer, William McEuen, they did a marathon recording with many of the "greats" in country like Roy Acuff, Maybelle Carter, Merle Travis, Earl Scruggs, and Doc Watson. Many of their fans bought the record simply on their reputation and name but as a by-product were introduced to some of the giants of country music. ♪

The Oak Ridge Boys, after going through many personnel changes in the 1960s, became controversial in the gospel field with their long hair, flashy apparel, mix of secular and gospel material, and sexy choreography on stage. They began incorporating some country songs into their Las Vegas show in the 1970s and eventually produced hits in the country market such as "Y'all Come Back Saloon," "Leaving Louisiana in the Broad Daylight," "Trying to Love Two Women," and the biggest hit of all, "Elvira." This was a 1950s-style rockabilly tune that vaulted to the top of the country chart, crossed over into pop radio, and won them a Grammy. The Oak Ridge Boys were pretty open about wanting to be the first group to ever win CMA's Entertainer of the Year Award. Despite all their accolades, this goal was never attained. The first group to achieve this feat was the much less experienced band Alabama. ♪

"Buck" Owens was born Alvis Edgar Owens Jr. in Sherman, Texas, on August 12, 1929. He was a musician, singer, songwriter, and bandleader who had twenty-one number-one hits on the *Billboard* country music charts with his band the Buckaroos. More than any other artist of his time, Owens brought the bandstand into the production of his records. He and his band pioneered what would become known as the Bakersfield Sound, a reference to Bakersfield, California, a place Owens called home. He originally used fiddle and retained pedal steel guitar into the 1970s, but his sound on records and onstage was always more stripped down. He always wanted to incorporate more elements of rock and roll in his music. Beginning in 1969, Owens co-hosted the TV series *Hee Haw* with Roy Clark, but he left the cast in 1986. The accidental death of Rich, his best friend, in 1974, devastated him for years and abruptly halted his career until he performed with Dwight Yoakam in 1988. Owens died on March 25, 2006, shortly after performing at his Crystal Palace restaurant, club, and museum in Bakersfield. ♪

Brad Paisley moved to Nashville in the mid-1990s, where he would enroll in Belmont University's music business program. In 1999, he recorded his first Arista CD, *Who Needs Pictures*, on which he played all the guitar parts and wrote all the songs. Several songs on this album received airplay, but the biggest hit on this album was "Me Neither." He was inducted into the Grand Ole Opry in 2001. ♪

Dolly Rebecca Parton was born in Sevier County, Tennessee, on January 19, 1946, and is a singer-songwriter, instrumentalist, actress, author, businesswoman, and philanthropist known primarily for her work in country music. She began writing serious songs when she was about seven years of age. Her career began as a child performer on the radio and then by recording a few singles at the age of thirteen. Relocating to Nashville at age eighteen in 1964, her first commercial successes were as a songwriter. Her songs during this period were covered by numerous artists, including Bill Phillips and Kitty Wells. She rose to prominence in 1967 as a featured performer on Porter Wagoner's weekly syndicated TV program; their first duet single, a cover of Tom Paxton's "The Last Thing on My Mind," was a top ten hit on the country singles chart and led to several successful albums before they ended their partnership in 1974. Moving toward mainstream pop music, her 1977 single "Here You Come Again" was a success on both the country and pop charts. A string of pop-country hits followed into the mid-1980s, the most successful being her 1981 hit "9 to 5" (from the film of the same name) and her 1983 duet with Kenny Rogers, "Islands in the Stream," both of which topped the U.S. pop and country singles charts. A pair of albums recorded with Linda Ronstadt and Emmylou Harris were among her later successes. In the late 1990s, she returned to classic country/bluegrass with a series of acclaimed recordings. Non-musical ventures include Dollywood, a theme park in Pigeon Forge in the Smoky Mountains of Tennessee, and her efforts on behalf of childhood literacy, particularly her Imagination Library, as well as Dolly Parton's Dixie Stampede and Pirates Voyage. Parton is the most honored female country performer of all time. Achieving twenty-five RIAA-certified gold, platinum, and multiplatinum awards, she has had twenty-five songs reach number one on the *Billboard* Country charts, a record for a female artist. She has forty-one career top-ten country albums, a record for any artist, and she has 110 career charted singles over the past forty years. All-inclusive sales of singles, albums, hits collections, and digital downloads during her career have topped one hundred million worldwide. She has garnered eight Grammy Awards, two Academy Award nominations, ten Country Music Association Awards, seven Academy of Country Music Awards, and three American Music Awards and is one of only seven female artists to win the Country Music Association's Entertainer of the Year Award. Parton has received forty-six Grammy nominations, tying her with Beyoncé for the most Grammy nominations for a woman and placing her in eighth place overall. In 1999, she was inducted into the Country Music Hall of Fame. She has composed more than three thousand songs, the best known of which include "I Will Always Love You" (a two-time U.S. country chart-topper for Parton, as well as an international pop hit for Whitney Houston), "Jolene," "Coat of Many Colors," "9 to 5," and "My Tennessee Mountain Home." Parton is also one of the few to have received at least one nomination from the Academy Awards, Grammy Awards, Tony Awards, and Emmy Awards. As an actress, she starred in *9 to 5*, *Rhinestone*, *A Smoky Mountain Christmas*, *Steel Magnolias*, *Wild Texas Wind*, *Gnomeo and Juliet*, *Straight Talk*, *Unlikely Angel*, *Blue Valley Songbird*, and *Joyful Noise*. Parton especially moved into bold territory never before occupied by women singers when she played the role of a madam in *The Best Little Whorehouse in Texas*. Some did not approve of her taking that role, but she and Loretta Lynn spoke up many times for the right of women to be free and honestly expressive in their artistic ventures. During the mid-1970s, Dolly Parton was a highly successful mainstream country artist who mounted a high-profile campaign to cross over into pop music. This effort came to fruition with her 1977 hit "Here You Come Again," which topped the U.S. country singles chart and also reached number three on the pop singles charts. Parton's male counterpart, Kenny Rogers, came from the opposite direction, aiming his music at the country charts after a successful career in pop, rock, and folk music. He achieved success the same year with "Lucille," which topped the country charts and reached number five on the U.S. pop singles charts. Parton and Rogers would both continue to have success on both country and pop charts simultaneously well into the 1980s. Artists like Crystal Gayle, Ronnie Milsap, and Barbara Mandrell would also find success on the pop charts with their records. ♪

Elvis Presley began his career in the rockabilly genre, as rock and roll was not yet in existence, but it was during this period that Elvis Presley would convert to country music with the hit "Heartbreak Hotel." In 1958, Elvis Presley acknowledged the influence of rhythm and blues on his style, saying, "The colored folk have been singin' and playin' it just the way I'm doing it now, man, for more years than I know." Elvis also admitted that his music was just "hopped-up country." The musical style blended the traditions of both black and white music. ♪

Jim Reeves signed a recording contract with an independent label in 1952 and spent the next several years touring, recording honky-tonk songs, and performing on the *Louisiana Hayride*. After recording a few hits such as "Mexican Joe," he was asked to join the Grand Ole Opry and signed a recording contract with RCA. At RCA, producer Chet Atkins added backup vocals and a sleeker, more sophisticated arrangement to go along with his smooth vocals. The formula that Atkins used seemed to work, and in 1957, Reeves had his first crossover hit with "Four Walls." This recording topped the country charts and went to number eleven on the pop charts. The formula of downplaying the twang, steel guitar, and honky-tonk elements was essentially the same formula of the teen crooner artists whose music crossed over to pop. ♪

Charlie Rich was a country singer with an eclectic style that was hard to classify in any one category. His music style included a little rockabilly, jazz, blues, country, and gospel. He eventually acquired the nickname the "silver fox" and is perhaps best remembered for a pair of 1973 hits, "Behind Closed Doors" and "The Most Beautiful Girl." "The Most Beautiful Girl" topped the country singles charts as well as the pop singles charts and earned him two Grammy Awards. ♪

LeAnn Rimes (Cibrian) was born as Margaret LeAnn Rimes in Jackson, Mississippi, on August 28, 1982. She is known professionally in country music as LeAnn Rimes. When she released her sophomore studio record in 1997, *You Light up My Life: Inspirational Songs*, she moved toward country-pop material. With this album, she would set the trend for a string of albums released into the next decade. Even though she grew up in a family that was not afraid of hard work, at the age of eighteen, she went through a bitter breakup with her father over a contractual dispute. She made the tough decision to "go it alone" and assume control over her blossoming career. Similar to the Dixie Chicks and Martina McBride, Rimes has done a few songs that champion social or political issues. Her song "Probably Wouldn't Be This Way" tells the story of a young widow nursing a broken heart. Although the song is somewhat ambiguous with military service not being mentioned, audiences have interpreted it as talking about a war widow.

Rimes has won many awards, including two Grammys, three ACMs, a CMA, 12 *Billboard* Music Awards, and one American Music award. She has released ten studio albums and three compilation albums and two greatest hits albums, one released in the United States and the other released internationally, through her record label of thirteen years, Curb Records, and placed more than forty singles on American and international charts since 1996. She has sold more than 37 million records worldwide, with 20.3 million album sales in the United States according to Nielsen Soundscan. *Billboard* ranked her as the seventeenth artist of the 1990–2000 decade. Rimes has also written four books: two novels and two children's books. ♪

Tex Ritter grew up in Texas and became interested in cowboy songs and folklore while studying at the University of Texas. It was here that he met prominent folklorist John Lomax. After college, Ritter moved to New York City to pursue a theater career. By 1932, he began to record for Art Satherley and American Record Corporation; by 1933, he was hosting his own radio program of old cowboy songs. One of his big hits was "Get Along Little Dogies" (1935), an actual cowboy song that was often dumped amid different Hollywood movies. A year later, he signed with a start-up movie studio as their singing cowboy star and began producing the same sensationalized cowboy movies and songs that Gene Autry and Roy Rogers had been making famous. ♪

Jimmie Rodgers, born on September 8, 1897, near Meridian, Mississippi, is widely revered as the "Father of Country Music." Rodgers found a string-band trio from Bristol, Tennessee, called the Tenneva Ramblers. He quickly took over leadership of the group and dubbed them the Jimmie Rodgers Entertainers. He was the son of a railroad man and later worked for the railroad himself but, after contracting tuberculosis, used his sickness as an excuse to leave the railroad and do music full time. Rodgers and his group began to fuse hillbilly, country, gospel, jazz, blues, pop, cowboy, and folk styles into his compositions. His original tune, "Blue Yodel," sold more than a million records and established him as the premier singer in the early years of country music. ♪

Kenneth Donald "Kenny" Rogers, a member of the Country Music Hall of Fame, was born in Houston, Texas, on August 21, 1938. He has charted more than 120 hit singles across various music genres. Though most of his success has been with country audiences through the years, he was a pop singer early in his career but made a very wise move to country music in the 1970s. His gritty voice was perfectly suited to the story songs of country music. He has topped both the country and pop album charts for more than two hundred individual weeks in the United States alone and has sold more than one hundred million records world-wide. This fact alone makes him one of the best-selling music artists of all time. He was voted the "Favorite Singer of All-Time" in a 1986 joint poll by readers of both *USA Today* and *People*. He has received numer-ous AMAs, Grammys, ACMs, and CMAs, as well as a lifetime achieve-ment award for a career spanning six decades in 2003. Later success for Rogers includes the 2006 album release, *Water and Bridges*, which hit the Top 5 in the *Billboard Country Albums* sales charts, also charting in the Top 15 of the *Billboard* 200. The first single and big hit from the album was "I Can't Unlove You." As a popular entertainer worldwide, the following year he completed a tour of the United Kingdom and Ire-land, and told *BBC Radio 2* DJ Steve Wright his favorite hit was "The Gambler." He has also acted in a variety of movies and television shows. Some of his most notable title roles include *Kenny Rogers as The Gam-bler*, the MacShayne series, and his appearance on *The Muppet Show*. Even though his good looks have attributed to some of his popularity, his singing style, above all, has been the chief source of his success. Kenny Rogers is first and foremost a storyteller, with an intimate and unique style that commands the listener's attention. ♪

Blake Tollison Shelton, known as "Blake Shelton," was born in Ada, Oklahoma, on June 18, 1976, and is a country music singer/television personality who helps to keep country music's present connected to its past with honky-tonk traditionalism and contemporary vocals. In 2001, he made his debut with the single "Austin." The lead-off single from his self-titled debut album, "Austin" spent five weeks at number one on the *Billboard* Hot Country Songs chart. The gold-certified debut album also produced two more top-twenty hits ("All over Me" and "Ol' Red"). Although the album was released on Giant Records Nashville, he was transferred to Warner Bros. Records Nashville after Giant closed in late 2001. His second and third albums, *The Dreamer* (2003) and *Blake Shelton's Barn and Grill* (2004), were each certified gold as well. His fourth album, *Pure BS* (2007), was reissued in 2008 with a cover of Michael Bublé's pop hit "Home" as one of the bonus tracks. His fifth album, *Startin' Fires*, which had an appearance by his then-girlfriend Miranda Lambert, was released in November 2008. It was followed by the extended plays (EPs) *Hillbilly Bone* and *All about Tonight* (2010) and the albums *Red River Blue* (2011), *Based on a True Story . . .* (2013), and *Bringing Back the Sunshine* (2014). Overall, Blake Shelton has charted twenty-four country singles, including eleven number ones. The eleventh number one ("Doin' What She Likes") broke "the record for the most consecutive No. 1 singles in the Country Airplay chart's 24-year history." He is a five-time Grammy Award nominee. Shelton is also known for his role as a judge on the televised singing competitions *Nashville Star*, *Clash of the Choirs*, and *The Voice*. He has been on *The Voice* since its inception, and four out of the seven seasons (2–4, 7) his teams have won. He was the ex-husband of country singer Miranda Lambert; they divorced in 2015. ♪

Ricky Lee Skaggs, born on July 18, 1954, wedded country music and bluegrass, working in the industry as a singer, musician, producer, and composer to become one of the most influential mainstream stars of the 1980s. He primarily plays mandolin; however, he also plays fiddle, guitar, mandocaster, and banjo. Skaggs was born in Cordell, Kentucky, and started playing music at age five after he was given a mandolin by his father, Hobert. At age six, he played mandolin and sang on stage with Bill Monroe. At age seven, he appeared on television's Martha White country music variety show, playing with Lester Flatt and Earl Scruggs. He also wanted to audition for the Grand Ole Opry at that time but was told he was too young. In his mid-teens, Skaggs met a fellow teen guitarist, Keith Whitley, and the two started playing together with Whitley's banjo-playing brother Dwight on radio shows. By 1970, they had earned a spot opening for Ralph Stanley, and Skaggs and Keith Whitley were thereafter invited to join Stanley's band, the Clinch Mountain Boys. Skaggs later joined the Country Gentlemen in Washington, D.C., and also played with J. D. Crowe's New South. In 1976, Skaggs formed progressive bluegrass band Boone Creek, including members Vince Gill and Jerry Douglas. For a few years, Skaggs was a member of Emmylou Harris's Hot Band. He wrote the arrangements for Harris's 1980 bluegrass-roots album, *Roses in the Snow*. In addition to arranging for Harris, Skaggs sang harmony and played mandolin and fiddle in the Hot Band. ♪

Roy Rogers (aka Leonard Slye) was a member of Sons of the Pioneers. In 1938, when Gene Autry fell into a contract dispute with Republic Pictures, the film company slipped Leonard Slye into a couple pictures in small roles and then gave him the starring role in *Under Western Stars*. He changed his name to Dick Weston and then again to Roy Rogers. With some encouragement from the movie producers, Art Satherley quickly launched a campaign that promoted Roy Rogers as a solo cowboy singer. They knew that a hit record would improve the movie's success and that the movie would propel the success of the record. Roy Rogers was eventually known as "King of the Cowboys" and is probably most famous for his hit song "Happy Trails." ♪

The Statler Brothers started touring with Johnny Cash in 1964 and stayed with him for eight and a half years. Although known as a gospel quartet, they always performed a variety of styles. Cash negotiated their first recording contract with Columbia, and their third release was eventually the mega-hit and Grammy Award winner "Flowers on the Wall." Beginning in 1970, the Statler Brothers were named CMA's Vocal Group of the Year for seven years in a row. They reawakened memories of small-town radio with spoofs about amateur country bands on their recording "The Saturday Morning Radio Show." With an emphasis on traditional values, patriotism, and nostalgia, they struck a chord with Americans during the 1970s that eventually reached around the world. ♪

George Strait, a genuine cowboy, was born on May 18, 1952, and grew up on a ranch near Pearsall, Texas. He is known as the "King of Country" and one of the most influential and popular recording artists of all time. Although surrounded by country music as a youth, he did not sing publicly until his stint with the army in the late 1970s. When he was just starting out, he bought a cheap, old guitar and a bunch of songbooks with a little chart on the guitar that showed him where to put his fingers. Then he began to study the greats like Hank Williams, Merle Haggard, and George Jones. Later on, while pursuing a college degree in agriculture and ranch management at Southwest Texas State University, he put together his Ace in the Hole Band and started playing clubs. He is known for his neotraditionalist country style and cowboy look and for being one of the first and main country artists to bring country music back to its roots and away from the pop-country era in the 1980s. He never got into the outlaw mania, even though Austin was only thirty miles away. Instead, he wanted his music to reflect the shuffle beat and Texas swing rhythms he had grown up with, including the vocal stylings of men like Ray Price, George Jones, and Merle Haggard. Strait's success began when his first single, "Unwound," was a hit in 1981. During the 1980s, seven of his albums reached number one on the country charts. In the 2000s, Strait was named Artist of the Decade by the Academy of Country Music, was elected into the Country Music Hall of Fame, and won his first Grammy Award for the album *Troubadour*. Strait was named CMA Entertainer of the Year in 1989, 1990, and 2013, and ACM Entertainer of the Year in 1990 and 2014. He has been nominated for more CMA and ACM Awards and has more wins in both categories than any other artist. In 2009, he broke Conway Twitty's previous record for the most number-one hits on *Billboard*'s Hot Country Songs chart when his forty-four number-one singles surpassed Twitty's forty. Counting all music charts, Strait has amassed a total of sixty number-one hits, breaking a record also previously set by Twitty and giving him more number-one songs than any other artist. Strait has sold more than one hundred million records worldwide, making him one of the best-selling artists of all time. His certifications from the RIAA include thirteen multi-platinum, thirty-three platinum, and thirty-eight gold albums. His best-selling album is *Pure Country* (1992), which sold six million (6x platinum). His highest-certified album is *Strait out of the Box* (1995), which sold two million copies (8x platinum due to being a box set with four CDs). According to the RIAA, Strait is the twelfth best-selling album recording artist in the United States overall. ♪

Sugarland, a country music duo, is composed of singers, songwriters, and actors Jennifer Nettles (lead vocals) and Kristian Bush (background vocals, lead vocals, mandolin, acoustic guitar, and harmonica). Sugarland was founded in 2002 by Kristen Hall with Bush and became a trio after hiring Jennifer Nettles as lead singer. Signed to Mercury Nashville Records in 2004, Sugarland broke through that year with the release of their debut single "Baby Girl," the first single from their multi-platinum debut album *Twice the Speed of Life*. The trio became a duo in 2006, when they also released their second album, *Enjoy the Ride*. This album produced their first two number-one singles (in the United States), "Want To" and "Settlin'," and won the duo a Grammy for "Stay." In 2008 they released their third album, titled *Love on the Inside*. This album produced three more number-one singles with "All I Want to Do," "Already Gone," and "It Happens." Their fourth album, *The Incredible Machine*, was released on October 19, 2010, in both a standard and deluxe edition. Upon *The Incredible Machine* being certified platinum, Sugarland had sold in excess of fourteen million records. Besides songs written with Kevin Griffin, Nettles and Bush write all of the band's songs. In 2012, after recording a series of tours, the duo went on hiatus due in part to Nettles taking a maternity leave; during the hiatus, both she and Bush recorded solo projects. ♪

Taylor Swift first became widely known in 2006 when her debut single, "Tim McGraw," was released when Swift was sixteen. In 2006, Taylor released her first studio album, *Taylor Swift*, which spent 275 weeks on *Billboard* 200, one of the longest runs of any album on that chart. In 2008, Taylor Swift released her second studio album, *Fearless*, which gave her the second-longest number one charted on *Billboard* 200 and the second best-selling album (just behind Adele's *21*) within the past five years. At the 2010 Grammys, Taylor Swift was twenty and won Album of the Year for *Fearless*, which made her the youngest artist to win this award. Swift has received seven Grammys already. Buoyed by her teen idol status among girls and a change in the methodology of compiling the *Billboard* charts to favor pop-crossover songs, Swift's 2012 single "We Are Never Ever Getting Back Together" spent the most weeks at the top of *Billboard*'s Hot Country Songs chart of any song in nearly five decades. The song's long run at the top of the chart was somewhat controversial, as the song was largely a pop song without much country influence, prompting disputes over what constitutes a country song;

many of Swift's later releases, such as "Shake It Off," were released solely to pop audiences. ♪

Randy Bruce Traywick, otherwise known professionally as **Randy Travis,** is a singer, songwriter, guitarist, and actor who was heralded as being the bright new hope of traditionalism. His sound is somewhat reminiscent of Lefty Frizzell. With encouragement from manager Libby Hatcher, whom he later married, he moved to Nashville in 1981 and started pitching his material to recording studios and publishers. In May 1986, "On the Other Hand" jumped to the number-one position on the *Billboard* Country charts, and in May 1990 he had a string of eleven number-one hits and two that went to number two. He won the CMA Horizon Award in 1986 and Male Vocalist of the Year from the CMA, Academy of Country Music, and the *Music City News* in 1987 and 1988. Since 1985, he has recorded twenty studio albums and charted more than fifty singles on the *Billboard* Hot Country Songs charts, and sixteen of these were number-one hits. Considered a pivotal figure in the history of country music, Travis broke through in the mid-1980s with the release of his album *Storms of Life*, which sold more than four million copies. This was the album that established him as a major force in the neotraditional country movement. Travis followed up his successful debut with a string of platinum and multi-platinum albums. He is known for his distinctive baritone vocals delivered in a traditional style that has made him a country music star since the 1980s. In 1993, Travis recorded an album of western songs called *Wind in the Wire*. As a cowboy at heart, he said he would know that he had made it when he became a member of the Grand Ole Opry. By the mid-1990s, Travis saw a decline in his chart success. In 1997, he left Warner Bros. Records for Dream Works Records and changed his musical focus to gospel music. Although the career shift produced only one more number-one country hit, "Three Wooden Crosses," Travis went on to earn several Dove Awards, including Country Album of the Year five times. In addition to his singing career, he pursued an acting career, appearing in numerous films and television series, including *The Rainmaker* (1997) with Matt Damon, *Black Dog* (1998) with Patrick Swayze, *Texas Rangers* (2001) with James Van Der Beek, and seven episodes of the *Touched by an Angel* television series. Travis has sold over twenty-five million records and has earned twenty-two number one hits, six number-one albums, six Grammy Awards, six CMA Awards, nine ACM Awards, ten American Music Awards (AMA) Awards, eight Dove Awards, and a star on the Hollywood Walk of Fame. ♪

Shania Twain was born in Windsor, Ontario, as Eileen Regina Edwards on August 28, 1965. She adopted her name from her stepfather, an Ojibwe Indian named Jerry Twain, who raised her after her father deserted the family. Jerry Twain and her mother were killed in an automobile accident and Shania was left to raise her younger siblings. As a child she often appeared on Canadian television shows singing Emmylou Harris and other leading female country stars. She worked as an entertainer at Deerhearst Resort in the Huntsville, Ontario, area prior to breaking into the country music industry. Twain's second studio album, 1995's *The Woman in Me*, made her the best-selling female country artist of all time. It sold nine million in the United States and a total of twenty-one million units worldwide, spawning hits such as "Any Man of Mine" and earning her a Grammy Award. Twain's third album, *Come on Over*, became the best-selling studio album of all time by a female act in any genre and the best-selling country album of all time, selling around forty million copies worldwide. *Come on Over* produced several singles, including "You're Still the One," "From This Moment On," and "Man! I Feel Like a Woman!" earning Twain four Grammy Awards. Her fourth and latest studio album, *Up!*, was released in 2002 and, like her previous two albums, was also certified diamond in the United States, spawning hits like "I'm Gonna Getcha Good" and "Forever and for Always." Twain has received five Grammy Awards, twenty-seven BMI Songwriter Awards, stars on Canada's Walk of Fame and the Hollywood Walk of Fame, and an induction into the Canadian Music Hall of Fame. She is the only female artist in history to have three consecutive albums certified diamond by the RIAA. Altogether, Twain is ranked as the tenth best-selling artist of the Nielsen Soundscan era. In 2004, Twain retired from performing and retreated to her home in Switzerland. In her 2011 autobiography, she cited a weakening singing voice as the reason for not performing publicly. When both her singing and speaking were affected, Twain consulted the Vanderbilt Dayani Center in Nashville. Specialists discovered lesions on her vocal cords and diagnosed her with dysphonia, all treatable with careful rehabilitation. In 2012, Twain returned to the concert stage in her critically acclaimed show *Still the One*, exclusively at the Colosseum at Caesars Palace. ♪

Carrie Underwood was born in Muskogee, Oklahoma, but was raised in nearby Checotah, where her family owned a farm. She started singing in church as a child and performed all through high school. Underwood earned a journalism degree from Northeastern State University and, while in college, competed in beauty pageants and continued to sing in local venues. In 2005, Underwood rose to fame as the winner of the fourth season of *American Idol* and has since become one of the most prominent recording artists of past ten years, with worldwide sales of more than sixty-four million records and six Grammy Awards. With her first single, "Inside Your Heaven," Underwood became the only solo country artist to have a number-one hit on the *Billboard* Hot 100 chart in the 2000–2009 decade and also broke *Billboard* chart history as the first country music artist ever to debut at number-one on the Hot 100. Underwood's debut album, *Some Hearts*, became the best-selling solo female debut album in country music history, the fastest-selling debut country album in the history of the SoundScan era, and the best-selling country album of the past ten years, being ranked by *Billboard* as the number-one country album of the 2000–2009 decade. She has also become the female country artist with the most number-one hits on the *Billboard* Hot Country Songs chart in the Nielsen SoundScan era (1991–present) with twelve and breaking her own *Guinness Book* record of ten. In 2007, Underwood won the Grammy Award for Best New Artist, becoming only the second country artist in history (and the first in a decade) to win it. She also made history by becoming the seventh woman to win Entertainer of the Year at the Academy of Country Music Awards and the first woman in history to win the award twice, as well as the first to win it twice consecutively. *Time* has listed Underwood as one of the one hundred most influential people in the world. ♪

Porter Wagoner was a country music singer from West Plains, Missouri, known for his flashy Nudie and Manuel suits and blond pompadour hairdo. In 1967, Wagoner introduced a young Dolly Parton to the world on his long-running television show, and they were a well-known vocal duo throughout the late 1960s and early 1970s. Porter Wagoner, known as "Mr. Grand Ole Opry," charted eighty-one singles from 1954 to 1983. He was elected to the Country Music Hall of Fame in 2002. ♪

Kitty Wells's hit "It Wasn't God Who Made Honky Tonk Angels" was the first number-one song recorded by a woman since *Billboard* began tracking country records in January 1944. Interestingly enough, some radio stations would not play it because of its suggestive topic; and for a brief time, Wells was barred from singing the song not only on NBC's "Prince Albert" spot but also on the entire Opry program. Wells's recording of this song was an outspoken defense of women who had formerly been cast down as "bad girls," but in interviews she was quick to deny any staunch feminist views. It is ironic that she also always liked to talk about her role as a wife and mother and even published several cookbooks. Wells soon became the most well-known female honky-tonk singer of the 1950s. ♪

Hiram "Hank" Williams started singing in church sitting beside his mother on the organ bench at Mount Olive West Baptist Church in south Alabama. He filled out his western suits like a scarecrow and was known to all the world as "Hank" Williams. By age eleven, he began drinking hard liquor and performing in the streets for pocket change. In his early teens, he met a fiftyish black street musician by the name of Rufus Payne. "Tee Tot," as he was commonly known, played the blues and captivated a young Hank Williams. Hank even said at a later time that all of his musical training had come from him. Hank was shining shoes and following Tee Tot around to get him to teach him to play guitar. At thirteen, he was singing for his supper twice a week in fifteen-minute programs on WSFA in Montgomery, Alabama. He was known by his listeners as "the singing kid." ♪

Randall Hank Williams, better known as Hank Williams Jr. or Boce-phus, was born in Shreveport, Louisiana, on May 26, 1949. His musical style is considered to be a blend of southern rock, blues, and traditional country. He is the son of legendary country singer Hank Williams and began his career by following in his father's footsteps, singing his father's songs and imitating his style. His style slowly evolved as he struggled to find his own voice and place within the country music industry. A near-fatal fall off of the side of a mountain in Montana in 1975 required massive plastic surgery, including the complete rebuilding of his face. Even though this event interrupted his career, after an extended recovery, he challenged country music with a blend of country, rock, and blues. He enjoyed a great deal of success in the 1980s, both inside and outside of the country music industry. Williams is a multi-instrumentalist with skills in the following instruments: guitar, bass, upright bass, steel guitar, banjo, dobro, piano, keyboards, harmonica, fiddle, and drums. From 1989 until 2011, a version of his song "All My Rowdy Friends Are Coming over Tonight" was used as the opening for broadcasts of *Monday Night Football*. ♪

Tammy Wynette was born Virginia Wynette Pugh in Tremont, Mississippi, and grew up picking cotton alongside her grandparents. She married before her high school graduation but by age twenty-three was a divorced mother of three working at a hair salon. She frequently appeared on Birmingham, Alabama's WBRC6 morning segment called "The Country Boy Eddie Show" before anyone knew her name. Her friendship with a Birmingham DJ led to her first trip to Nashville. While visiting Nashville, Opry star Porter Wagoner heard her and offered her a spot singing on one of his tours. Wynette then moved to Nashville in 1965 and signed with Billy Sherrill, a producer with Epic Records and the person responsible for shaping the "classic" country sound. She was called the "First Lady of Country"; her first hit was "Apartment No. 9," but her best-known song was "Stand by Your Man." This song was one of the best-selling hit singles by a country female until Dolly Parton came out with "9 to 5." Many of her hits dealt with classic themes of loneliness, divorce, and the difficulties of man-woman relationships. During the late 1960s and early 1970s, Wynette charted twenty-three number-one songs. Along with Loretta Lynn and Dolly Parton, she is given credit for defining the role of women in country music during the 1970s. Wynette's marriage to country music singer George Jones in 1969 created a country music couple, following the earlier success of Johnny Cash and June Carter Cash. Even though Jones and Wynette divorced in 1975, they recorded a sequence of albums and singles that hit the charts throughout the 1970s and early 1980s. ♪

Trisha Yearwood, a banker's daughter from Monticello, Georgia, became one of the most respected vocalists in country music when she launched her first album and single in 1991. This first hit in 1991 was a mid-tempo story song called "She's in Love with the Boy." Before she had a record deal with MCA, she worked as a demo singer and as a receptionist at MTM Records. Yearwood was one of five female artists in 1998 to account for 52 percent of all number-one hits on *Billboard*'s Hot Country Singles and Tracks. The other female artists besides Yearwood who were responsible for these hits were Reba McEntire, Faith Hill, Shania Twain, and Martina McBride. Trisha Yearwood married longtime friend, fellow country artist, and musical collaborator Garth Brooks in 2005. ♪

The Zac Brown Band consists of Zac Brown (lead vocals, guitar), Jimmy De Martini (fiddle, vocals), John Driskell Hopkins (bass guitar, guitar, baritone guitar, banjo, ukulele, upright bass, vocals), Coy Bowles (guitar, keyboards), Chris Fryar (drums), Clay Cook (guitar, keyboards, mandolin, steel guitar, vocals), Matt Mangano (bass guitar), and Daniel de los Reyes (percussion). The band has released four studio albums, three of which have been in collaboration with Atlantic Records, along with two live albums, one greatest hits album, and two EPs. They have also charted sixteen singles on the *Billboard* country singles charts, of which ten have reached number one: "Chicken Fried," "Toes," "Highway 20 Ride," "Free," "As She's Walking Away," "Colder Weather," "Knee Deep," "Keep Me in Mind," "Goodbye in Her Eyes," and "Sweet Annie." Their first Atlantic album, *The Foundation*, is certified triple-platinum by the RIAA, while its follow-ups, *You Get What You Give* and *Uncaged*, are certified platinum. Artists with whom they have collaborated include Alan Jackson, Jimmy Buffett, Kid Rock, Amos Lee, Trombone Shorty, Joey + Rory, Jason Mraz, Dave Grohl, and Chris Cornell. ♪

GLOSSARY

affiliated writers: Songwriters who are affiliated with a publisher because they have signed single-song agreements but are not signed as exclusive writers to that company.

Americana: A style defined by the American Music Association as contemporary music that incorporates various elements of American roots music. Some of these elements include country, roots-rock, folk, bluegrass, R&B, and blues. This amalgamation results in a distinct roots-oriented sound that is entirely different from each of the genres from which it draws. Acoustic instruments are often present and a vital part of this particular sound, but Americana can also use a full electric band. Americana is a blend or coming-together of the various musical traditions that make up the characteristic spirit of the United States.

ASCAP: The American Society of Composers, Authors, and Publishers (ASCAP) is an American not-for-profit performance-rights organization (PRO) with a membership of 575,000 U.S. composers, songwriters, lyricists, and music publishers of every kind of music. ASCAP protects its members' musical copyrights by monitoring public performances of their music, whether via broadcast or live performance, and compensating them accordingly. Licensees encompass all who want to perform copyrighted music publicly.

backing vocals/background vocals: The supporting vocal tracks that are present on a recording behind, or in the background of, the lead recording artist.

backup (drive): The external hard drive on which audio engineers save a copy of a recording session.

band hits: Rhythmic hits for the entire band that are usually notated on a rhythm chart or rhythm stave of a full musical score.

bluegrass: A related genre of country music and a form of American roots music. Influenced heavily by the music of Appalachia, bluegrass also has roots in Irish, Scottish, Welsh, and English traditional music and was later influenced by the music of African Americans by incorporating elements of jazz.

blues: A musical form that originated in rural plantation African American communities in the Deep South of the United States around the end of the nineteenth century. The genre developed from traditional African music combined with European American folk music. Blues incorporated spirituals, shouts, chants, work songs, field hollers, and rhymed simple narrative ballads. The blues form, found frequently in jazz, rhythm and blues, and rock and roll, is characterized by the call-and-response pattern, the blues scale, and specific chord progressions, including the most common form, twelve-bar blues. The blue notes, which are often the thirds or fifths, are an important part of the sound of this genre and are flatter in pitch than in other music styles. Blues shuffles or walking bass are elements of blues that incorporate a trance-like rhythm and form a repetitive effect throughout the song that is otherwise known as the groove.

BMI: Broadcast Music, Inc. (BMI) is one of three U.S. performing-rights organizations, along with ASCAP and SESAC. It collects license fees on behalf of songwriters, composers, and music publishers and distributes them as royalties to those members whose works have been performed. BMI was founded in 1939 by forward thinkers who wanted to represent songwriters in emerging genres, like jazz, blues, and country, and protect the public performances of their music. Operating on a non-profit-making basis, BMI is now the largest music rights organization in the United States and is still nurturing new talent and new music. BMI is the bridge between songwriters and the businesses and organizations that want to play their music publicly.

As a global leader in music rights management, BMI serves as an advocate for the value of music, representing more than 10.5 million musical works created and owned by more than 700,000 songwriters, composers, and music publishers.

boogie (or boogie-woogie): A repetitive swing note or shuffle rhythm "groove" or pattern used in blues that was originally played on the piano in boogie-woogie music. The characteristic rhythm and feel of the boogie was then adapted to guitar, double bass, and other instruments. The earliest recorded boogie-woogie song was in 1916. By the 1930s, swing bands led by Benny Goodman, Glenn Miller, Tommy Dorsey, and Louis Jordan all had boogie-woogie hits. By the 1950s, boogie became incorporated into rockabilly and rock-and-roll styles. In the late 1980s and early 1990s, country bands released songs they called "country boogies."

chord chart: A form of musical notation that describes the basic harmonic and rhythmic information for a song or tune. It is the most common form of notation used by professional session musicians playing jazz or popular music. It is intended primarily for a rhythm section (usually consisting of piano, guitar, drums, and bass). In these genres the musicians are expected to be able to improvise the actual notes used for the chords and the appropriate ornamentation, countermelody, or bassline. In many chord charts, the harmony is given as a series of chord symbols above a traditional musical staff. The rhythmic information can be very specific and written using a form of traditional notation, sometimes called rhythmic notation, or it can be completely unspecified using slash notation, allowing the musician to fill the bar with chords or fills any way he or she sees fit. This type of playing is called "comping." In Nashville notation, the key is left unspecified on the chart by substituting numbers for chord names. This facilitates the convenience of on-the-spot key changes to songs.

chord progression: A series of musical chords or chord changes that establishes a tonality founded on a key, root, or tonic chord. Chord progressions are based upon a succession of root relationships. Chords and chord theory are generally known in the musical community as harmony.

clavicular breathing: The drawing of minimal breath into the lungs, usually by drawing air into the chest area using the intercostal muscles rather than throughout the lungs via the diaphragm. In upper lobar breathing, clavicular breathing, or clavicle breathing, air is drawn predominantly into the chest by the raising of the shoulders and collarbone (clavicles) and simultaneous contracting of the abdomen during inhalation. Maximum amount of air can be drawn this way only for short periods of time since it requires a lot of effort.

commercial voice: The term that refers to any type of singing or study of the singing voice that involves the various popular styles that are intended for commercial consumption.

comping: When a musician fills in the chord changes on a chart improvisationally but with a rhythmic pattern.

compression: An electronic effect unit that reduces the volume of loud sounds or amplifies quiet sounds by narrowing or "compressing" an audio signal's dynamic range. Compression is commonly used in sound recording and reproduction, broadcasting, and live sound at music concerts and in some instrument amplifiers (usually bass amps). Audio compression reduces loud sounds above a certain threshold while leaving quiet sounds unaffected. In the 2000s, compressors became available as software plug-ins that run in digital audio workstations of audio recording software. A dedicated electronic hardware unit or audio software that applies compression is called a compressor. In recorded and live music, compression parameters may be adjusted to change the way the effect sounds. Compression and limiting are identical in process but different in degree and perceived effect. Attack, release, knee, threshold, and gain are common compression parameters that can be adjusted.

copyright: A form of intellectual property applicable to certain forms of creative work. Under U.S. copyright law, legal protection attaches only to fixed representations in a tangible medium that can be documented. It is often shared among multiple authors, each of whom holds a set of rights to use or license the work. These authors are commonly referred to as "rightsholders." These rights frequently include reproduction, control over derivative works, right of first refusal, distribution, public performance, and "moral rights" such as attribution.

cowpunk: Cowpunk or country punk is a subgenre of punk rock. It began in the United Kingdom and California in the late 1970s and early 1980s. It combines punk rock or new wave with country music, folk music, and blues in musical sound, subject matter, attitude, and style. Many of the musicians who are connected with this genre have now become affiliated with the genre of alternative country or the roots rock music scene.

crooning: "Crooner" is a term given to male singers of jazz standards, mostly from artists who attempt to sing out of the Great American Songbook. These "crooners" are usually either backed by a full orchestra, a big band, or a piano. Originally it was an ironic term often describing an emotional singing style made possible by the use of microphones. Some performers did not accept the term. Frank Sinatra said in an interview that he did not consider himself or Bing Crosby "crooners."

crossover artist: A term applied to performers appearing on two or more of the record charts that track differing musical tastes or genres. If the second chart combines genres, however, such as a Hot 100 list, the performer is not a crossover artist.

crossover hits: A term applied to works appearing on two or more of the record charts that track differing musical tastes or genres. If the second chart combines genres, however, such as a Hot 100 list, the work is not a crossover hit.

DAW (digital audio workstation): An electronic device or computer software application for recording, editing, and producing audio files. These files might be songs, musical pieces, human speech, or sound effects. DAWs come in a wide variety of configurations from a single software program on a laptop, to an integrated stand-alone unit, all the way to a highly complex configuration of numerous components controlled by a central computer such as ProTools. Modern DAWs have a central interface that allows the user to alter and mix multiple recordings and tracks into a final produced stereo mix of recorded material.

demonstration recording (or demo): A recording of an original song shortly after it has been written. This is a recorded version of the song that can be as simple as a guitar/vocal or as complex as a fully produced track.

echo: A reflection of sound arriving at the listener's ear some time after the direct sound. Typical examples of this reflection are the echoes produced by the bottom of a well, by a building, or by the walls of an enclosed, empty room. A true echo is a single reflection of the sound source. The time delay is the extra distance divided by the speed of sound.

exclusive writers: A songwriter who is signed to an exclusive contract with one publishing company for a specified period of time. All songs written by this writer during the term of the contract belong to the publisher that holds the exclusive agreement with the songwriter.

external hard drive: A hard drive that can be bought separately and housed outside of a computer and connected with a USB cable. These types of drives are the best way to store recorded session files that need to be transported from studio to studio.

fan base: A group of people who support and are loyal followers of a particular artist. Artists usually keep a contact list of their fan base and send a regular newsletter updating their fans about their upcoming itineraries and new music.

flip side: A term that refers to a recorded song that for many years was on the "flip side" or other side of a radio single when issued on vinyl by the record label.

gig: Any public or private performance by a musical artist.

Great American Songbook: This songbook is also known as "American Standards." It is a collection of the most influential and important American popular songs and jazz standards from the early twentieth century.

hold: The act of an artist putting a song on "hold" or reserve for an upcoming recording. The publisher is supposed to stop pitching it to other artists once the song is placed on "hold."

honky-tonk: The term "honky-tonk" has been used to describe various styles of twentieth-century American music. A honky-tonk refers to a type of bar that provides country music as entertainment to its patrons. Bars of this kind are common in the southern and southwestern regions of the United States, where country music is most popular. Many country music legends, such as Loretta Lynn, Merle Haggard, Patsy Cline, and Ernest Tubb, began their careers as amateur musicians in honky-tonks. The first music genre to be commonly known as honky-tonk music was a style of piano playing related to ragtime but emphasizing rhythm more than melody or harmony. This style developed in response to an environment where the pianos were not taken care of, usually out of tune and having some keys that did not work. This honky-tonk music was an important influence on the formation of the boogie-woogie piano style. During the pre–World War II years, the music industry began to refer to hillbilly music being played from Texas and Oklahoma to the West Coast as honky-tonk music. In the 1950s, honky-tonk entered its golden age, with the massive popularity of Webb Pierce, Hank Locklin, Lefty Frizzell, Faron Young, George Jones, and Hank Williams.

instrumental solo: The moment in a recording or performance when one of the instrumentalists plays an improvised "solo" while the artist is not singing.

instrumental tracks: The individual tracks in a recording that contain all the different band instruments' audio and data.

instrumentation: The type of instruments an artist decides to use on a particular song whether for live performance or recording.

intro: The beginning of a song before the artist starts singing. An intro can be one to sixteen measures in length but is normally eight or fewer.

line dance music: Music that is used in dance halls and clubs for the patrons to form a line and do the same dance all together across the floor.

livestream: Refers to a performance that is broadcast live over the Internet via a webcam or smartphone.

Logic: A popular digital audio workstation software that was invented more for programmers but also functions quite well as a recording platform.

lyric: The words of a song.

master recordings: Recordings that are intended to be distributed to the public for mass appeal. These recordings are usually always mastered by a mastering engineer, hence the use of the term "master" recordings.

meter markings: The markings on a musical chart that tell the musician or the performer in which meter the song is to be played. Examples include 2/4, 3/4, 4/4, 6/8, 9/8, 12/8, and so on.

mix stage: The stage in the recording process when all the recorded tracks have been cleaned up and are finally given to a mixing engineer in order to blend all the tracks together so that everything can be heard as desired. A mix engineer uses a variety of techniques to achieve the perfect mix, including equalization, compression, and simple volume control.

music copyist: Someone who takes the orchestrator's score and separates all the different instrument staves into individual parts so that each musician can have a copy of his part on his own personal music stand during the recording session. Music copyists used to do this by hand with a calligraphy pen, but now with music notation software like Finale, it can be done with the click of a mouse. The music copyist is usually also responsible for printing out the copies for each musician and taping the pages together so that the pages can be easily managed or flipped during the recording session.

octavo vocal sessions: Sessions where eight singers are hired to record the vocals for a production that usually accompanies a printed version of the recording for the choral marketplace.

outro: The last few measures of a song, usually just instrumental after the artist is done singing, but occasionally the artist will sing a bit more over the outro as a "tag."

phasing: What occurs when the microphones are not placed correctly: the waveforms will begin to reduce the level of the audio because the instruments are "out of phase" with each other.

phonation: The process by which the vocal folds produce certain sounds through vibration. Phonation, or voicing, occurs when air is expelled from the lungs through the glottis, creating a pressure drop across the larynx, at which point the vocal folds start to oscillate, producing vibrations and ultimately what we perceive as sound.

processing: Refers to any type of effect that an engineer might put onto an audio signal during the recording, mix, or mastering stage in the recording studio.

programmer: A musician who uses virtual instruments in various digital audio workstations (DAWs) to create programmed tracks that sound as close as possible to live acoustic instruments recorded in the studio.

ProTools: A digital audio workstation software, developed and manufactured by Avid Technology, that lets you record, arrange, compose, edit, mix, and master professional-quality audio and MIDI for music, video, film, and multimedia for Microsoft Windows and OS X.

ragtime: A musical genre that enjoyed its greatest amount of popularity between the years of 1895 and 1918. Its fundamental trait is its syncopated, or "ragged," rhythm. Years before ever being published in sheet music form for piano, the genre had its origins in African American communities such as St. Louis. Ernest Hogan (1865–1909) was a pioneer of ragtime music and the first to publish a piece in the musical genre. He is also credited with coining the term "ragtime." Ben Harvey, a white Kentucky native, has often been credited for introducing the music to the general market. His ragtime compositions helped popularize the genre throughout America. Ragtime was also a close cousin to the march made popular by John Philip Sousa with additional polyrhythms coming from African music. The ragtime composer Scott Joplin (c. 1868–1917) became famous through the publication of the "Maple Leaf Rag" (1899) and a series of ragtime hits such as "The Entertainer" (1902). Sadly, he was later forgotten by all but a small, dedicated community of ragtime aficionados until the major ragtime revival in the early 1970s. For at least twelve years after its publication, "Maple Leaf Rag" heavily influenced later ragtime composers with its melody lines, harmonic progressions, and metric patterns.

reggae: A music genre that originated in Jamaica in the late 1960s. The term also represents the modern popular music of Jamaica and the Jamaican people. While sometimes used in a broad sense to refer to most types of popular Jamaican dance music, the term "reggae" more properly describes a particular music style that was strongly influenced by traditional mento music of the nineteenth century and calypso music. Other influences include American jazz and rhythm and blues, especially the New Orleans R&B practiced by Fats Domino and Allen Toussaint. Reggae evolved out of the earlier genres ska and rocksteady. Reggae usually relates news, social gossip, and political comment. Reggae spread into a commercialized jazz field, being known first as "rudie blues," then ska, and later "blue beat" and rocksteady. It is most usually recognizable from the counterpoint between the bass and drum downbeat and the rhythm section playing the offbeat.

resonating chambers: A term used in voice pedagogy to describe the areas of the body that resonate during vocal phonation, including the oropharynx (mouth), nasopharynx (nose), and laryngopharynx (throat).

reverberation: In acoustics, the persistence of sound after a sound is produced. A reverberation, or reverb, is created when a sound or signal is reflected causing a large number of reflections to build up and then decay as the sound is absorbed by the surfaces of objects in the space. These objects could include furniture, people, and air. This is most noticeable when the sound source stops but the reflections continue, decreasing in amplitude, until they reach zero amplitude. Reverberation is frequency dependent as the length of the decay, or reverberation time, receives special consideration in the architectural design of spaces, which need to have specific reverberation times to achieve optimum performance for their intended activities. In comparison to a distinct echo that is a minimum of 50 to 100 milliseconds after the initial sound, reverberation is the occurrence of reflections that arrive in less than approximately 50 milliseconds. As time passes, the amplitude of the reflections is reduced until it is reduced to zero. Reverberation is not just limited to indoor spaces as it also exists in forests and other outdoor environments where reflection exists. Reverberation occurs naturally when a person sings, talks, or plays an instrument acoustically in a hall or performance space with sound-reflective surfaces. In modern-day settings, the sound of reverberation is often electronically added to the vocals of singers in live sound systems and sound recordings by using effects units or digital delay effects.

ritard (or ritardando): A marking in music notation that indicates the tempo should slow down gradually.

rockabilly: One of the earliest styles of rock and roll music, dating to the early 1950s in the United States, especially the South. As a genre it blends the sound of western musical styles such as country with that of rhythm and blues. This led to what is considered "classic" rock and roll. Some have also described it as a blend of rock and roll with the bluegrass style. The term "rockabilly" itself is a combination of "rock" (from "rock 'n' roll") and "hillbilly." Hillbilly is a reference to the country music that was called "hillbilly music" in the 1940s and 1950s. Other important influences on rockabilly include Western swing, boogie-woogie, jump blues, and electric blues.

scratch vocal: A vocal performance that a singer records to provide a reference track that music producers and audio engineers can use as they craft other pieces of the recorded song. It is primarily used for timing purposes. It may also provide an idea of how the vocalist may ultimately perform the vocal, making it easier to add matching musical embellishments. A scratch vocal is often recorded quickly, and the singer may mark the song rather than hit more difficult notes. The singer ultimately rerecords the vocal performance.

SESAC: Originally called the Society of European Stage Authors and Composers, this is a performing-rights organization (PRO) in the United States. Since the organization stopped using its full name in 1940, it is now known exclusively as SESAC. The organization was founded in 1930, making it the second-oldest and also the fastest-growing PRO in the United States. Based in Nashville, SESAC deals with all aspects of the business, from creation to licensing and administration. The company also has offices in New York City, Los Angeles, London, Atlanta, and Miami. Since being established in 1930, SESAC Performing Rights has become the nation's most innovative PRO with a stellar roster of affiliates including Bob Dylan, Mumford and Sons, Neil Diamond, Green Day, Mariah Carey, Lady Antebellum, and Alt-J among many others. A leader in technology, SESAC Performing Rights was the first and only PRO to offer monthly royalty payments to songwriters and publishers. As the United States' only music rights organization, SESAC has now acquired Rumblefish, a leader in microlicensing, and the Harry Fox Agency (HFA), the leading U.S. mechanical rights organization.

session: A term referring to a recording session or a session in a studio where musicians are recording.

sound reinforcement: The combination of microphones, signal processors, amplifiers, and loudspeakers that makes live or prerecorded sounds louder and may also distribute those sounds to a larger or more distant audience. Occasionally, a sound reinforcement system is also used to enhance or alter the sound of the sources on the stage, typically by using electronic effects, as opposed to simply amplifying the sources.

speech-level singing: The voice pedagogy concept of getting the singing voice on the same easy level as speaking. This term was coined by Los Angeles–based voice coach and technician Seth Riggs.

story song: A song whose lyric tells a story from beginning to end.

string band: A term used in bluegrass to describe a band that is made up of string instruments only.

square dance: A square dance is a dance for four couples arranged in a square, with one couple on each side facing the middle of the square. Square dances were first documented in seventeenth-century England but were also quite common in France and throughout Europe. They came to North America with the European settlers and have undergone considerable development. In some countries and regions, square dances have attained the status of a folk dance. The Western American square dance may be the most widely known for its association with the American cowboy and his romanticized image. Square dancing is, therefore, strongly associated with the United States. In most American forms of square dance, the dancers are prompted or cued through a sequence of steps by a caller. The caller may be one of the dancers or musicians but is more likely to be onstage, giving full attention to directing the various steps of the dancers.

subglottal back pressure: Refers to an unnecessary, undesired amount of breath pressed from the underside of the vocal folds that causes excessive pressure and unnecessary tension at the laryngeal level during singing.

template: Refers to a generic session "template" an engineer will create in a DAW software like ProTools or Logic in order to be able to quickly create a session that already contains some of his favorite plug-ins and routing system.

tempo: The speed or pace of a given piece of music (or subsection).

upper bridge: A commercial or popular vocal term that refers to the upper "break" or *passaggio* in the female voice.

vaudeville: A theatrical genre of variety entertainment. It was especially popular in the United States and Canada from the early 1880s until the early 1930s. A typical vaudeville performance is made up of a series of separate, unrelated acts grouped together on a common program, otherwise known as a bill. Types of vaudeville acts have included popular and classical musicians, singers, dancers, comedians, trained animals, magicians, female and male impersonators, acrobats, illustrated songs, jugglers, one-act plays or scenes from plays, athletes, lecturing celebrities, minstrels, and movies. Vaudeville developed from many sources, including the concert saloon, minstrelsy, freak shows, dime museums, and literary American burlesque. Sometimes known as the "heart of American show business," vaudeville was one of the most popular types of entertainment in North America for several decades.

venue: The place where an artist or band performs.

vocal folds (or vocal cords): Twin infoldings of mucous membrane stretched horizontally. They lie from back to front, across the larynx and vibrate, modulating the flow of air being expelled from the lungs during phonation.

vocal improvisation: Singing with wordless nonsense syllables or without words at all. It is a technique that requires singers with the ability to sing improvised melodies and rhythms using the voice as an instrument rather than a speaking medium.

vocalise: A vocal exercise without words, usually sung on one or more vowel sounds.

vocal pedagogy: The study of the art and science of voice instruction. It is used in the teaching of singing and assists in defining what singing is, how singing works, and how proper singing technique is accomplished.

vocal tracks: Refers to the particular channels in digital audio workstation software that contain the recorded vocal tracks.

vocal tract: The cavity in human beings where sound that is produced at the laryngeal level (at the source) is filtered. It consists of the laryngopharynx (throat), the oropharynx (mouth), and the nasopharynx (nose). Unlike most instruments, the vocal tract is not a fixed-bore instrument, meaning that its shape can be easily manipulated. The estimated average length of the vocal tract in adult male humans is 16.9 centimeters and 14.1 centimeters in adult females.

vocal tuning: The act of adjusting, through vocal editing, the notes of a recorded vocal (with a software program like Melodyne or Auto-Tune) to the correct pitches, thus adjusting the voice to be "in tune."

vocal twang: The bright-sounding forward placement that is commonly used in singing country music. One of the hallmarks of the style.

waltz: A ballroom and folk dance in triple time.

yodeling: A form of singing that involves repeated and rapid changes of pitch between the lower-pitched chest register and the higher-pitched head register (or falsetto).

BIBLIOGRAPHY

Berry, Chad, ed. *The Hayloft Gang: The Story of the National Barn Dance.* Urbana: University of Illinois Press, 2008.

Boyd, Jean A. *The Jazz of the Southwest: An Oral History of Western Swing.* Austin: University of Texas Press, 1998.

Brown, Maxine. *Looking Back to See: A Country Music Memoir.* Fayetteville: University of Arkansas Press, 2005.

Bufwack, Mary A., and Robert K. Oermann. *Finding Her Voice: Women in Country Music, 1800–2000.* Nashville: Vanderbilt University Press, 2013.

Cantwell, Robert. *Bluegrass Breakdown: The Making of the Old Southern Sound.* Urbana: University of Illinois Press, 1984.

Carlin, Richard. *Country Music: The People, Places, and Moments That Shaped the Country Sound.* New York: Black Dog & Leventhal, 2006.

Chertkow, Randy, and Jason Freehan. *The Indie Band Survival Guide: The Complete Manual for the Do-It-Yourself Musician.* New York: St. Martin's Press, 2008.

Cox, Patsi Bale. *The Garth Factor: The Career behind Country's Big Boom.* New York: Center Street, 2009.

Cusic, Don. *Discovering Country Music.* Westport, CT: Praeger, 2008.

Dicaire, David. *The First Generation of Country Music Stars: Biographies of 50 Artists Born before 1940.* Jefferson, NC: McFarland and Company, 2007.

Ellison, Curtis. *Country Music Culture: From Hard Times to Heaven.* Jackson: University Press of Mississippi, 1995.

Escott, Colin. *Hank Williams: The Biography*. Boston: Little, Brown and Company, 1995.

———. *Lost Highway: The True Story of Country Music*. Washington, DC: Smithsonian Books, 2003.

Frascogna, Xavier M., and H. Lee Hetherington. *This Business of Artist Management: A Practical Guide to Successful Strategies for Career Development in the Music Business for Musicians, Managers, Music Publishers and Record Companies*, 3rd ed. New York: Billboard Books, 1997.

Goodman, David. *Modern Twang: An Alternative Country Music Guide and Directory*. Nashville: Dowling Press, 1999.

Green, Douglas B. *Singing in the Saddle: The History of the Singing Cowboy*. Nashville: Country Music Foundation Press and Vanderbilt University Press, 2002.

Greenway, John. "Jimmie Rodgers—A Folksong Catalyst." *Journal of American Folklore* 70, no. 277 (July–September 1957): 231–34.

Hall, Tom T. *The Storyteller's Nashville*. Garden City, NY: Doubleday, 1979.

Haslam, Gerald W. *Workin' Man Blues: Country Music in California*. Berkeley: University of California Press, 1999.

Hooper, David, and Lee Kennedy. *How I Make $100,000 a Year in the Music Business: Without a Record Label, Manager or Booking Agent*. Nashville: Kathode Ray Music, 2003.

Huber, Patrick. *Linthead Stomp: The Creation of Country Music in the Piedmont South*. Chapel Hill: University of North Carolina Press, 2008.

Jensen, Joli. *The Nashville Sound: Authenticity, Commercialization, and Country Music*. Nashville: Vanderbilt University Press, 1998.

Jones, Margaret. *Patsy: The Life and Times of Patsy Cline*. New York: Da Capo Press, 1999 (originally published New York: Harper Collins, 1994).

Kienzle, Rich. *Southwest Shuffle: Pioneers of Honky-Tonk, Western Swing, and Country Jazz*. New York: Routledge, 2003.

Kingsbury, P. *The Grand Ole Opry History of Country Music: 70 Years of the Songs, the Stars, and the Stories*. New York: Villard Books, 1995.

Kingsbury, P., and A. Nash, eds. *Will the Circle Be Unbroken: Country Music in America*. New York: DK Publishing, 2006.

Krasilovsky, M. William, Sydney Schemel, John M. Gross, and Jonathan Feinstein. *This Business of Music: The Definitive Guide to the Business and Legal Issues of the Music Industry*, 10th ed. New York: Watson-Guptill Publications, 2007.

Laird, Tracey E. W. *Louisiana Hayride: Radio and Roots Music along the Red River*. New York: Oxford University Press, 2005.

Lewis, George H., ed. *All That Glitters: Country Music in America*. Bowling Green, OH: Bowling Green State University Press, 1993.

Lynn, Loretta, with George Vecsey. *Loretta Lynn: Coal Miner's Daughter*. New York: Warner Books, 1976.

Malone, Bill C. *Don't Get above Your Raisin': Country Music and the Southern Working Class*. Urbana: University of Illinois Press, 2002.

Malone, B. C., and J. R. Neal. *Country Music, USA*, 3rd ed. Austin: University of Texas Press, 2013.

Mazor, Barry. *Meeting Jimmie Rodgers: How America's Original Roots Music Hero Changed the Pop Sounds of a Century*. New York: Oxford University Press, 2009.

McCusker, Kristine M. *Lonesome Cowgirls and Honky-Tonk Angels: The Women of Barn Dance Radio*. Urbana: University of Illinois Press, 2008.

Nash, Alanna. *Dolly: The Biography*, updated ed. New York: Cooper Square Press, 2002.

Neal, J. R. *Country Music: A Cultural and Stylistic History*. New York: Oxford University Press, 2013.

Passman, Donald S. *All You Need to Know about the Music Business*, 9th ed. New York: Simon & Schuster, 2015.

Pecknold, Diane. *The Selling Sound: The Rise of the Country Music Industry*. Durham, NC: Duke University Press, 2007.

Porterfield, Nolan. *Jimmie Rodgers: The Life and Times of America's Blue Yodeler*, rev. ed. Jackson; University Press of Mississippi, 2007.

Rosenberg, Neil V. *Bluegrass: A History*, rev. ed. Urbana: University of Illinois Press, 2005.

Sisk, Eileen. *Buck Owens: The Biography*. Chicago: Chicago Review Press, 2010.

Spellman, Peter. *The Musician's Internet: Online Strategies for Success in the Music Industry*. Boston: Berklee Press, 2002.

Stanley, Ralph. *Man of Constant Sorrow: My Life and Times*. New York: Gotham Books, 2009.

Streissguth, Michael. *Eddy Arnold: Pioneer of the Nashville Sound*. Jackson: University Press of Mississippi, 2009.

———. *Johnny Cash: The Biography*. Cambridge, MA: Da Capo Press, 2006.

Wolfe, Charles K. *Classic Country: Legends of Country Music*. New York: Routledge, 2001.

———. *A Good Natured Riot: The Birth of the Grand Ole Opry*. Nashville: Country Music Foundation Press, 1999.

Wolff, Kurt, and Orla Duane. *Country Music: The Rough Guide*. London: The Rough Guide, Ltd., 2000.

Zwonitzer, Mark, and Charles Hirshberg. *Will You Miss Me When I'm Gone?* *The Carter Family and Their Legacy in American Music.* New York: Simon & Schuster, 2002.

INDEX

ABOUT THE AUTHOR

Dr. Kelly K. Garner is an assistant professor of commercial voice at Belmont University. She presently teaches applied voice and performance seminars in the commercial music program. Dr. Garner taught Commercial Vocal Styles II/III (Pop-Rock/Country) and the Pop/Rock ensemble, *Phoenix*, during her previous years of employment at Belmont University from 2001 to 2006.

Dr. Garner earned a bachelor of science in education degree with a major in mathematics from Auburn University in 1990. In 1992, Dr. Garner graduated with a bachelor of music degree from Belmont University in commercial voice with a performance emphasis and began her career in Nashville as a nationally distributed recording artist/writer in the gospel music industry. She wrote and co-produced her debut release for the record label Brentwood-Benson and has been singing, writing, and producing ever since. From 1998 to 2003, she was signed as an exclusive staffwriter for Centergy Music Group, garnering Dove and BMI Award nominations for Song of the Year and Most Performed Gospel Song for "I Stand Redeemed," recorded by Legacy Five. As a session singer, Kelly was awarded two RIAA Certified Gold Records in 2001 for her work in Nashville as a background vocalist on major artist recordings. In the same year, she agreed to accept a position on the commercial voice faculty at Belmont University and began to pursue a master of arts degree in jazz studies from Middle Tennessee State University, graduating in 2004. She remained on Belmont's voice faculty until she resigned in 2006 to manage Big Dog Studios in Franklin, Tennessee, and found Kelly Garner Productions, LLC. She continued to develop and produce independent artists covering a variety of styles from jazz to R & B, gospel, country, and rock. She also currently owns and operates Nashville-based Yellow Tree Music Group, a music publishing company that provides southern gospel, worship, CCM, jazz, and country songs to the music community and has recently started a print division, Yellow Tree Press. Dr. Garner has served for the past five years as a publisher on BMI's Gospel Songwriter Showcase Committee.

In May 2014, Kelly completed a doctor of musical arts degree in jazz voice performance with a cognate in music technology from the Frost School of Music at the University of Miami. While a doctoral student at Frost, Dr. Garner was the recipient of six prestigious Student Downbeat "DB" Awards including three individual awards for Outstanding Graduate Jazz Vocal Soloist, Outstanding Graduate Jazz Arrangement (for her jazz vocal arrangement of "East of the Sun"), and Outstanding Graduate Blues/Pop Rock Soloist. She received three additional awards for Outstanding Large Vocal Ensemble as a group member of Jazz Vocal Ensemble I and Winner/Outstanding Small Vocal Ensemble as a member of the Frost sextet, Extensions. Dr. Garner's dissertation is entitled "Vocal Recording Techniques for the Modern Digital Studio." She also presented a clinic at the Jazz Education Network 2013 in Atlanta entitled "Studio Recording Techniques for Jazz Vocal Ensembles: Getting the Most out of Your Vocals without Compromising Musical Integrity."

Dr. Garner has worked with the following artists as vocal coach: Denver Bierman (Denver and the Mile High Orchestra), Ricky Braddy (top-twelve finalist for *American Idol*), Seth Costner (Lauren Alaina Band), Kiley Phillips (High Road), Erinn Bates (The Darlins), Jenny Lee Riddle (Revelation Song), Sam Allen (No Other Name), Jason and Lena Cox (Ragdoll), Mike and Kelly Bowling (The Bowlings), Tara Crabb Penhollow (The Crabb Family), Joseph Habedank (The Perrys), Michaela and Adam Brown (The Brown Family), Wes Smith (The Dixie Echoes), Jordan LeFevre (The LeFevre Quartet), Valerie Ruppe Medkiff (The Ruppes), Sara Beth Geoghegan (indie pop artist), Ella Glasgow Binion (indie pop/urban artist), Troy Peach (The

Bowling Family), Sarah Peacock (country/pop artist), Alvin Love (indie pop artist), Michelle Rene (country artist), Jessa and Jordan Anderson (indie artists), Sarah Silva (indie pop artist), Brett McLaughlin (indie pop artist), Nanami Morikawa (jazz artist), Adam Tell (indie pop artist), Claudia Lopez (indie Latin artist), Keith Waggoner (Tribute Quartet), Taylor Begert (indie artist), and Dakota Green (pop artist).

Kelly Garner has recorded or edited vocals for the following artists in the studio: Sunny Wilkinson, Lauren Kinhan (New York Voices), Kate Reid, Jim Van Cleave and Mountain Heart (tour with Alison Krauss), Kara Reynolds (Forte Femme), Broken Wire (bluegrass artist), Sarah Peacock (country/pop artist), Kiley Phillips (High Road), Jana Long (Avalon), Ronnie Freeman, Cindy Morgan, Michael Boggs (former lead singer of FFH), Mike, Faye, and Melody Speck (The Specks), The Booth Brothers, Legacy Five, The Keffer Family, Paul Lancaster (indie gospel artist), Matt Huesmann (Lifeway Press), Jessa and Jordan Anderson (indie CCM artist), Dakota Green (indie pop artist), Jonathan and Emily Martin (worship artists), and many others.

Dr. Garner has sung backup vocals for the following artists: Marie Osmond, Ray Stevens, George Benson, Gloria Estefan, New York Voices, Steve Miller Band, Billy Ray Cyrus, Michael W. Smith, Karrin Alyson, Roseanna Vitro, Pam Thum, and Point of Grace. She has shared the stage or done session work with the following artists/studio singers: Gail Farrell (The Lawrence Welk Show), Mandisa, Jaime Paul (Wynonna Judd), Shaun Groves (worship artist), Steve Wiggins (Big Tent Revival), Melissa Greene (Avalon), Travis Cottrell (Living Proof Live), Chance Scoggins, Russ Taff, Paul Lancaster (The Martins), Mac Powell (Third Day), Guy Penrod (Gaither Vocal Band), Wendy Foy Green (Sierra), Mike Eldred, Bev Darnell, Mary Bates George, Lisa Cochran-Kmecik, Kirk Kirkland, Ellen Musick, Jane Scherberg, John Scherberg, Mark Ivey, Bill George, Amy Joy Williamson Weimer, Leann Albrecht, Lisa Bevill, Melodie Crittenden Kirkpatrick, Lisa Stewart, Stephanie Hall, and Leah Taylor.

Dr. Garner has had songs recorded by the following artists: Vestal Goodman, Legacy Five, Gold City, The Martins, The Perrys, The Crist Family, The Kingsmen, The Whisnants, Brian Free and Assurance, Karen Peck and New River, Three Bridges, The Talleys, The Webbs, The Lesters, Jaidyn's Call, Sarah Peacock, The Diplomats, The Dixie

Echoes, The Dixie Melody Boys, Greater Vision, Lillenas Publishing, Word Music Publishing, Brentwood-Benson Music Publishing, and Lifeway Music Publishing, just to name a few.

Dr. Kelly Garner has four nationally distributed recordings, *Confession of Love* (Diadem Records/Brentwood-Benson Distribution), *Undivided Heart* (Independent), *I Stand Redeemed* (Maze Records), and as a featured artist-writer on the *Left Behind II (Adult Contemporary)* motion picture compilation recording (Butterfly Records/Diamante Distribution). She is currently working on an album of original compositions and a Christmas album of original arrangements and is a member of the jazz sextet Music City Six.